FAMILY LAW IN CANADA: NEW DIRECTIONS

Edited by Elizabeth Sloss

November 1985

CANADIAN ADVISORY COUNCIL ON THE STATUS OF WOMEN

Cover Design: John Stevenson

Prepared for the
Canadian Advisory Council on the Status of Women
Box 1541, Station B
Ottawa, Ontario
K1P 5R5

Available in Canada by mail from:
Canadian Council on Social Development
55 Parkdale Avenue
Ottawa, Ontario K1Y 1E5

Catalogue No. LW31-22/1985E
ISBN 0-660-11925-0
Canada: $4.95
Price subject to change without notice.

Cette publication est aussi disponible en français.

Table of Contents

Acknowledgements

This book was a project of the Research Department of the Canadian Advisory Council on the Status of Women. I would like to thank Jennifer Stoddart, who was the Director of Research in the initial stages, and Marylee Stephenson, the current Director.

I would also like to thank the staff of the CACSW who have participated in the preparation of this book, particularly Micheline Savoie, Director of Communications and editorial staff members, Jim Young, Catherine Rancy, and Claire Rochon.

E.S.

Introduction

— Elizabeth Sloss

Family law is that area of the law which defines the rights and obligations of family members to each other. In its traditional role, it regulates marriage, the legitimacy of children, adoption, separation, divorce, support, and child custody. The parameters of what we have considered family law are constantly being extended by such things as the increased incidence of "common-law" relationships and new parental relationships resulting from rapidly advancing reproductive technologies.

Legislation pertaining to the family plays a complex role in society. Because it regulates social relations it must reflect social norms, and it must also keep pace with social change. On one hand it must be the guardian of certain social values and on the other it must take a leadership role in advancing the rights of the parties to whom it applies. As real social change often precedes legislative change, the distinction between the role of guardian or protector and that of perpetuator of a social myth is often obscure.

Women have a particular interest in the way family relations are defined by the law. Historically, a woman's identity was linked directly to that of her family, or more particularly to that of the "man in her life" — her father or her husband.

Women have fought a long and arduous battle to change both society and the law in areas that they see as particularly crucial. A major step forward was taken on April 17, 1985, when the equality provisions of the *Charter of Rights and Freedoms* came into effect. Sexual equality is now a constitutionally guaranteed right for Canadian women. The Charter will undoubtedly be used to challenge the validity of Canadian laws, and to ensure that women and men are treated equally before and under the law.

Changing legislation to ensure that both men and women are given the same legal rights and obligations, however, will not in itself ensure that men and women are, in fact, substantively equal. For example, the fact that women are as eligible for job training grants as men are means little if mothers cannot find or afford day care for their children.

Women have come a great distance since the time when they had no legal status independent of their husbands', but statistics show that a woman's relationship to her family is still a powerful factor in determining her life and her opportunities. In 1982, approximately one in every three marriages ended in divorce[1] — an increase of 130 per cent since 1968 when the present *Divorce Act* came into effect. Between 1971 and 1981 the number of single-parent families rose by almost 50 per cent.[2] Of those single-parent families, 85 per cent are headed by women — and 47 per cent of these families are living below the poverty line.[3] In contrast, only 14 per cent of single-parent families headed by men were defined as low-income.

Given these grim statistics, how the law acts to try to alleviate some of the pressure on single mothers requires examination. First, the amounts ordered by courts for the support of ex-spouses and children are as a rule very low indeed.[4] In addition, a recent study notes that "the few studies available indicate that . . . between 50 per cent and 85 per cent of maintenance orders are in default and many of them are substantially behind in payment."[5] Inadequate enforcement of maintenance orders is the result of faulty legislation. The law in this case is not responding to the needs of the people it is intended to protect.

The Canadian Advisory Council on the Status of Women organized a forum on family law in the spring of 1985, with the goal of furthering an exchange of information among people involved in different facets of family law across the country. Representatives of federal and provincial governments, family law practitioners, academics, individuals who work within the family law process, and representatives of women's groups attended the conference. This book is a selection of the background papers prepared for the Family Law Forum. We hope this collection will provide useful resource material for readers interested in contemporary issues in family law. Very little Canadian material is available on many of these subjects, particularly from a feminist perspective. The papers published here attempt to fill that gap by giving descriptive and analytic priority to the understanding of women's own experience in their discussion of family law.

Judge Rosalie Silberman Abella delivered the opening address at the forum, and the text of her speech opens this volume. In her thought-provoking general introduction to problems of family law, Judge Abella raises many of the issues elaborated upon and debated by other contributors to this volume. The variety of approaches taken by forum participants makes it clear that there are no simple or definitive answers to the many questions raised here. Yet it is equally clear that the questions are being addressed with particular intensity at this point in history.

Shelagh Day, in "The Charter and Family Law", looks at the *Charter of Rights and Freedoms* and its potential for challenging legislation relating to the family. It may be that issues raised in this chapter have become non-issues in certain provinces, as some have introduced omnibus bills to bring their legislation into line with the Charter since the time of writing. The importance of the paper remains, however, in reminding the reader that the *Charter of Rights and Freedoms* will have an impact on many facets of our lives. The Charter constitutes part of the "supreme law of the land" and all legislation passed by any level of government must comply with its terms. Where legislation is not appropriately amended by governments, it will be up to those women wishing to invoke their rights to see that the law does respect the Charter's equality provisions.

Economic power in the family is most frequently held by the male wage-earner. Exceptions to the principle of independent taxation in the Canadian *Income Tax Act* reinforce this economic power. Louise Dulude, in "Tax and Family Laws: A Search for Consistency", examines the effect of taxation on the economics of the family, and suggests that rather than exacerbate the economic differential between the spouses, our tax system should attempt to balance that power as much as possible.

There is growing concern that the Canadian judicial system, which is adversarial in nature — pitting one party against another in a win/lose battle — is particularly inappropriate for settling family law disputes. In order to help dissipate the tension and emotional trauma that accompanies courtroom battles, the judicial system is in the process of creating its own alternative mechanisms. Mediation and assessment (termed "dejudicialization" because they relieve the court of much of the decision-making responsibility) are such mechanisms, and both are being used frequently to determine the outcome of these disputes. In "Dejudicialization of Family Law: Mediation and Assessments", the problems of instituting such alternative forms of dispute resolution without adequate research and adequate standardization of practices are discussed by Harriet Sachs.

Another win/lose situation to which much attention has been devoted over the last decade concerns the awarding of custody of children following a separation or divorce. Joint custody has been widely proposed as a solution to the problems inherent in custody battles and decisions. Feminist groups in the United States initially lobbied quite heavily, and successfully in certain states, for the inclusion of a presumption of joint custody in the law; in other words, for the assumption that custody by both parents is always the best arrangement. This leaves the onus on the parent or other party to convince a court that sole custody is in the best interests of the child(ren) involved in any particular case.

Based on recent experiences in states where a presumption of joint custody is the law, however, arguments against this presumption are currently taking the foreground among feminists. Joint custody itself is a multifaceted phenomenon, the understanding of which requires a historical context and some definitional fine-tuning. In "Joint Custody", Renée Joyal-Poupart examines this form of custody and explains the debate over the benefits of legislation preferring joint custody.

The questions of mediation and of joint custody have both been raised in discussions of the *Divorce and Corollary Relief Act* tabled by the Progressive Conservative government in May 1985. These issues are not being dealt with directly by the federal government at this time, but they may well be within the relatively near future. It is therefore important that women be prepared to prevent the enactment of legislation which would make the already difficult position many women face after divorce even more difficult.

Matrimonial property law, discussed in "The Ideal Marital Property Regime — What Would It Be?", plays a vital role in the distribution of economic power between the spouses. In most families there is an earning power differential between the spouses. The role of each spouse in the family constitutes a valuable contribution each makes to the functioning of the unit. In ideal terms one would see marriage as a partnership of equals: each with his or her own responsibilities and each making his or her own contribution. Freda M. Steel examines various alternative matrimonial property regimes and explains what sorts of reforms are needed to ensure that the law adequately reflects this notion of equality.

The protection afforded legally married couples with respect to matrimonial property does not apply for couples living "common-law". In "To Marry or Not to Marry? A Study of the Legal Situation of

Common-Law Spouses in Canadian Law", Suzanne P. Boivin examines the legal treatment of common-law spouses and argues that the law must provide some mechanism to protect the rights of those living in these relationships.

In "The Surname of the Married Woman and of Children", Suzanne P. Boivin looks at the tradition whereby women assume their husband's surname upon marriage. Until recently women rarely challenged this custom. Society put strong pressure on women to conform to this practice, although they were not legally obliged to do so. Only in recent years has change of name legislation been enacted by the provinces, to formalize the procedures for changing one's name. These procedures either make it more complicated for a woman to retain her own surname upon marriage or, in the case of Quebec, prevent her from taking that of her husband.

A change in her name when she marries means that a woman's personal identity is decided by her marital status. Ms. Boivin argues that this is both inefficient and unnecessary in our society, leading her to conclude that the solution codified by the Quebec legislature is the most appropriate: women should for all legal purposes retain their own surnames.

The book concludes with a look at the rapidly growing area of reproductive technologies. This is a completely new area of science and technology, with enormous social, moral, and legal implications. In the very near future, Canadian legislatures will have to deal with issues such as: who can benefit from artificial insemination and *in vitro* fertilization? Should the reproductive technologies be available to single people? Gay people? Does each of us have a constitutional right to procreate? Who decides when a foetus is in danger and needs medical attention? In a possible conflict of rights between the mother and the foetus, whose are primary?

In "Women and the Reproductive Technologies", Bartha Maria Knoppers describes legislative proposals and policy considerations that have been raised by law reform organizations in various countries. The implications of any Canadian legislation in this area will be of extreme importance to women. With increased medical intervention in the reproductive process, women stand to lose an enormous amount of control over their own bodies. Because of the speed at which these technologies are advancing, legislative guidelines are vitally needed and women must participate in their formulation.

Jurisdiction over issues in family law is split between the federal and the provincial governments. Many issues fall in the "grey area" between the two, such that both levels of government have room to legislate. The papers in this collection deal with issues clearly within provincial jurisdiction, as well as with those in the federal jurisdiction and the "grey area". Although each paper deals with a very different subject, they all demonstrate how important the implications of law relating to the family are to women.

As a federal advisory council, we have taken this opportunity to provide our readers with an overview of legislation across the country and a feminist critique of that legislation — or its absence. It is vital that women participate in the law reform process to ensure that our rights are adequately protected. It is up to women to define what sort of legislation will satisfy our needs and to see that it is enacted.

The law reform process is a very long one. We hope that this collection will be a valuable contribution to the contemporary debates within and around family law, and of use to those involved in the process of its reform.

Notes

1. Canada, Statistics Canada, *Marriage and Divorce, Vital Statistics, Vol. II*, cat. no. 84-205 (Ottawa: Supply and Services Canada, 1982).

2. From the Census of Canada for 1966, 1971, and 1981. Information provided by Statistics Canada.

3. Canada, Statistics Canada, *Income Distribution by Size in Canada, 1982* (Ottawa: Supply and Services Canada, May 1984), cat. no. 13-207, p. 67, table 19, and p. 167, table 86.

4. Louise Dulude, *Love, Marriage and Money . . . An Analysis of Financial Relations Between the Spouses* (Ottawa: Canadian Advisory Council on the Status of Women, 1984).

5. Eve Finnbogason and Monica Townson, *The Benefits and Cost Effectiveness of a Central Registry of Maintenance and Custody Orders* (Ottawa: Status of Women Canada, March 1985).

Opening Address

— *Judge Rosalie Silberman Abella*

More than any other area of law, family law has a pervasive influence on the way society functions. To dissect family law is to begin to understand the dynamics of laws, traditions, and culture. It is also to begin to appreciate the dynamics and components of social change.

The premises underlying the law of the family over the past several generations are no longer tenable. The primary purpose of the law was to keep the family together. This was most successfully done by keeping the marriage together, and this, in turn, was accomplished by forbidding divorce. Even when divorce was later permitted as a judicial remedy, any attempt to depart from marriage was usually met with the stern disapprobation of the court. This usually translated into punitive monetary consequences — either loss of income for a guilty wife or the reduction of a guilty husband's income for the financial benefit of his innocent wife. These economic sanctions were intended not only to maintain the home, they acted in addition as "immorality prophylactics" by attempting to prevent the occasional sinful lapse which threatened the structure and integrity of the family. The economic sanctions more successfully prevented the iniquities of wives than of husbands. A husband was the only source of income a wife had, and her reluctance to jeopardize this source was understandable. Since abstention was a lesser evil than destitution, most wives stayed faithful to the social expectations and to their husbands.

The second function of family law was to provide a system for the distribution of assets and children in the event of a marriage breakdown. The concept of equity, though well developed in other areas of law, was not a feature of the law of the family. On the contrary, there existed a series of theories in family law which effectively challenged any notion of fairness.

These unfair legal maxims were often nothing more than symbiotic reflections of unfair community maxims. The regime of separate property is an example of this fusion. Under separate property, property was to be divided according to title unless a spouse could show a direct monetary contribution to an asset not in his or her name. This approach to the marital economy was borrowed from the secular economic milieu, the milieu spawned by the industrial revolution and by what C.B. Macpherson called "possessive individualism". It was appropriate to the marketplace but entirely incongruous with the domestic sphere. Although the right to own property was eventually granted to wives, censorious social conventions ensured that they were not able to earn the money with which to buy the property or to make a direct contribution. They stayed home, performing valuable but unlucrative jobs.

Consequently, the right to own separate property given to wives by the series of *Married Women's Property Acts* in the late nineteenth century could well be considered the right to accumulate separate penury. Wives remained economically dependent and this reinforced their social dependence.

A study of custody laws over the years shows that children were first entrusted by the courts to their fathers, then to non-adulterous mothers, particularly if the children were of tender years and female, then to mothers, then again to fathers if mothers (even if non-adulterous) caused the separation. Along the way, the theory of the welfare of the child was propounded but it tended to be subject to the presumptions of gender and morality to which I have just referred.

In effect, to summarize these introductory comments, family law was intended as a means of maintaining the family and, if the family would not be maintained, it was a means of retributive reconstruction.

This is the context against which the recent changes in family law must be examined. Today's laws may not be less arbitrary, but they are certainly more committed to the promotion of equitable premises.

While there is no doubt that the whole issue has become very complicated, there is a nostalgic preoccupation with the erosion of time-honoured values and traditions. This has generated a communal malaise which seems to be dominated by fears that the traditional family has fragmented into a number of undefined and redefined entities. How should the law respond appropriately? It is evident that old laws have to be replaced in order to synchronize the law with new social norms; but it is not so evident what these norms now are.

In looking at what seems to be happening to families, I have some trouble understanding the "wailing jeremiahs" who fear for the imminent collapse of society in general or the family in particular. I can understand that it is disillusioning and traumatic to find that some of the firmly held goals and expectations of successive generations suddenly no longer have credibility. For example, it is frightening to wonder whether a commitment made to a marriage partner will be honoured throughout the increasingly debilitating passages of adulthood and old age. This, after all, was what the family used to be all about — a permanent sanctuary in which the personalities often multiplied but were never replaced.

But I think we exaggerate both the romance of the traditional family and the neuroses of the modern version. The traditional family was not, by virtue of its indivisibility, necessarily productive of emotional well-being. It was, as literature often points out, quite possible to have the tortured family relationships of *The Little Foxes* or *Long Day's Journey into Night.* This is not to suggest that these artistic hyperboles represented the typical family, but it is true that in mourning the passing of the old family, little time has been spent analysing the emotional welfare of the old unit or its members. It is only in recent times that we have done more than factual assessments of our ancestors. We know the hows and whys of their lives, but only recently have we begun to scrutinize their psyches. Again, I lay no claim to ours being a better *Zeitgeist*; I point out simply that before we rush to judgement we should remember that we are looking at the past with incomplete data.

One thing was, however, clear about the traditional family — the characters and their roles were easily discernible. Upon breakdown, there was always a clearly identifiable victim and villain, and the legal framework was sympathetically vindictive.

Today, in what many consider to be our trendy sophistication, families disintegrate before bewildered eyes and no one seems to know why. The traditional reasons, like boredom and alternative sexual partnerships, still exist. But now, instead of the innocent versus guilty theory of spousal accountability, there is a new approach in which both spouses are considered equally innocent victims. This is what I like to call the Titanic theory of marriage breakdown — that adultery, cruelty, or desertion represent only the tip of the iceberg against which the marriage has crashed. The real collision, according to the more humane no-fault approach to marriage breakdown, occurs through an irrepressible combination of factors beyond any one party's control.

However, it is ingenuous to rely entirely upon the theory of the irresistible impulse to separate. I certainly think the legal trend away from fault analysis is salutary, but not because we may or may not have discovered new causation theories about marriage breakdown. Marriage breakdown may not be attributable to boredom or adultery, but on the other hand it may very well be. We seem to need to justify our efforts to decriminalize divorce by referring to the behavioural science theories which exculpate both sides. This then gives us the licence to develop a more humane no-fault system of family law since to punish the guilty spouse, as our primordial instincts would have us do, is to ignore modern psychology, which supposedly says in a marriage breakdown, no one may be guiltier than anyone else.

This is a case of syllogism with the right conclusion but the wrong premises. The reason the law should make no distinctions between faultor and faultee in marriage is because it is none of the law's business. What is the law's business is, in family law, one of the most intriguing issues and vital in any assessment of whether family law is successful in meeting the needs it was intended to satisfy. To what extent has the State through its legal process the right to intervene in the internal politics of a group of people who collectively constitute a family, whether or not they are legally married?

There can be no doubt that the State has an interest in what happens to families. As scholars like Donzelot and Eeckelaar have shown, the family operates in and is an outgrowth of society. The two entities, family and society, have a vested interest in each other's welfare.

Notwithstanding this tautology, the issue to unravel is whether to respect the sanctity of the family as an independent social unit, a refuge from society, or whether to respect, as a more compelling value, the State's overriding interest in maintaining consistency and order. The latter philosophy, which necessarily entitles the State to investigate and rearrange the family, results in such things as strict divorce laws, punitive maintenance and custody awards, and "Scarlet Letters". The former philosophy which stresses the independence of the family, results in a laissez-faire system whereby, provided no family member's rights fall below an acceptable minimum standard, the family and its members are left to determine such items as its longevity and economic infrastructure. It also results in liberal divorce laws, marriage contracts, and legally sanctioned non-married conjugal partnerships.

This emphasis on the independence of the family is the direction of most family law. There are those like Christopher Lasch who feel even now that the family is still besieged by well-intentioned experts and State representatives who undermine the integrity of the family unit. But the direction is clear — if not in implementation, then certainly in intent.

The present function of family law is no longer primarily to maintain the marriage. Society's survival instinct has shifted from the need to preserve marriages to the need to preserve families — serially if necessary. It has come from a recognition that saving a marriage may in fact be destroying the members of the family. The messianic ambitions of family law have therefore been replaced by more practical, therapeutic ones in the interests of promulgating the rights of the family and of its constituent members.

The matter is not resolved by accepting the primacy of the family. In many ways, this approach to the family greatly complicates the pursuit of an appropriate legal model. Even after severing to some extent the family's rights from society's rights, one is still left with having to apportion between family members such rights as they have, not only in relation to each other, but to society as well. In the days of the categorical imperatives of family law, when society made golden rules which were intended to apply universally (as opposed to equally, between men and women), any given family situation led to relatively predictable results. The rights of the family members were subject to the rights of the community to expect and sanction certain kinds of behaviour. The law operated on what political scientists would call a Hobbesian philosophy: that laws were necessary to prevent us from exercising our natural selfish impulses and to encourage us to live together in a way consistent with the common good.

When furthering freedoms from society, and particularly from social expectations, one has to contend with a myriad of arguably equally compelling yet competing rights. The State has the right to demand adherence to those values it considers necessary for its survival and the family has the right to insist on implementing those values it considers necessary for its survival.

Here starts the modern dilemma of family law. Who is to say which rights within a family are most deserving of protection? Once it has been called upon to intervene in an otherwise private unit, how does the State decide to what extent it should interfere?

If we accept the fact that family law has, as one of its functions, the establishment of minimum standards of expectations and conduct, then we have to consider what those expectations and conduct should be. Though this function may not be totally desirable, it grows from a recognition that there will be circumstances in which a family will be unable on its own to respond to disruptive crises. It will then seek, voluntarily or involuntarily, the assistance of the State and its laws in resolving internal disputes. At this point, the law should be able to respond with a coherent philosophy which attempts to balance the parties' rights, interests, and needs. This is where the need for minimum standards applies, and this need is particularly important to remedy historic injustices for women.

The courts realized earlier than statutes that women were unfairly consigned to what was designated as "dependent status". Even this label is erroneous because women's economic contribution to the family and the economy has always been significant. However, this contribution has not been recognized in the gross national product (the measure of economic output) because it was not made in the market sector and was therefore not remunerated by direct payment.

In his dissent in the notorious 1973 *Murdoch* decision, Chief Justice Laskin referred to the inequities of the then operative system of separate property, which recognized only the direct financial contributions of a spouse. He therefore developed in that dissent the applicability of constructive trusts, or the doctrine of unjust enrichment, to matrimonial property law. He argued that it was unfair to allow one spouse, namely the male, to benefit exclusively from the non-monetary contribution of his wife. The theories in his dissent became part of the majority judgement of the court five years later in the *Rathwell* decision. Justice Brian Dickson, speaking for the majority of the court, observed that the courts had to be more sensitive to the many forms in which spouses could contribute to the marital relationship.

There followed a series of provincial statutes across Canada which recognized that the traditional contributory theories in family law were neither relevant, fair nor accurate in responding to what actually went on in a family. Under the new laws, contributions to a marriage were considered equal whether the function was performed within or outside the home. The barometer was not whether money was contributed, but whether there was a division of labour. We have yet to move to the next obvious stage, the equal division of assets accumulated during marriage, but one hopes that this too will come to pass.

If the laws are interpreted as they appear to have been intended, spouses will obtain support if they need it from their spouses who are able to contribute. The court must look at what went on during the history of the marriage to decide what is fairest upon separation. The court will look at what functions the spouses performed during the marriage to determine what functions they are capable of performing after the marriage.

A spouse who has remained at home to care for the household will no longer be prejudiced on separation if he or she caused the relationship to terminate. If in making a contribution to the subsistence of the family the spouse removed himself or herself from the labour force where there would have been direct remuneration, the court is entitled to consider rehabilitative support payments, to allow the spouse to put himself or herself into the same position he or she would have been in, had the family responsibilities not been undertaken.

In other words, the redistribution of assets upon dissolution of the marriage will depend on the extent to which the individual's economic situation was negatively affected by the assumption of family responsibilities, not on a judgemental assessment as to who caused the relationship to unravel. To the extent that the spouse could claim that the marriage damaged his or her economic well-being, there would be rehabilitative support. If the family relationship resulted in no economic dependency, then the breakdown of the marriage would result in no economic consequences and no support.

This theory, as commendable as it is, must however be realistically applied. Spousal independence and the degree of economic impact will vary according to the age, solvency, and employment situations of the spouses, the number and ages of the children, the duration of the relationship, the division of functions within the partnership, and the state of the economy generally. We must be wary, in attempting to encourage speedy economic recovery and financial independence, about finite support orders that bear no relationship to a spouse's history.

The notion of spousal independence is a salient part of the new vocabulary in family law. For this generation (and possibly the next one), it has more value as an esoteric, but highly commendable principle than as a reflection of reality, and as a principle which promotes androgynous choices in future marriage partners.

However, we still must be considerate of the traditional sentiments which are on their face antithetic to the modern legislative directives of new *Family Law Reform Acts*. It is hard to be an independent equal when one is not equally able to become independent. Independence will not be possible for everyone; it should therefore not be used, as it has sometimes been, prematurely. It should not be used, in other words, where the realities of the marketplace and community combine to make it impractical. The pattern of a given marriage is critical to the possibility of independence.

It is impossible to fix the length of time such a process should take. Before the passage of acts like the *Family Law Reform Act* in 1978,

15

women entered adulthood and marriage confident that they need not seek ways to become self-sufficient — marriage brought a legal guarantee of financial support. On the basis of this socially accepted and legally sanctioned bargain, women made certain educational and social decisions. These often resulted in no, or poorly paid, jobs. Their economic well-being was in being married.

It is a facile and futile exercise to be judgemental about such decisions and expectations; they existed and continue to exist. And the longer a woman stayed married, the less likely were her chances of ever matching her husband's ability to earn an income. The years when the husband was increasing his educational and career prospects were years which increasingly diminished the wife's prospects in the labour force.

It is therefore difficult to see how any time limit can be put on her economic reconstruction. If she is lucky enough to find a job it will likely not be lucrative, given her lack of marketable skills. If she decides to re-educate herself, this will take several months or years of non-income-producing activity. In both cases, it will be some time before she will be able to entrench herself in the paid labour force in such a way that she can earn something that begins to approximate her husband's income. Nor will she likely have the benefit of the indispensable support of child care. She will probably never catch up.

There is no reason why a stronger economic partner should not continue to support an economically weaker one for as long as the latter is unable to contribute independently to the needs the stronger one helped create. There is nothing offensive about support as an indefinite payment if one accepts that the partnership has for one partner created an economic disability which may continue indefinitely. The economics of indefinite support flow naturally from the economics of many current marriage partnerships.

If there are children, then just as with spousal support, the post-marriage economy should reflect the partnership standards. Ideally, enough support should be received in the children's home so that they can continue the same standard they enjoyed while the parents lived together in the same household.

This is sometimes resisted on the grounds that it results in an unintended economic benefit to a former spouse who may not otherwise qualify for economic assistance. This approach ignores the obvious economic symbiosis between the custodial spouse and the child. To separate the allowance between adult and infant beneficiary may have some psychological value, but its economic value is dubious and largely arbitrary in effect. If a choice must be made as a matter of policy, it must be in favour of the children suffering less economically than either adult. This will almost inevitably result in monetarily benefitting the spouse with whom the children live. The inequity of an indirect allowance to a former spouse is overwhelmed by the justice of trying to cause the children as little economic disruption as the circumstances will allow.

The tangential benefits to the children's custodian, moreover, give partial recognition to the performance of additional duties no longer undertaken by the absent parent. Support for children should thus be global assessments of the needs of the household in which they reside based on the marital standard of living rather than on artificial budgets for each individual family member. Children's needs have also been created by this former lifestyle and cannot be assessed in the abstract.

As for children, some of the most drastic redefinition of rights in the realm of family law have been of those connected with custody. Almost all of these legal developments have been a direct result of the development of the behavioural sciences which have, on the whole, practically discredited the historical premises upon which custody cases had been decided.

The traditional shortcuts to custody decisions, which involved rewarding innocent spouses, the tender years doctrine, and the non-separation of siblings doctrine, have now been replaced by the doctrine known as the "best interests" of the child. The older doctrines have been relegated to the status of considerations rather than operative presumptions.

What has replaced them is the notion that the only test that should be applicable is what is in the best interests of the child. For some time, the courts indicated that the welfare of the children was a paramount consideration; but they then went on to circumscribe that paramountcy with reference to other circumstances, such as the moral conduct of the spouses or the ages and genders of the children.

Not until the statutory delineation of the best-interests test did the court take the position that what is in the child's best interests is the only test. It is an approach which sees custody as a matter to be looked at from the perspective of the child upwards rather than from the adults down. The courts became, as a result, obliged to consider, apart from stock theories, in each particular case what a particular child needs and which of the adults before the court seeking custody can best meet most of those needs. This has in turn resulted in the development of a number of concomitant phenomena.

It has come to be recognized, for example, that children do best after divorce when their lives most closely approximate what went on during the subsistence of the family relationship. In many families today, both parents take an equal role in parenting the children.

The changed social and economic environment which resulted in many more mothers being in the work force has also resulted in a growing trend to shared care of the child during the subsistence of a family. Studies such as those at the Child Studies Institute at the University of Maryland have shown that there is no psychiatric evidence or behavioural studies that establish the superior parenting ability of one sex over the other. Experts do agree, however, that there is importance in a male as well as a female role model for children in daily activities. All of these factors have combined to make the notion of joint custody an important one.

The purpose of joint custody is to continue as far as possible after a family breakup what went on while the family was together. Its theory is much more compelling than the courts have thus far acknowledged. There can be no doubt that a father who walks away from a divorce with just visiting rights and support payments often stops visiting and often stops paying support. Either event is harmful to the child. Professor Joseph Goldstein suggests that perhaps judges should issue cigarette package warnings in custody and access orders which read: "Denial of visits or failure to cooperate in making your custody agreement work may be detrimental to your child."

It should be conceded that joint custody cannot work if one parent is consistently unreasonable in dealing with issues around the child. However, one cannot easily measure the future capacity of parents to cooperate at that point in their relationship when they are shaking on the fault line of marital discord. It appears that in most cases joint custody would disrupt the parent/child relationship less than any other custody alternatives. If one acknowledges that the best interests of the child are what the exercise is all about, joint custody is a presumption devoutly to be wished, as a normal rather than an exceptional post-marital arrangement.

It is worth examining, however, whether the concept of custody itself and its legal premises are worth retaining. It is a term that at its best is amorphous and at its worst represents ossification. It connotes victory and loss, which in turn suggest winners and losers.

Since joint custody has not found much favour with the Canadian courts to date, those parents who cannot agree on this form of arrangement are limited to the winner-take-all proposition that the term "custody" historically and jurisprudentially symbolizes. It represents psychological as well as physical vindication of the position necessarily taken at trial that the non-custodial parent was less fit to parent the child than the parent to whose care the child was entrusted by the court.

The impact of such a decision on the non-custodial parent is often devastating. He or she is relegated to the status of a visiting relative who has no enforceable voice in the decision-making process of raising the child, notwithstanding the fact that up to the time of separation, parenting was presumed to be a joint responsibility.

This means that instead of divorce representing a termination of only the spousal relationship and status, it also effectively terminates the exercise of the status of parent. Raising a child then becomes a process that has inherent and inchoate rights of parental obsolescence rather than being a process that lasts as long as the child continues to be legally dependent and entitled to the care of adults.

Most of the behavioural scientists are suggesting that, except in extreme circumstances, children are entitled to the benefit of co-parenting for the duration of childhood. The law should somehow be able to synchronize its tenets with these common-sense observations. The cessation of a parent-child relationship upon divorce is arbitrary and unfair from the perspective of the child.

The status of child is independent of the relationship between his or her parents and should be preserved notwithstanding their physical separation. Rather than developing laws and procedures that encourage the notion of sole custody, the direction should be towards developing processes and laws that enhance the possibility of the continuance of parenting.

Aside from the routine order of joint custody, and aside from the elimination of semantics such as "awards" of custody, one way might be to have hearings to determine a child's residence instead of custody. No parent would be "awarded" custody. The hearing would determine simply where the child should live and would delineate what the respective rights and obligations of both parents are. One parent would necessarily have the final say, but there would be on the part of the parent with whom the child does not live, the right to information about the child, the right to be advised and consulted about major decisions affecting the child, as well as the right to access at times that are mutually agreed upon.

This would, in many cases, cauterize the psychological wounds that result from the notion of "losing" custody. It would not then become a question of the competing rights of each parent to have custody of the child or the right of the child to be cared for by one of the two competing parents, but rather would be a residence hearing to assess where the child should live. The court would make the assessment on the basis of evidence from all parties and would in the end declare the location of the child's home rather than the winner of the custody dispute.

These "residence hearings" may appear to be nothing more than semantic distinctions, but in matters such as these, the terminology may be critical to the psychological future of the former members of the family.

Another aspect of custody law which has recently developed follows logically, given that most of our new approaches are based on social science theories. This development is the role of the expert in custody proceedings. In *Before the Best Interests of the Child*, the authors describe a prime function of the law to be "to prevent one person's truth . . . from becoming another person's tyranny." There must therefore be a complement to judicial speculation in custody decision making. No one suggests that the expert is any more or less infallible than is the judge, but these experts are trained in assessing emotional and behavioural probabilities. Judges are not.

The expert provides a funnel through which a judge can pour his or her legal and practical observations. The result is a more informed decision, one more likely to accommodate the child's needs than a decision based exclusively on either a judge's or an expert's exclusive perception.

Independent expert assessments are as much an admission on the part of the judicial system that it lacks omniscience in custody matters as they are a recognition that the adversarial system with its partisan emphasis cannot always be relied upon to present a full picture to the court. They are also acknowledgements that the adversarial system, while adept at gleaning historical or antecedent facts, is less well able to encourage the evocation of social or consequential facts.

Since custody involves the formulation of policies and prognoses about the mental and physical well-being of the child, mere facts about the child's background may be insufficient information upon which to base a decision about the child's future placement. What is required in most of these cases is an analysis of emotional, factual, and psychological factors, only some of which a judge is able to ascertain from the perceptions of the parties or their supporters. It is for these reasons that the adversary process has entrenched the use of impartial expert assessments that investigate skillfully those facts that it could not otherwise ascertain.

The presence of an expert in the courtroom represents a classic clash of cultures. There has been very little cross-educational pollination between the professions of law and behavioural science. As a result there is limited comprehension, on both sides, of the objectives and semantics of the other profession. Psychiatrists and psychologists are frequently unsympathetic to being subjected to devastating scrutiny through cross-examination when their purpose is simply to explain a scientific conclusion in as objective a way as possible. Lawyers and judges, who perceive themselves to be commonsensical, are suspicious of what they perceive to be impractical behavioural sophistry. The discomfort of experts in a courtroom setting, matched as it is by a sceptical reception to their expertise, represents an inadequate partnership.

Psychiatrists are now learning to appreciate the significance of legal process to those who are legally skilled, and to understand that the respect given to procedures does not indicate an insensitivity to the issues presented.

The legal profession, on the other hand, is now learning to pay more deference to the diagnostic skills of those who are expert in problems of human behaviour. At the very least, these experts have had the benefit of experience and information that are not part of the regular legal or judicial educational diet.

Since the test in custody is "best interests" and since the evidence required must necessarily go beyond materially demonstrable perceptions, it is difficult to see how informed judgements can be made about the best interests of children without at least the assistance of a non-partisan qualified expert who can better attempt to evaluate the competing emotional claims that underlie the pursuit of legal remedies. Since the jurisprudential mandate includes assessing a child's emotional needs, the courts should make this assessment on the basis of the most complete evidence available. This often necessitates authoritative exploration of these needs, which is not a usurpation of the judicial function but an indispensable contribution to its proper exercise.

21

No one suggests that the expertise provided is of uniform quality. There is the additional reality of the multiplicity of theories and approaches which percolate through the behavioural sciences — one expert's hypothesis is another expert's antithesis. But these may simply be unavoidable tangents of an unavoidably human process. They accentuate the benefit of some aspects of the adversary system, like the right to cross-examine or to call contradictory evidence. However vulnerable the injection of experts is to the charge of fallibility, it is a credible and vital part of a process which ultimately minimizes the weaknesses of the expert's role and relies on its strengths.

Whereas the judicial process results in the imposition of a decision upon the parties, mediation attempts to achieve a consensus. Mediation is a process whereby a third person attempts to resolve a dispute by creating an environment of empathy and openness in the hopes of assisting the parties to understand each other's position and effect an agreement between them. It has a persuasive rather than coercive *ambiance*.

The benefits of mediation are obvious. Notwithstanding any refinements to the adversarial process, the better solution to resolving disputes between family members lies in achieving consensus rather than imposing judgement. In the short term, the benefit of mediation, if properly performed, is that it provides the parties with a better understanding of themselves, the issues, and the position of the other party.

It also gives to the parties the sense that their privacy and family autonomy have remained sacrosanct. In the long term, this awareness may assist the parties in resolving future disputes in a flexible manner. The brittleness that may result from the imposition of an unfavourable decision can easily encourage the continuation of the kind of intractability that resulted in the initial litigation. This has the tendency of proliferating litigation by encouraging reliance on the court process in resolving grievances.

The benefits for children in such a process are equally compelling. If adults can appreciate the nuances in their own gestures or those of their former partners, and if they are helped through conciliation to protect themselves from any negative impact of the nuances, then they will be better able to set aside their own irrational tendencies in the interest of furthering the well-being of their children.

Since parents are generally in the best position to know and accommodate their children's needs, they, rather than a judge, are the best people to make decisions about them. Where they are handicapped by emotional disabilities resulting from injuries sustained in the fall from a spousal relationship, they may need some assistance in regaining the ability to make these decisions. Mediation provides this assistance and avoids the need for judicial intervention.

Based on the assumption that a good bargain is better than a good fiat, mediation will and should continue to be increasingly relied upon in assisting parties to settle disputes.

The other commonly accepted theme that has now been implemented, unfortunately in only five provinces, is the suggestion that family law can function best if it functions as a specialized superior court with only one judicial level of expert judges having jurisdiction over all family law matters.

There have been a number of reports on these Unified Family Courts, all of them indicating that the predictions for success were warranted. The Unified Family Court structure proved to be most expeditious for the parties in dealing with family law disputes. Most of these Unified Family Courts have non-legal resources available either on the premises or by arrangement with community resources, and the legal and behavioural aspects operate in tandem. It is a critical institutional improvement over the truncated multi-level court approach and should be adopted all across Canada.

There remains the problem of an appropriate confluence of family law and social policy. Having isolated outmoded attitudes towards women as one of the dramatic bequests of family law, is the passage of legislation likely to remedy the parochialism of the past?

If one accepts the notion that changed laws lead to changed behaviour which leads to changed attitudes and conditions, then new legislation, as the statutory endorsement of new norms, will have a profound effect.

But it cannot be expected that in the few years since the new legislation was passed society will have overcome the complacency of a century's assumptions about men and women. It is axiomatic that most people absorb values and self-images from the family, often touted as the fundamental unit in society. If the family historically treated wives as chattels in the possession and service of husbands who controlled their conduct with the threat of penury, can one be surprised that this attitude towards women pervaded the marketplace, the public sphere, and women's own attitudes about themselves?

Can this attitude not explain such otherwise inexplicable phenomena as paying two people who do the same work different wages because one is male and the other female? And does it not explain why, in the face of a stampede by mothers to join the paid labour force, it is still considered that society's obligation for the quality care of the young does not precede a child's sixth birthday? How else to explain the absence of universally accessible child care except that society seems unwilling to pay for a service that it expects mothers to perform for free?

Given all of this, where does responsibility lie for appropriate changes in legal principles? Does it rest with the legislative assembly as the accountable democratic expression of public consensus, or does it rest with the appointed judiciary as the expression of justice?

How wary must one be of crossing what Lord Devlin referred to as the "Rubicon that divides the judicial and legislative powers"? And wherever one places the onus for changing the law, should the law-makers be anticipating or merely reflecting social trends? To what degree must a concept be socially entrenched before it is legally articulated by either a court or a legislature? Was Lord Devlin correct when he treated the law as a valve for the competing host of new ideas "galloping around the outskirts of society's thought"? Or is there a role for the court as the conscience of the community, giving expression to ideas as a means of educating and directing society's thoughts?

The responsibility lies primarily with the legislature, but the courts should intervene to update parts of the law if the government is not keeping pace with social changes. As Chief Justice Bora Laskin pointed out:

> The legislatures (are) occupied with economic planning, with managing resources, with social welfare policies, with administering the province or country as the case may be (and) may, hence, properly rely on the courts to share in the burden of law-making in those areas congenial to judicial legislation.[1]

The courts, he said, become "institutionalized" thereby "into a partnership, albeit a junior one, with the legislature." By this theory, if they must redress a glaring deficiency, the courts will step in. The partnership thrives on a powerful, self-serving, and dynamic instinct on the part of both institutions to maintain credibility with the third partner — public consensus.

There may be no unequivocal solution to the dilemma of when and how to implement new assumptions. Certainly before it is enunciated in either jurisprudential or statutory form, a social principle will require at least a degree of entrenchment or it runs the risk of starving from cultural malnutrition. One cannot in fairness castigate a mirror for the image it reflects. Both judiciary and legislature draw water from the same well of public opinion. The cultural assumptions in family law that have resulted in over a century of gender stereotyping were tolerated by the public or they would not have survived. They were tolerated notwithstanding the fact that they were not and probably could not be empirically justified. That they not only survived but affected every aspect of our secular lives, remains their most profound legacy.

Only when they were roundly challenged, bruised, and emasculated (most vocally by a population galvanized into awareness by the decision in *Murdoch v. Murdoch*) were these assumptions replaced by the massive social reform of the provincial *Family Reform Acts*. This social reform was and is, like every social metamorphosis, a spectacle confusing to observers and poignant to participants. But it was a metamorphosis whose time had come.

The policy triumvirate — legislature, judiciary, and public consensus — is undoubtedly chiselling new assumptions out of a cultural mould. It remains to be seen whether it will provide the legislative, institutional, and conceptual machinery required to make the law of the family as fair and humane in practice as it was intended to be in principle.

Judge Rosalie Silberman Abella is a judge in the Ontario Provincial Court, Family Court. Currently the Chairman of the Ontario Labour Relations Board, Judge Abella was the Commissioner of the federal Commission of Inquiry on Equality in Employment.

Note

1. Bora Laskin, *The Institutional Character of the Judge* (Jerusalem: Magnes, 1972), pp. 17-18.

The Charter and Family Law

— *Shelagh Day*

The new Canadian Charter of Rights and Freedoms offers an opportunity to reform family law, thereby reducing inequalities which particularly affect women. Historically, the status and legal rights of women have been subsumed under those of their husbands. Over the last century, however, women have gradually won improvements with regard to rights over property, maintenance, custody, divorce, and other issues.

The author examines the various sections of the Charter and how they may be used to effect change in family law. A sample of current legislation (pertaining to a variety of issues) which appears to violate the Charter is presented and discussed. The author argues that existing inequality in Canadian society, and how it operates, must be understood when changes to the law are being proposed and drafted. It must also be recognized that simply making legislation "gender neutral" does not always remove the inequality: challenges invoking sections 15 and 28 of the Charter must result in actual equality, not merely juridical equality. Care must also be taken not to allow the limitations sections to be used to render the Charter guarantees meaningless.

Introduction

The new *Charter of Rights and Freedoms* is expected to have a great impact on family law in Canada. The Charter will be used to mount challenges to current discriminatory legislation; however, the success rate of these challenges will vary.

Family law is a branch of law of prime importance to women since decisions regarding marriage, separation, divorce, family property, and the care of children directly affect women's equality, independence, security, and economic status.

Although traditionally the family has been viewed as woman's sphere, the place in which she "held sway", the law governing the family has been the principal instrument for subjugating women. Women's lack of status in the family has provided the negative model for the treatment of women in every other sphere.

Both Napoleonic law and British common law, from which Canadian law is derived, deprived married women of legal personhood, independence, and equality. The traditional status of married women at law is summarized in Blackstone's famous aphorisms: "Husband and wife are one person and the husband is that one", and "The very being or legal existence of the woman is suspended during marriage."

Upon marriage, a woman's property customarily passed to her husband. Monies she earned, gifts she was given, or property she inherited all belonged to her husband.[1] A married woman had no right to contract or to make a will, nor could she sue or be sued independently.

Marriage also resulted in a woman's physical person and her sexuality becoming her husband's property. He had the right to physically "correct" her, to rape her, to control her physical movement, and to determine her domicile and place of residence.

Children were also entirely in the control of the husband, as he was the sole legal guardian of them, with the right to make all decisions regarding their care, discipline, and education.

Married women assumed the names and nationalities of their husbands, and lost their own. The husband was responsible for any illegal actions of his wife. She could not testify in court against her husband, nor could she sue him for actions against her.

A married woman could not divorce and only in extreme circumstances could she live apart from her husband. Her only basic legal right was to have her husband supply the necessities of life.[2]

In nineteenth century Canada, this was the state of the law. Reform of the law has required constructing a legal personality for married women and introducing equality for women inside the family law scheme.

Over the last century, women have gained the rights to own separate property, to make contracts, to obtain maintenance when separated from or deserted by their husbands, to have custody and parental authority with respect to their own children, to retain their own citizenship, to be dealt with as separate persons by the criminal and civil law, and to divorce and separate from their husbands.

Despite a century of change, reform is not complete; family law still trails clouds of patriarchy. At the core of woman's inequality in the family is her economic dependency. The reforms which have occurred have not altered this basic inequality, and economic inequality may render some of the reforms ineffective.

Married Women's Property Acts did not force husbands to share the family's wealth, but provided that men and women could each own their own property. Since, in general, women performed unpaid labour and men owned the property and earned the money, this reform had little effect on the lives of most women.

Nor did laws giving women equality with respect to the care and control of children alter the greater power of the father which flows from his greater financial resources and physical strength.

North American divorce laws in the twentieth century have allowed women to leave marriages, but they have not addressed the financial and emotional impact that divorce has on women, whose living standards are likely to drop and whose employment prospects are limited.

The husband's former right to "correct" his wife is now recognized as simple assault. However, women who are economically dependent may not be free to press charges against their husbands.[3]

There is no question that family law reform has improved women's equality, independence, and security; however, on average, women remain poorer than men and are often economically dependent. Giving women the same legal rights as men when they do not start from the same position of advantage may not address the continuing problems of women's inequality in the family and at marriage breakdown.

As Frances Olsen summarizes in her article "The Family and the Market; A Study of Ideology and Legal Reform", "cosmetic change

. . . fails to eliminate the ideology of sexual inequality because merely formal gender neutrality does not address actual conditions of economic dependency."[4]

Canadian women may now look to the *Charter of Rights and Freedoms* for assistance in continuing the reform of family law. In considering the changes which may be brought about through the Charter, it is important to note that achieving gender neutrality where it does not currently exist in statute law will probably be relatively easy and uncontroversial. In some circumstances, simple neutrality on the face of the law will be exactly what women want to achieve. But the contraventions of the Charter which lend themselves to this "quick fix" are, in the main, insignificant. In the most important circumstances, simple gender neutrality on the face of the law will provide only an appearance of equality. Ultimately, judicial interpretations of the Charter which will deliver actual equality and not merely juridical equality will be needed if the central issues are to be touched.

The Charter

Substantive and Interpretive Sections

There are two sections of the Charter which relate directly to equality rights for women. These are sections 15 and 28.

Section 15 of the Charter provides:

> (1) Every individual is equal before and under the law and has the right to equal protection and equal benefit of the law without discrimination based on race, national or ethnic origin, colour, religion, sex, age, or mental or physical disability.

> (2) Subsection (1) does not preclude any law, program or activity that has as its object the amelioration of conditions of disadvantaged individuals or groups including those that are disadvantaged because of race, national or ethnic origin, colour, religion, sex, age or mental or physical disability.

This is the principal section which provides equality guarantees to women. It is the substantive equality rights section.

Women played a vital role in the formulation of the language of this section of the Charter. They could not be satisfied with the simple repetition of the *Bill of Rights* guarantees of "equality before the law" and "protection of the law"[5] which was originally proposed. During the 1970s, women lost several vital challenges to discriminatory laws with the *Bill of Rights* language.[6] Because of these losses, women insisted during the Committee hearings on the Constitution that the guarantees of "equality under the law" and "equal benefit of the law" be added.

The Supreme Court's interpretation of section 15's four guarantees will determine their meaning. However, the history of the development of the section gives some clues.

According to Mr. Justice Ritchie in the 1974 *Lavell; Bedard* decision, "equality before the law" means equality in the administration and application of the law by law enforcement authorities and courts.[7] "Equality under the law", as he distinguished it then, requires equality on the face, in the provisions of the laws themselves.[8]

"Equal protection of the law" lends itself to two possible interpretations. The first is that the law must extend equal protection to all groups. It cannot, for example, protect men but not women. The second interpretation is that the laws must operate in such a way as to provide equal protection for all groups. This interpretation may allow women to claim, for example, that they do not receive "equal protection of the law" if police do not respond with equal concern to assaults on wives as to assaults on others. "Equal protection" seems to address both the coverage or reach of the law, and the operation of the law.

"Equal benefit of the law" appears to be the broadest of the guarantees. It will certainly address literal examples of failure to provide equal benefits, as contested in the *Bliss*[9] case. However, beyond addressing laws which deal with literal benefits, such as unemployment insurance and pension benefits, it is to be hoped that "equal benefit of the law" will come to be a guarantee that the results which flow from law must be equal for comparable groups.[10] If the Charter can deal with laws that have a discriminatory impact, but are not discriminatory on their face, it will probably be through this guarantee.[11]

In any particular case, it is likely that more than one of the guarantees will come into play. A gender distinction on the face of a law will violate the guarantee of "equality under the law". It may also violate the guarantee of "equal protection of the law" because it protects women but not men, or vice versa.

In addition to the four equality guarantees, section 15 has another important feature. It guarantees equality "without discrimination, *and in particular*, without discrimination based on race, national or ethnic origin, colour, religion, sex, age, or mental or physical disability." This wording has led commentators to conclude that access to the section 15 guarantees is not limited to those whose claims relate to the named grounds. It seems clear that section 15 is open-ended, and that claims can be brought that concern discrimination because of marital status, sexual orientation, criminal record or any other ground of discrimination.[12]

Section 15(2) of the Charter recognizes the validity of affirmative action programs and policies as a method to overcome the disadvantages that are experienced by groups within Canadian society because of sex, race, and disability, for example. Section 15(2) makes it impossible to argue that programs designed to end discrimination are themselves discriminatory.

Section 28 of the Charter is a vital guarantee and was included in the Charter at women's insistence.[13] It provides:

> Notwithstanding anything in this Charter, the rights and freedoms referred to in it are guaranteed equally to male and female persons.

This section has been called Canada's Equal Rights Amendment since it makes equality between sexes a fundamental value of the Constitution.

While sections 15 and 28 address sex equality issues most directly, women's rights as parents, and the rights of children[14] will also be addressed through section 7:

> Everyone has the right to life, liberty and security of the person and the right not to be deprived thereof except in accordance with the principles of fundamental justice.

The "liberty" guarantee provided in section 7 is important to women and to children since it is through this that parents may challenge State interference with the family and children may gain rights to fair procedures when they are removed from their parents or when their liberty is restricted by the State.[15]

For women and children, as for others in our society who are physically vulnerable or of lower status, such as prisoners, the mentally disabled, and the physically disabled, the protection of "security of the person" is particularly important. "Security of the person" has been interpreted to mean that one cannot be physically harmed or interfered with and may protect from interference with privacy. It may also be interpreted to include a protection for economic security.[16]

It should be noted that subsection (2) of section 32 of the Charter provides that section 15 comes into force three years after the proclamation of the Charter, on April 17, 1985. The purpose of the three-year moratorium was to allow governments to examine existing legislation and determine whether amendments needed to be made in light of these new equality guarantees.[17]

Limitations Sections

The substantive rights in sections 15 and 7 are not absolute. The Charter limits these rights through two sections: section 1 and section 33.

Section 1 provides:

> The Canadian Charter of Rights and Freedoms guarantees the rights and freedoms set out in it subject only to such reasonable limits prescribed by law as can be demonstrably justified in a free and democratic society.

The burden of proving that a limit on rights is "reasonable" and "demonstrably justified" is likely to be on the party wishing to maintain the limit. Courts may go through a two-stage analysis.[18] In the first stage, the onus will be on the party challenging an inequality in law or practice to show that an infringement of a right has occurred. In the second stage, the onus will shift to the party wishing to maintain the limit on a right to show that the limit is "reasonable" and "demonstrably justified in a free and democratic society."[19]

The other limitation section in the Charter is section 33, which provides:

> (1) Parliament or the legislature of a province may expressly declare in an Act of Parliament or of the legislature, as the case may be, that the Act or a provision thereof shall operate notwithstanding a provision included in section 2 or sections 7 to 15 of this Charter.
>
> . . .
>
> (3) A declaration made under subsection (1) shall cease to have effect five years after it comes into force or on such earlier date as may be specified in the declaration.

(4) Parliament or a legislature of a province may re-enact a declaration made under subsection (1).

This section has been dubbed the "notwithstanding" or "override" clause. It allows governments to remove laws from the purview of the Charter by exercising this legislative override. Governments can expressly declare that a law will operate notwithstanding section 15 (for example) of the Charter. If the override is used, it is valid for five years and then must be re-enacted if a government wishes to continue the law which conflicts with Charter guarantees.

This clause allows governments to keep in place existing laws which conflict with the Charter and to enact new ones which do so. However, it would be politically unwise for governments to do this in any wholesale fashion. It is generally agreed that any use of section 33 by governments should be watched carefully, since its use can render the Charter guarantees meaningless.

To date, only Quebec has used section 33. Because of Quebec's rejection of the Constitution, it has used section 33 to override the application of the Charter to all Quebec laws and practices. The Quebec *Charter of Rights and Freedoms*, which is the equivalent of other provincial human rights legislation, is Quebec's only protection for human and civil rights.

Application Section

Section 32 of the Charter provides:

(1) This Charter applies

(a) to the Parliament and government of Canada in respect of all matters within the authority of Parliament including all matters relating to the Yukon and Northwest Territories; and

(b) to the legislature and government of each province in respect of all matters within the authority of the legislature of each province.

It is clear from this section that the Charter applies to both federal and provincial governments in their law-making and administrative capacities. In addition, since municipal governments are creatures of statute it is generally accepted that the Charter will apply to municipal governments in their by-law-making and administrative capacities. Hospitals, universities, and school boards operating under statute are also likely within reach of the Charter's provisions, as are federal and provincial Crown corporations.[20]

There is debate among legal experts in Canada as to how far the Charter can reach into the "private sector".[21] However, in the area of family law the significant point is that the Charter applies to all laws, including the common law, that is, to the traditions of law built up through court decisions, as well as to the statutes.[22]

Enforcement Sections

There are two enforcement sections in the Charter: sections 24 and 52.

Section 24 provides:

> (1) Anyone whose rights or freedoms, as guaranteed by this Charter, have been infringed or denied may apply to a court of competent jurisdiction to obtain such remedy as the court considers appropriate and just in the circumstances.

This section allows a person whose rights have been infringed or denied to seek a personal remedy for the infringement of their rights.[23]

Section 52 provides:

> (1) The Constitution of Canada is the supreme law of Canada, and any law that is inconsistent with the provisions of the Constitution is, to the extent of the inconsistency, of no force or effect.

This section allows any person, whether their rights have been denied or not, to seek a declaration from a court that a law is unconstitutional because it does not meet the requirements of the Charter. In such a case, a personal remedy is not sought, but rather the striking down of a discriminatory or otherwise improper law.

In summary, family law will be affected by the application of equality rights, as expressed in sections 15 and 28, and by guarantees of liberty and security of the person, as expressed in section 7. These rights are not absolute but may be limited if the limits are "reasonable" and "demonstrably justified". The onus for proving that the limits are "reasonable" will likely rest with those who wish to maintain a limit. Charter guarantees can be overridden by governments using section

33, but they are expected to be cautious in doing so. Both personal remedies for infringements of rights and declarations that laws are unconstitutional can be sought under the Charter's provisions.

Application of the Charter to Family Law

Any discussion of particular applications of the Charter must be purely speculative at this time. Because of the moratorium which ended on April 17, 1985, only a few interpretations of sections 15 and 28 have been made by the courts. Some interpretations of section 7 have been made by courts, but section 7 interpretations applying to family law are still scanty.[24]

Some of the possible Charter violations identified here are simple ones that can be easily corrected; others are more complex and more controversial. For each of the Charter violations which is suggested there will be contrary arguments that they are not violations. Some of those contrary arguments may well carry the day should these issues come to court.

It has not been possible in preparing this paper to do a complete statute audit of all family law provisions in all Canadian jurisdictions. The provisions identified here are intended to be illustrative, not encyclopaedic. Where a provision of law which may violate the Charter has been identified in one jurisdiction, it is cited. Similar provisions may exist in other jurisdictions, or they may not. In addition, other provisions which have not been identified may also violate Charter guarantees.

Marriage

■ *Mental and Physical Disability*
Marriage acts in most jurisdictions prohibit or place restrictions on the marriage of mentally disabled persons.[25] *The Marriage Act* of Saskatchewan prohibits the marriage of persons who are mentally retarded or mentally ill or who have a specified communicable disease. Members of the clergy and marriage commissioners are required to refrain from performing marriages if they have any reason to believe that one of the couple is mentally retarded or mentally ill, and those marriage officials are guilty of an offence if they do not refrain.

These provisions appear to be straightforward violations of the section 15 guarantees of equality under the law without discrimination because of mental or physical disability. They are archaic parts of the law, based on outmoded and unfounded concerns.[26] The discussion paper issued by the Government of Saskatchewan on *Compliance of Saskatchewan's Laws with the Canadian Charter of Rights and Freedoms* recommends repeal of these provisions.[27]

■ *Consanguinity and Affinity*

Canadian marriage laws prohibit marriage between persons who are too closely related by blood (consanguinity) or too closely related by marriage (affinity). These prohibitions are derived from church law and the prohibitions are extensive.[28] The Canadian prohibitions are different from the English and the American, and the list may be over-inclusive.[29]

It may be open to a person prohibited from marrying another because of consanguinity or affinity to argue that the guarantee of equality under the law without discrimination should allow them to marry and that persons with their particular relationship to each other are being discriminated against unnecessarily.[30]

This is a more difficult Charter argument. It requires establishing the courts' acceptance of the open-ended nature of section 15 and establishing that the particular blood or marriage relationship between the persons proposing to marry is not a reasonable basis for prohibiting their marriage.

There may be an argument made under section 1 in this case, since governments will want to maintain some restrictions on who can marry whom. Restrictions *per se* will probably be considered reasonable limits. However, the onus is expected to be on governments to show that the restriction is a reasonable limit in the case of the particular relationship which a challenger presents.

■ *Sexual Orientation*

Canadian marriage is heterosexual. Marriages between persons of the same sex are not legal. Under section 15 of the Charter it may be open to lesbian women and homosexual men to contest this prohibition against marriage between persons of the same sex.

As with the argument regarding consanguinity and affinity, this will be a more difficult challenge. It will require establishing that grounds other than those named in section 15 are covered by the equality guarantees. It will also require answering section 1 arguments which will undoubtedly be made by governments interested in maintaining marriage as a heterosexual institution.[31]

Canadian legislators and courts have not been champions of the rights of gay people. This challenge will be a difficult one, not just because of some legal hurdles, but because of the political climate in which it will be made.

Maintenance and Divorce

■ *Sex Discrimination in Maintenance Acts*

The Saskatchewan *Deserted Wives' and Children's Maintenance Act* provides that a wife who has been deserted can apply to the court for maintenance for herself and her children. Under the *Dependant's Relief Act*, a wife can apply for an amount from the estate of her deceased husband which will provide maintenance for herself and her children.

Since these laws were originally enacted to extend by statute the one basic legal right of the wife in common law to be provided with the necessaries of life by her husband, the same rights to maintenance and relief were not given to deserted or dependent husbands.[32]

Like the prohibitions against the marriage of mentally or physically disabled persons in the Saskatchewan *Marriage Act*, the gender distinctions here are straightforward facial violations of the section 15 guarantee of equality under the law without discrimination because of sex. In this case, it is men who are discriminated against because they cannot claim maintenance as women can. However, amending the law to include men can also be seen to be removing the discriminatory common law presumption that women are always the dependants of their husbands. The *Saskatchewan Discussion Paper* recommends changing the wording in both instances from "wife" to "spouse" so that both men and women can use the provisions of these Acts as necessary.

■ *Adultery Bars*

Section 11 of the Saskatchewan *Deserted Wives' and Children's Maintenance Act* provides that no maintenance order can be made to assist a wife who has committed adultery. It also provides that a maintenance order can be rescinded if adultery occurs after the order is made.[33]

Again, these provisions are a simple facial violation of section 15 since they apply to wives but not to husbands and consequently violate the guarantee of "equality under the law" without discrimination based on sex.

There are two possible ways to amend these laws. The first would be to apply the same provisions to deserted spouses, male and female, as does the Newfoundland *Maintenance Act*.[34] The other, and better, alternative is repeal of these provisions so that neither a man nor a woman can be denied maintenance because of adultery.

The history of these provisions lies in the presumption that a married woman, and her sexuality, are the property of her husband. This sexist tradition is not corrected by extending its indignity to men.

The *Saskatchewan Discussion Paper* recommends repeal in these words:

> (Section 11) is inconsistent with the spirit of section 15. Firstly, its absolute nature results in harsh results (sic) and secondly, it reflects an archaic view of married women as property. Retention of the bar based on adultery would not in itself be contrary to the Charter as long as it applied equally to both husbands and wives. However, for reasons of public policy it would be preferable to repeal the section.[35]

The same problem arises in Saskatchewan law under certain sections of the *Queen's Bench Act* which allow the court to make awards of alimony and maintenance where a decree of nullity, judicial separation, restitution of conjugal rights or alimony is sought.[36] A wife who has committed adultery which is not condoned by her husband is barred from receiving an alimony award. Making the same bar apply to husbands would satisfy the Charter's requirements, but repeal is clearly preferable.[37]

■ *Maintenance for Common-Law Spouses*

There are two issues here, both of which are difficult. The first is that in some jurisdictions there do not appear to be any provisions allowing common-law spouses to claim maintenance when the spouses separate.[38] While married spouses can (or, in the case of Saskatchewan, wives can) claim maintenance on desertion or separation, common-law spouses can not.

It may be possible for common-law spouses in these jurisdictions to claim that they do not receive the 'equal protection' or 'equal benefit of the law' because of their marital status.

This may be a difficult challenge. It must be brought under the open-ended guarantee in section 15, since marital status is not a named ground. It requires making a comparison between two groups — married spouses and common-law spouses. Finally, to be effective, it requires applying the guarantees of "equal protection" and "equal benefit of the law" in such a way as to bring into existence protections for common-law spouses which do not presently exist in those jurisdictions.[39] The fact that other jurisdictions provide for maintenance for common-law spouses in their family maintenance legislation may assist in making this challenge.

The second issue regarding maintenance for common-law spouses is that in the jurisdictions where they can claim it, their right to maintenance is based on certain cohabitation periods, limitation periods during which they must apply, and, in some cases, on the presence of a child of the common-law parents.

The definitions and restrictions vary. In Ontario, for support purposes, spouses include "a man and woman not married to each other but who have cohabited continuously for a period of not less than five years, or are in a relationship of some permanence where there is a child born of whom they are the natural parents and who have so cohabited within the preceding year."[40] The most restrictive definition appears to be in Manitoba's *Family Maintenance Act* of 1978. Common-law spouses were defined there as "an unmarried man and woman who have cohabited for one year and have a child and who apply while still cohabiting or within a year of the cessation of cohabitation."[41] On July 11, 1985, the Manitoba provision was amended to bring it into compliance with section 15.[42]

Probably not all restrictions on common-law spouses are challengeable. Even if common-law spouses have to cohabit for a defined period of time, when married spouses can, technically at least, claim for maintenance the day after the wedding, this will probably be seen to be reasonable. It will be necessary to determine when a relationship between two unmarried persons becomes a relationship that should be treated like a marriage.[43]

However, some restrictions, such as the former Manitoba requirement that there be a child before there can be any claim for maintenance,[44] and the Ontario requirement of five years of cohabitation, would be challengeable.

Where provisions entitling common-law spouses to maintenance are in the law, but, it can be argued, those provisions treat common-law spouses differently and unfairly, challenges can be brought and will be easier than where laws do not address common-law spouses' right to maintenance.

Property

■ *Equality of Status of Married Persons*

Married Women's Property Acts were enacted originally to cure the common law disabilities of women with respect to holding and administering separate property and contracting independently. However, not all the common law disabilities of women have been cured. The *Saskatchewan Discussion Paper* indicates that the Saskatchewan *Married Person's Property Act* does not go far enough and needs to be replaced by a new act.

Examples of outstanding problems given in the Saskatchewan paper are:

> The domicile or permanent residence of a married woman is deemed to be that of her husband even if she is living separate and apart from him. A second example is furnished by a number of tort actions available to a husband but not to a wife. These include the right to sue a person who entices a married woman from her husband's home, who harbours or shelters her while she is away from her husband or who causes the wife injury which deprives the husband of his matrimonial rights.[45]

The inability of a married woman to establish her own domicile or permanent residence is a section 15 violation, a contravention of the guarantee of equality under the law without discrimination based on sex. The cure here is improvement of the Act which was intended to alter the common law. Men and women should have the same ability in law to establish domicile and residence.

However, the tort actions referred to raise policy questions similar to those regarding adultery being a bar to maintenance or alimony awards. Is it better to make these actions available to both men and women, or to prohibit them for both sexes?

These tort actions are claims for "loss of consortium" against a third party who commits adultery with a man's wife,[46] entices her away from her husband, or harbours or shelters her in a place separate from her husband's home.[47] "Consortium" has been said to comprise any or all of "companionship, love, affection, comfort, mutual services, and sexual intercourse".[48]

These tort actions for adultery, enticement, and harbouring are rooted in the presumption that the person and the sexuality of a woman are her husband's property. As with adultery bars, the extension of the availability of legal actions, which are inherently sexist, in the name of equality does not appear to be progress. It is preferable to prohibit these actions entirely, as Manitoba has done.

There is another right of action for "loss of consortium". This is the claim for compensation for "loss of consortium" when a spouse is injured by a third party. Where one spouse is wrongfully injured, the other spouse is able to claim, among other losses, compensation for the loss of, or damage to, the marital relationship. This action is not offensive and it may have some practical value. In Saskatchewan, this claim is presently available only to men; it should be available to spouses of both sexes.[49]

■ The Division of Matrimonial Property
The division of property at the time of marriage breakdown is a central issue for women. Since the *Murdoch* case,[50] all Canadian jurisdictions have reformed their laws respecting matrimonial property. The earlier law, as expressed in *Married Women's Property Acts*, was a separate property system dealing only with women's rights to separate holdings and separate earnings. The *Murdoch* case dramatically illustrated the unfairness of a marriage property scheme which did not recognize years of work in the home and on the farm as entitling a wife to an equal share of the property acquired during the time of the marriage.

The matrimonial property laws enacted since 1978 are an improvement. However, women are still not receiving equal shares of property at marriage breakdown.[51]

In Quebec, there are two matrimonial property schemes. Wives can opt out of the basic matrimonial property regime by becoming parties to a marriage contract. Their property rights are then determined by their contract. For those who have not opted out, the Quebec rule is:

> "Everything that spouses owned before their marriage, or acquired at any time by way of gift or inheritance, as well as personal items and tools used in their trade or profession, are separate properties that are not shared between them at any time; everything else (with the exception of pension rights) is shared equally between them at the time of their divorce."[52]

This appears to be the best scheme in the country.

The laws in other provinces have their own idiosyncracies, but they are designed according to certain standard principles which Louise Dulude describes in *Love, Marriage and Money . . . An Analysis of Financial Relations Between the Spouses*.[53] The Acts provide for

1) the equal sharing of certain categories of assets, with the categories varying from province to province; 2) entitlement to a share in a business or farm because of monetary or work contributions to it; 3) discretion for the courts to vary the shares from equal division, or to include assets in the calculation which are not in the equal sharing category.[54]

In all provinces, the principal residence and its contents, the automobile, and leisure goods fall into the category of goods to be shared. The rights to a retirement pension and registered retirement savings plans belong to the same category in some provinces and not in others.[55]

However, it is with the category of business assets and farms that there is the most difficulty. Women who are traditional home managers and child raisers are still not recognized as partners making equal contributions to the family through their unpaid labour. Only if women work outside the home or on the farm or without pay in their husbands' businesses will they be awarded half the property.[56]

The matrimonial property acts meet the guarantees of the Charter on their face, because the same provisions apply to men and women and the ostensible principle, at least with some assets, is equal sharing.

However, it may be possible to mount a Charter challenge against the categories of assets which are not subject to the equal sharing principle. For example, Ontario's scheme exempts so-called "non-family" assets from the equal sharing regime. The non-owning spouse is not entitled to any share unless she has made a direct contribution to the "acquisition, management, maintenance, operation, or improvement of (non-family) property."[57]

It can be argued that this restriction fails to provide women with the "equal protection" and "equal benefit of the law" and has a negative impact on women who are most likely to be the ones who remain at home to care for children and household management and less likely to make a direct contribution to the "non-family" assets. In order for this challenge to win, it will be necessary to persuade the courts that failing to entitle women who work in the home to an equal share of the business assets acquired during the time of marriage amounts to sex discrimination.

■ *Division of Property for Common-Law Spouses*
While common-law spouses are recognized in some jurisdictions as having a right to claim maintenance when a common-law marriage

ends, in no Canadian jurisdiction do matrimonial property schemes recognize common-law relationships.

It is not inconceivable that there are couples who have lived together in a common-law relationship for some years, accumulated property, cared for children and households, and contributed to the acquisition of assets in the same way as legally married spouses. When such a relationship ends, should the same principles for dividing the assets apply to them as apply to married persons?

A common-law spouse in such a circumstance could challenge the appropriate matrimonial property act on the grounds that it discriminates because of marital status, by not providing the same protection and benefit of the law to common-law spouses that it provides to married spouses.

As with other challenges based on common-law status, there is the difficulty of applying that part of section 15 which provides open-ended equality guarantees, since marital status is not a named ground of protection. Section 1 arguments will undoubtedly be made defending the restriction of access to these schemes to married persons.[58]

■ *Illegitimacy*
In some jurisdictions there are distinctions in law between legitimate and illegitimate children.[59]

Historically, the illegitimate child was considered at law the "child of nobody". Subsequently, the illegitimate child came to be considered the child of the mother exclusively. This status affects the illegitimate child's rights to inherit from the parents and to receive support.

The most recent commentator on this aspect of law in British Columbia is Lynn Smith.[60] She notes that while "B.C. statutes do contain a number of scattered provisions alleviating some of the harsh consequences of the common law . . . nevertheless . . . the status of illegitimacy continues to have a significant effect on rights to inheritance, to support and to recovery of damages for the death of a family member."[61]

It is Smith's view that the different and negative treatment of illegitimate children in British Columbia law will be challengeable under section 15 of the Charter.[62] Like the challenges regarding common-law status, this one will be brought under the open-ended protections of section 15 and will assert that illegitimate children do not receive "equal protection" and "equal benefit of the law".

■ *Protective Legislation Regarding Property*

The Saskatchewan *Homesteads Act*[63] and the British Columbia *Land (Wife Protection) Act*[64] prevent a husband from transferring his interest in property to anyone other than his wife without his wife's consent. This legislation is intended to protect wives from the loss of property rights.

The legislation offends section 15 since it deals with men and women differently. Since there are no similar restrictions on women, they can transfer property without the consent of their husbands.

The *Saskatchewan Discussion Paper* indicates that this Act should be amended to make it gender-neutral or it should be repealed.[65]

■ *The One-Year Rule*

In enforcing orders for maintenance, the courts have applied a "one-year rule".[66] In general, they will not order the payment of arrears of maintenance beyond one year.[67]

It may be possible to challenge this practice on the grounds that wives who are their husbands' creditors are treated differently from other creditors. Where there are court-ordered payments due, it is not usual practice to apply a "one-year rule" to the collection of payments which are in arrears.

Since the negative impact of this rule falls mainly on women, they can argue that they are not treated equally before the law nor do they receive "equal protection" or "equal benefit of the law" while this practice persists.

Custody, Access, and Adoption

■ *Custody for Fathers*

A Statistics Canada report indicates that in 85 per cent of Canadian divorces, custody of children is awarded to the mother. This has not changed over the last ten years.[68] It may be the result of judicial bias in favour of mothers, or it may reflect the agreement of both parents to the mother's custody.

In any case, it will be open to men to invoke the Charter in individual custody cases in order to argue that their right to custody must be dealt with on a footing of equality and without discrimination because of sex.

These claims will be for the protection of the guarantee of "equality before the law", since the decisions regarding custody are an exercise of the courts' discretion and any discrimination results from judicial administration of the law, not from the law itself.

■ Custody for Lesbian or Homosexual Parents

Lesbian and homosexual parents fear judicial bias against awarding custody to them. Revelation of lesbian or homosexual activity can damage parents' chances of being awarded custody of their children.[69]

It will be open to lesbian or homosexual parents in individual custody cases to invoke the Charter in order to argue that their right to custody must be dealt with without discrimination on the basis of sexual orientation. Since "sexual orientation" is not a named ground in section 15, these claims will rely on the open-ended protections and the guarantee of "equality before the law".

■ Unwed Fathers

In a recent article, Nicholas Bala and J. Douglas Redfearn argue that the section 7 protection of "liberty" is an important guarantee for both parents and children.[70]

It is their view that the concept of "liberty" means more than freedom from physical restraint. It includes the "freedom to enjoy family life" without interference by the State or others. "Liberty" can be seen to protect both the integrity of the family as an autonomous unit in society, and the right of parents to exercise parental control over their children without outside interference.[71]

The terms of section 7 of the Charter require that this "liberty" of exercising parental rights cannot be taken away "except in accordance with the principles of fundamental justice". At the very least, the principles of fundamental justice require procedural due process, which means an impartial adjudicator of the issue, adequate notice, and an opportunity to be heard.[72]

One of the applications of these section 7 liberty rights which Bala and Redfearn suggest is to the rights of unwed fathers. They refer, for example, to section 16(f) of the Manitoba *Child Welfare Act*, which provides that a child in need of protection is "a child born to parents not married to each other whose mother is unable or unwilling to care for him". The ability or willingness of the father to care for the child is not considered.[73]

Bala and Redfearn also point out that legislation regarding adoption in British Columbia and Saskatchewan requires the consent of the mother to the adoption of a child born out of wedlock, but there is no requirement that the father be notified, let alone consent.[74]

Provisions of this kind which were not made gender-neutral by April 17, 1985, can be challenged on section 15 grounds; they can also now be challenged on section 7 grounds. The section 15 argument will assert that whatever parental rights unwed mothers enjoy, unwed fathers should enjoy equally. The section 7 argument asserts that unwed fathers have a "liberty interest" in their natural parental right and they should not be deprived of it without notice and without the right to be heard on the issue of the care of their children.

The combination of these two Charter arguments seems to mean both that discriminatory provisions can be struck down and that unwed fathers can assert their right to be notified and heard when there are decisions to be made regarding the custody, protection, or adoption of their children.

■ *Foster Parents*
Bala and Redfearn suggest that foster parents who have a stable relationship with a child may also be able to assert a section 7 right not to have the child removed from their care without notice and a hearing before an impartial adjudicator. Those who care for children but are not their legal guardians have had few rights; section 7 may assist them to have their interests considered.[75]

■ *Adoption and "Protection" of Native Children*
Native peoples in Canada have been concerned for years by the practice of placing native children in non-native adoptive homes.[76] The loss of native ethos, culture, religion, and language is damaging to the children and, it is argued, undermines the strength of native communities since these children tend to lose their native identity.[77]

Native peoples may be able to challenge the placement of native children with non-native parents on the grounds that this practice does not meet the section 15 guarantees of "equal protection" and "equal benefit of the law" without discrimination because of race. Challengers can argue that the practice has the effect of discriminating on the basis of race because it damages the cultural identity of the individual child and weakens native people as a group within the Canadian mosaic.[78]

Since these decisions are made on the basis of the "best interests of the child", it will be necessary to show that it is in the best interests of native children to be raised in a native environment and to have natural access to native customs and languages.

The same concerns arise when native children are taken into the care of the State and placed in foster homes and the same challenge may be available.

Child Welfare

■ *Undue Interference by the State*

As discussed earlier, Bala and Redfearn suggest that the section 7 right to "liberty" protects parents from undue interference by the State.

The State has an interest in the welfare of children and legislation gives the State the right to "interfere" or take the child away from its parents when the child is "in need of protection". Definitions of a child in need of protection are very broad and as one commentator says, "The extreme breadth of the section(s), while necessary to encompass possible problems, is also broad enough to admit of abuse."[79]

Clearly, some limits on the liberty of parents are reasonable. However, the breadth and vagueness of the State's powers to interfere cause Bala and Redfearn some concern. They cite, for example, the Ontario *Child Welfare Act* which allows the State to remove a child if the child is "living in an unfit or improper place" and the Saskatchewan *Family Services Act* which allows a court to dispense with a parent's right to consent to an adoption if this is "in the best interests of the child". These powers may be too broad in light of section 7 since even the procedural rights to notice and hearing seem to be dispensed with.[80]

In addition, Bala and Redfearn indicate concern regarding the onus and standard of proof in protection proceedings. In some cases, the onus seems to have fallen on parents to persuade the courts that there has not been "abuse", rather than on the child welfare agency to show that the child must be removed in his or her own best interests.[81]

In sum, Bala and Redfearn argue that parents have a constitutionally protected interest in their relationship with their children and that this "liberty interest" can and will be invoked by parents in protection proceedings.[82] However, children's countervailing right to security of the person is likely to be given equal weight in consideration by the courts.

■ *Children's Right to Due Process in Protection and Adoption Proceedings*

Children have rights too, though clearly their rights are subject to many age restrictions in law. However, Bala and Redfearn suggest that children also have "liberty interests" and that in some circumstances they can exercise their "liberty interests" against the State and their parents.[83]

They argue that in child protection proceedings, for example, children stand to lose their liberty to live with their parents and face the possibility of living until adulthood in State facilities or foster homes. In these circumstances, children should be afforded procedural due process, notice, and the opportunity to be heard.[84] "A child who has the capacity to participate in a protection hearing but who is denied the right to notice and participation may well be able to challenge the proceedings as violating his 'liberty' rights under section 7 of the Charter."[85]

A similar argument can be made regarding adoption proceedings. A child who has the capacity to participate should be able to do so, and at some age it should be the child's consent which determines whether he or she will be adopted.[86]

■ *Children's Right to Liberty and Due Process at School*

The "liberty interest" may be asserted in the school setting or with representatives of the State with whom children deal. A suspension or expulsion from school or the use of corporal punishment may allow a child to invoke section 7 if these interferences with liberty are undertaken without adhering to the principles of fundamental justice.[87] The prohibitions against unreasonable search and seizure and cruel and unusual punishment are also likely to apply in the school setting. However, if the Charter is not applied to the private sector, private schools will escape the obligations of providing these protections to children.

■ *Access to Birth Control*

The capacity of children to make decisions regarding their lives is a developing one; children's right to liberty should be recognized increasingly with their capacity.

Bala and Redfearn suggest that a 15-year-old, for example, may assert her right to decide whether or not to have an abortion against her parents' wishes. In such a case, they suggest, the capacity of the child should be recognized and she ought not to be deprived of her right to exercise her "liberty" without due process.[88]

■ *Forced Sterilization of Mentally Disabled Girls and Women*

The sterilization of girls and women who are mentally disabled raises both "liberty" and "security" issues.[89] In these cases, parents or legal guardians decide that sterilization is required, sometimes because they are concerned about their daughters becoming sexually active, sometimes because they do not wish to deal with physical problems of menstruation.[90] Sterilization is an interference with the "liberty" of a woman or a girl since her capacity to have children is removed; it is also an interference with her "security of person".

The right of parents or guardians of mentally disabled girls and women to authorize their sterilization seems to have been virtually unrestrained. Mentally disabled women and girls and their advocates will be able to rely on section 7 to prevent forced sterilization and on the prohibition against cruel or unusual punishment. In addition, they will be able to rely on the section 15 guarantee of "equal protection of the law, without discrimination based on mental or physical disability", since it is likely that the forced sterilization of so-called "normal" girls would be considered a criminal act.

Other Issues

■ *Assessment of Damages*

The Saskatchewan *Automobile Insurance Act* discriminates on the basis of sex in defining "dependants". Wives are defined as "primary dependants", but husbands are only considered "primary dependants" if they are physically or mentally infirm to the extent that they cannot provide themselves with the necessaries of life. These definitions determine the amount of damages which can be collected under the Act. The *Saskatchewan Discussion Paper* suggests several different ways of defining "dependant" in a gender-neutral fashion.[91]

However, the question of sex discrimination in the assessment of damages also arises in negligence cases. The sex discrimination arises because of the devaluing of women and their work; both men and women suffer losses because of it. Though the practice is declining, when a woman claims compensatory damages for losing her husband, her financial needs may still be assessed on the basis of her prospects for remarriage. On the other hand, when a man claims compensatory damages for losing his wife or for injury to her, he may find that the functions of child-raising and house-managing are not highly valued.[92]

Claimants may be able to invoke section 15 of the Charter where the amount of damages is determined in a discriminatory way.

■ *Responsiveness to Wife-Battery Complaints*

Until recently, neither the police nor the court dealt with wife-battery on the same footing as other assaults.[93] Women have insisted that the State must be prepared to intervene to stop assaults in the family in the way it intervenes elsewhere.[94]

Any lack of responsiveness by the police or the courts can be challenged under section 15, as well as under section 7. If assaults against wives are treated differently than other assaults, that differential treatment violates the guarantee of "equal protection of the law" without discrimination because of sex and marital status.

In addition, if the fact that a wife is native or an immigrant or poor affects the responsiveness of the police or the courts, then race, ethnic origin, and economic status could be additional grounds of challenge. However, such challenges to administrative practices would have to be based on carefully accumulated and established evidence.

■ *Change of Name Act and Vital Statistics Act*

Problems with these Acts arise from the common law presumption that a married woman will take her husband's name and that any child of a married couple will have the name of the father.

Under the Saskatchewan *Change of Name Act*, a married woman is required to follow a special procedure in order to change her name to anything other than her husband's surname.[95]

The Saskatchewan *Vital Statistics Act* requires that a child of a married woman be registered in the name of the woman's husband, unless the mother makes a declaration that her husband is not the father of the child. In the absence of such a declaration the child cannot be registered in the woman's name, nor can the child be registered with the names of both parents.[96]

These provisions discriminate on the basis of sex and will be actionable under section 15, since they treat married women differently from married men.

The *Saskatchewan Discussion Paper* proposes to repeal the special procedure in the *Change of Name Act* and to allow both married women and men to use the surname of their spouse or the legal surname they used prior to marriage.

The *Saskatchewan Discussion Paper* recommends that the *Vital Statistics Act* be amended to allow a child of a married woman to be registered in the name of either the woman or her husband or in a hyphenated name which is formed from both names.[97]

Conclusion

More than vestiges of its patriarchal roots remain in family law. The disabilities of married women have not yet been cured.

Acknowledging that assaults on wives are crimes, recognizing women's right to name their children, removing adultery bars, and prohibiting actions for enticing and harbouring seem simple steps in light of the Charter's guarantees. In the main, these require simple gender neutrality.

Some moves to gender neutrality, however, while correct and necessary, should cause women some unease. Amendments to definitions of "dependants" and provisions for husbands to make financial claims on their wives can give the false impression that men and women are on an equal economic footing. This juridical equality may obscure the fact of women's continuing economic dependency and vulnerability.

The possibilities of opening the institution of marriage or its protections to those who have been excluded and of giving children and parents improved protections and "liberty" are important and positive prospects.

However, the most vital issues, such as obtaining for women equal shares of property at marriage breakdown, may be the most difficult to address through the Charter.

Shelagh Day is President of the Canadian Human Rights Reporter and former Director of the Saskatchewan Human Rights Commission.

Notes

1. Some privileged women did have trusts established for them, which provided separate property for their use.

2. Sources for this introduction are Micheline D.-Johnson, "History of the Status of Women in the Province of Quebec" and Margaret E. MacLellan, "History of Women's Rights in Canada", in *Cultural Tradition and Political History of Women in Canada*, Studies of the Royal Commission on the Status of Women (Ottawa: Information Canada, 1971); and Frances E. Olsen, "The Family and the Market: A Study of Ideology and Legal Reform", 96 *Harvard Law Review* (1983), at 1497.

3. Olsen, *supra*, n. 2, at pp. 1532-1537.

4. *Ibid.*, p. 1541.

5. Section 1(b) of the *Canadian Bill of Rights* provides:

   > It is hereby recognized and declared that in Canada there have existed and shall continue to exist without discrimination by reason of race, national origin, colour, religion or sex, the following human rights and fundamental freedoms, namely . . . (b) the right of the individual to equality before the law and the protection of the law . . .

6. These two challenges were *Attorney General of Canada v. Lavell; Isaac et al. v. Bedard*, (1974) 38 D.L.R. (3d) 481; and *Bliss v. Attorney General of Canada*, [1979] 1 S.C.R. 183. The first of these was a challenge to section 12 (1)(b) of the *Indian Act*. 12(1)(b) provided that women lose their Indian status when they marry non-Indian men, but Indian men who marry non-Indian women confer their Indian status on them. Despite the blatant inequity of this provision, the Supreme Court of Canada found that there was no violation of the equality guarantees of the Bill of Rights. Justice Ritchie in his decision indicated that "equality before the law" was a procedural guarantee, a protection of equality in the administration of the law, not in the substance of the law. "Equality before the law" was protected, "equality under the law" was not.

   The second major challenge was the *Bliss* case. Stella Bliss's claim for regular unemployment insurance benefits was denied because she was pregnant, even though she qualified for regular benefits and was available for work. Bliss had the correct number of insured weeks for regular benefits, but not the correct number to qualify for UIC maternity benefits. Her claim for regular benefits was denied because she was pregnant and during the period before and after childbirth women were only entitled to collect maternity benefits. Bliss challenged the denial alleging that she was treated differently because she was a woman.

   The Supreme Court of Canada ruled that the denial of regular benefits did not violate Bliss's right to "equality before the law" because the distinctions made in unemployment insurance regulations "involved a definition of the qualifications required for entitlement to benefits."

   Apparently, because in this case a benefit rather than a penalty was at issue, "equality before the law" did not apply.

7. *Lavell; Bedard, supra*, n. 6, at p. 495. "Section 1(b) of the Bill of Rights is to be treated as meaning equality in the administration or application of the law by the law enforcement authorities and the ordinary courts of the land."

8. Walter S. Tarnopolsky, "The Equality Rights", in *Canadian Charter of Rights and Freedoms: Commentary*, eds. Tarnopolsky and Beaudoin (Toronto: Carswell, 1982), p. 421.

9. *Bliss v. Attorney General of Canada*, [1979] 1 S.C.R. 183.

10. Under money purchase pension plans and some optional forms of defined benefit plans, women who have made the same contributions as men similarly situated receive lower periodic pension benefits. There is a statistical probability that the 'average' woman will live

longer than the 'average' man, and therefore that the 'average' woman will receive benefits from pensions or annuities for a longer time. In order to deal with this, some plans calculate payments on the basis of sex-based mortality tables and reduce the amount of monthly benefit for women in order to adjust for the predicted total cost.

Some women live longer than the 'average' man; however, most do not. The practice of paying women lower periodic payments penalizes all women because of the small number of women who live longer. The need to predict the cost of plans for women as a class does not justify the unequal results of the practice for individual women.

Risk classification based on sex which results in higher premiums or lower periodic pension benefits to women has been challenged in the United States recently. See: *City of Los Angeles, Department of Water and Power et al. v. Marie Manhart et al.*, 16 E.P.D. 8250 (1978), and *Arizona Governing Committee for Tax Deferred Annuity and Deferred Compensation Plans v. Norris*, 103 S.Ct. 3492.

The only Canadian treatment of this issue is the 1976 decision of an Alberta Board of Inquiry in the matter of *Shandrowski v. Alberta Motor Association* (unpublished decision). All three decisions cited here ruled that using sex as a basis for risk classification results in discrimination. It seems clear that, where pension plans come within the purview of the Charter, the payment of lower periodic pension benefits to women is challengeable under section 15.

11. In numerous Canadian and American human rights decisions, discrimination has been identified by its impact, effect or results rather than by the motivation of the discriminator or the overt discriminatory nature of the impugned action. This allows the law to deal with practices which are neutral on their face, but discriminatory in practice.

Practices found to be discriminatory in this way are height and weight requirements for police officers, which have the effect of excluding the majority of women, and dress codes which have the effect of excluding members of the Sikh religion from work opportunities because of the Sikh religious requirement that they wear a turban.

These practices are not discriminatory on their face because they are seemingly neutral job requirements applied to everyone in the same manner. However, the effect of requirements that police officers be five feet nine inches tall and weigh 140 pounds or that security officers wear caps is to exclude the majority of women and Sikhs from these jobs.

It is to be hoped that an understanding of the discriminatory impact of practices which seem neutral will illuminate the courts' interpretation of section 15. Some legal provisions and government practices will only be challengeable if this definition of discrimination by impact, effect or results is applied.

For example, the provisions which apply to domestic workers in labour standards and human rights legislation have a discriminatory impact on women. In many jurisdictions, domestic workers are specifically exempted from labour standards or human rights legislation, or different and less stringent standards apply. Where this is the case, these workers do not enjoy the same protections with respect to minimum wage, hours of work, and protection from discrimination that other workers enjoy.

Since domestic workers are mainly women, the impact of these lesser protections is felt mainly by women. On the face of the law, "domestic workers" is not a sex-based classification; therefore, the law can be said to be neutral. The effect of the law, however, is to discriminate against women.

This discrimination can only be remedied under the Charter if "equal protection of the law" and "equal benefit of the law" are interpreted in such a way as to address the effects of laws as well as any lack of neutrality on the face of laws.

12. See, for example: Lynn Smith, "Charter Equality Rights: Some General Issues and Specific Applications in British Columbia to Elections, Juries and Illegitimacy", 18 *U.B.C. Law Review* (1984), at 405, and Dale Gibson, *Impact of Canadian Charter of Rights and Freedoms on Manitoba Statutes* (Winnipeg: Legal Research Institute of the University of Manitoba, 1982), p. 10.

13. For a brief history of the women's lobbying efforts to ensure the inclusion of section 28, see: Penney Kome, *The Taking of 28: Women Challenge the Constitution* (Toronto: Women's Press, 1983).

14. See: Nicholas Bala and J. Douglas Redfearn, "Family Law and the 'Liberty Interest': Section 7 of the Canadian Charter of Rights", 15 *Ottawa Law Review* (1983), at 274.

15. *Ibid.*

16. Gibson, *Impact of Canadian Charter, supra*, n. 12, at p. 7.

17. The fact that only section 15 was made subject to such a moratorium seems to indicate that governments felt there was considerable examination and revision to laws necessary to meet the requirements of the new equality guarantees. However, government performance on the audit and revision of laws is disappointing.

    By the end of 1984, only the government of Saskatchewan had published a discussion paper indicating which laws are in need of revision. Other governments provided no time for public comment or for lobbying for further reform before section 15 came into effect.

    In addition, the principal techniques which appear to have been used by governments are computer key word searches and simple scanning of statutes. These techniques are designed to identify discrimination which is explicit in the text of laws. Discrimination which occurs because of the impact or effect of laws is not likely to be identified by these means.

18. See: Mary Eberts, "Equality Rights under the Canadian *Charter of Rights and Freedoms* and the Statutes of Canada", Status of Women Canada, 1983 (unpublished document), pp. 57-58, and Herbert Marx, "Entrenchment, Limitations and Non-Obstante", in *Canadian Charter of Rights and Freedoms: Commentary*, eds. Tarnopolsky and Beaudoin (Toronto: Carswell, 1982), p. 73.

19. Eberts, *supra*, n. 18, at p. 58.

20. Dale Gibson, "The Charter of Rights and the Private Sector", 12 *Manitoba Law Review* (1982), at 213.

21. *Ibid.* See also: Smith, *supra*, n. 12, and Katherine Swinton, "Application of the Canadian *Charter of Rights and Freedoms*", in *Canadian Charter of Rights and Freedoms: Commentary*, eds. Tarnopolsky and Beaudoin (Toronto: Carswell, 1982), p. 41.

22. See: Smith, *supra*, n. 12, at pp. 354-364.

23. As distinct from section 52, section 24 allows for personal remedies to the victims of unconstitutional laws or practices. These remedies may include costs, damages, or any other measure which the court deems appropriate. It is to be hoped that remedial orders will include the institution of affirmative action programs as provided for in section 15(2).

24. In *Re: T and Catholic Children's Aid Society of Metropolitan Toronto*, May 14, 1984, 26 A.C.W.S. (2d) 86 (Ont. Prov. Ct. (Fam. Div.)), the court held that the rights to liberty and security of the person protected by section 7 include the right to individual privacy or family autonomy and the parental right to be free from State interference.

25. For discussion of this issue, see: Bret Mecredy-Williams, "Marriage Law and the Mentally Retarded", 2 *Canadian Journal of Family Law* (1979), at 63. Mecredy-Williams identifies prohibitive or restrictive provisions regarding the marriage of mentally disabled persons as follows: Prince Edward Island — *Marriage Act*, R.S.P.E.I. 1974, c. M-5, s. 23; Quebec — *Civil Code*, Title V, c. III, art. 142; Ontario — *The Marriage Act*, 1977, S.O. 1977, c.42, s.7; Manitoba — *The Marriage Act*, R.S.M. 1970, C. M-50, s.23 as amended by 1970, c.11; Saskatchewan — *The Marriage Act*, R.S.S. 1965, c.338, s.55, as amended by 1976-77, c.46, s. 21; Alberta — *The Marriage Act*, R.S.A. 1970, c.226, s. 27, as amended by 1975(2), c.64, s. 3; British Columbia — *Marriage Act*, R.S.B.C. 1960, c.232, s. 39.

26. Mecredy-Williams suggests that the prohibitions or restrictions upon the marriage of mentally disabled persons stem from society's contradictory attitudes towards mentally disabled persons' sexuality and from fears that mentally disabled persons will produce mentally disabled children. The move towards normalization and integration for mentally disabled persons should encourage us to accept their sexuality as part of normal living. In addition, the risk of mentally retarded children being born of mentally retarded parents is minimal. Mentally disabled persons who marry and have children may need community support systems to aid them with family life but prohibiting marriage or preventing reproduction is punitive and unnecessary.

27. *Compliance of Saskatchewan Laws with the Canadian Charter of Rights and Freedoms*, Discussion Paper released by the Honourable J. Gary Lane, Q.C., Minister of Justice and Attorney-General, September 1984.

28. Canadian prohibitions are based on Archbishop Parker's Table of 1563. See: *CCH Family Law Guide*, paragraphs 1195 and 2150 re: Capacity to Marry. The prohibitions are as follows: A man may not marry his grandmother, grandfather's wife, wife's grandmother, aunt, uncle's wife, wife's aunt, mother, step-mother, wife's mother, daughter, wife's daughter, son's wife, sister, granddaughter, grandson's wife, wife's granddaughter, niece, nephew's wife, wife's niece, or his brother's wife. A woman may not marry her grandfather, grandmother's husband, husband's grandfather, uncle, aunt's husband, husband's uncle, father, step-father, husband's father, son, husband's son, daughter's husband, brother, grandson, granddaughter's husband, husband's grandson, nephew, niece's husband, husband's nephew, or her husband's brother.

29. James G. McLeod, *Introduction to Family Law* (Toronto: Butterworth & Co., 1983), p. 10.

30. Gibson, *Impact of Canadian Charter, supra*, n. 12, at p. 127.

31. Marriage is on the one hand a matter of sentiment and, on the other hand, a matter of economics. Lesbian women or homosexual men may wish to marry for sentimental reasons or because they wish to gain the economic protections of maintenance and divorce laws and enjoy the benefits of income tax and inheritance provisions which apply between spouses.

The State does not prevent persons of the same sex from living together, having sexual relations, or sharing child care responsibilities and economic assets. However, governments may consider it threatening to the heterosexual family if these 'same-sex families' are deemed to be legitimate in law.

This issue is discussed by Harvey Brownstone in his article "The Homosexual Parent in Custody Disputes", 5 *Queen's Law Journal* (1980), at 236-237. He says: ". . . a growing faction of the homosexual community argues that access to the institution of marriage ought to be extended to homosexual couples. They contend that the traditional arguments against permitting gay marriages are no longer valid; the fundamental purposes of marriage extend beyond procreation. After all, sterile people are allowed to marry. Modern perceptions of the marital relationship characterize it as primarily an emotional and economic bond between two persons. Society's interest in promoting marriage derives from the notion that stability and moral order will be inherent consequences of monogamous partnerships. Gay activists are arguing that these same attributes of marriage can exist whether the parties are of the opposite sex or of the same sex . . ."

32. *Saskatchewan Discussion Paper, supra*, n. 27, at pp. 18-19.

33. *Ibid.*, p. 19.

34. *Maintenance Act*, R.S.N. 1970, c. 223, s. 7(1).

35. *Saskatchewan Discussion Paper, supra*, n. 27, at p. 19.

36. *The Queen's Bench Act*, R.S.S. 1978, C. Q-1, as amended, Ss. 29-38.

THE CHARTER AND FAMILY LAW

37. *Saskatchewan Discussion Paper*, *supra*, n. 27, at p. 22.

38. Neither the Northwest Territories nor Saskatchewan appear to provide for maintenance for common-law spouses.

39. This could be accomplished by the courts striking down the laws in these jurisdictions which deal with entitlement to maintenance, thereby forcing law reform on the appropriate legislators. Alternatively, it might be accomplished by the courts awarding remedies under section 24 to common-law spouses, thereby making it clear that Charter litigation can be avoided by amending the troublesome statute.

40. *Family Law Reform Act*, R.S.O. 1980, c. 152, s. 14(1).

41. *Family Maintenance Act*, S.M. 1978, c.25, s. 11.

42. See also: Robert Carr, "A Report on the State of Family Law in Manitoba, Recommendations for Change", Report prepared for the Honourable Roland Penner, Q.C., Attorney-General of Manitoba, May 1982, at p. 108-109. Carr finds the Manitoba provision regarding maintenance for common-law spouses "unduly harsh". He recommends that there should be circumstances where common-law spouses can apply for maintenance even when there is no child. However, he recommends following the Ontario model and requiring five years of cohabitation.

43. Section 1 arguments may be made on the grounds that distinctions should be kept between the obligations of married and common-law spouses. Some people choose not to marry for precisely the reason that they do not wish to become entangled in the web of State-defined obligations. Their choice would amount to no choice if the same obligations were imposed on them in any case. On the other hand, living in a common-law relationship should not allow spouses to avoid consideration of each other's economic needs as soon as the relationship is ended.

44. The Manitoba restriction on entitlement to maintenance for common-law spouses is also noted as a possible Charter violation by Dale Gibson in his book, *Impact of Canadian Charter of Rights and Freedoms on Manitoba Statutes*, at p. 78. However, his approach is slightly different. He suggests that the provision "would seem to be reasonable if the requirements of a year's cohabitation and a child were alternatives, but it is questionable whether it is a reasonable limit to deny a cohabitant spousal rights if there is a child, but a year has not elapsed."

45. *Saskatchewan Discussion Paper*, *supra*, n. 27, at p. 21.

46. Stella Bailey, "A Married Woman's Rights of Action For Loss of Consortium in Alberta", 17 *Alberta Law Review* (1979), at 513. At p. 523, Bailey quotes Mr. Justice McRuer's explanation in *Frampton v. Whiteman*, [1954] O.R. 32 (H.C.) of the rationale for not making this action available to women. "The adultery of the wife might impose a spurious issue upon the husband, which he might be called upon to dedicate a part of his fortune to educate and provide for; whereas no such injustice could result to his wife from the adultery of a married man."

47. At p. 525, Bailey quotes Mr. Justice Devlin in *Winchester v. Fleming* (1958 I.Q.B. 259) explaining the tort action for "harbouring": "the reason why harbouring was considered objectionable was because it interfered with the economic process by which a wife, refused food and shelter elsewhere than in the matrimonial home, would eventually be forced to return to it."

48. *Ibid.*, p. 530.

49. *Ibid.*, p. 531. Bailey concludes: "In 1973 a married woman in Alberta was given a statutory right of action for damages against a person who enticed away her husband, harboured him, committed adultery with him or injured him. In giving a married woman such a right of

action, one which her husband had enjoyed since 1927, the government gave little thought to why she should have it. It is submitted that had the government done a more complete analysis, it would have come to the conclusion that neither husband nor wife should have a right of action against a person who entices away, harbours or commits adultery with the other spouse, but that both spouses should have a right of action for loss of consortium where the other spouse has been injured by a third party."

Note, however, that S.M. Waddams in *The Law of Damages* (Toronto: Canada Law Book Ltd., 1983), at pp. 175-177 proposes a different resolution of the inequity of the action for injury being available only to husbands. "The action is available to a husband only, and its survival is undoubtedly out of keeping with the modern view of family relationships. The appropriate solution, as elsewhere, appears to be to permit the injured person to recover in full in her own right for lost earning capacity, with the consequence that the husband's action will become obsolete . . . . If an injured person of either sex, whether or not resident in the home, is able to recover in full for his or her lost earning capacity . . . then there is little justification for a separate action by the uninjured spouse. Even if the common law action were extended to both sexes, there would be difficulties, in the light of modern family relationships, in restricting recovery to spouses in the strict sense."

50. *Murdoch v. Murdoch* (1977) 26 R.F.L. 1.

51. Louise Dulude, *Love, Marriage and Money . . . An Analysis of Financial Relations Between the Spouses* (Ottawa: Canadian Advisory Council on the Status of Women, 1984), pp. 31-53.

52. *Ibid.*, p. 33.

53. *Ibid.*

54. *Ibid.*, p. 34.

55. *Ibid.*, p. 35. Pension rights are in the equal sharing category in British Columbia, Alberta, Manitoba, and New Brunswick, but not in Saskatchewan, Ontario, Quebec, Nova Scotia, Prince Edward Island, and Newfoundland. RRSPs are in the equal sharing category in British Columbia, Alberta, Saskatchewan, Manitoba, Quebec, and New Brunswick, but not in Ontario, Nova Scotia, Prince Edward Island or Newfoundland.

56. *Ibid.*, pp. 36-38.

57. McLeod, *supra*, n. 29, at p. 77.

58. *Supra*, n. 41. See also: Carr, *supra*, n. 44, at p. 109. Carr states his view that common-law relationships are not marriages and lesser protections for common-law spouses are reasonable.

59. Distinctions between legitimate and illegitimate children have been the subject of recommendations for law reform in British Columbia and Manitoba, but they have not been eliminated. See: *The Status of Children Born to Unmarried Parents*, Fifth Report of the Royal Commission on Family and Children's Law, Vancouver, British Columbia, 1975. See also: Carr, *supra*, n. 44, at pp. 5-15. See also: Gibson, *Impact of Canadian Charter, supra*, n. 12, at p. 66. It is also important to note that Douglas Sanders in *Family Law and Native People*, Background paper for the Law Reform Commission of Canada, 1975, and the British Columbia Royal Commission on Family and Children's Law indicate that provisions making distinctions between legitimate and illegitimate children create additional difficulties for native and Indian people, among whom the incidence of common-law marriages appears to be higher. In addition to other problems, Sanders indicates that illegitimacy affects a child's Indian status.

60. Smith, *supra*, n. 12, at p. 397.

61. *Ibid.*, p. 398.

62. *Ibid.*, p. 405. Smith notes, however, that some discrimination against illegitimate children arises from common law rules, not statutes; consequently, the view the courts take regarding sections 32 and 52 will determine whether challenges can be made to the discrimination which arises from the common law.

63. *Saskatchewan Discussion Paper*, p. 20.

64. R.S.B.C. 1979, c. 223.

65. *Saskatchewan Discussion Paper*, p. 20.

66. McLeod, *supra*, n. 29, at p. 23-24.

67. *Ibid.* McLeod explains that the purpose of the one-year rule is to prevent wives from 'hoarding' maintenance payments.

68. D.C. McKie, B. Prentice, and P. Reed, *Divorce: Law and the Family in Canada*, prepared for Statistics Canada (Ottawa: Supply and Services Canada, 1983), as cited in Dulude, p. 27.

69. See: Brownstone, *supra*, n. 31. Brownstone cites the *Case v. Case* (1974) 18 R.F.L. 132 (Sask. Q.B.), in which the court denied Mrs. Case custody of her children on the grounds that her social life, which included participation in gay organizations, would be detrimental to the children.

70. Bala and Redfearn, *supra*, n. 14. The decision in *Re: T*, cited at *supra*, n. 24, supports this view.

71. *Ibid.*, pp. 276-282.

72. *Ibid.*, pp. 282-288.

73. *Ibid.*, p. 289.

74. *Ibid.*

75. *Ibid.*, p. 291.

76. Sanders, *supra*, n. 59, at pp. 139-140.

77. For more recent comment on this issue, see: John A. MacDonald, "The Spallumcheen Indian Band By-law and Its Potential Impact on Native Indian Child Welfare Policy in British Columbia", 4 *Canadian Journal of Family Law* (1983), at 75.

78. The Charter provides support for this challenge in sections other than section 15. Section 27 provides that the Charter "shall be interpreted in a manner consistent with the preservation and enhancement of the multicultural heritage of Canadians." As well, sections 25, 35, and 27 all recognize aboriginal peoples as a distinct group with special needs and rights. These sections of the Charter indicate that the maintenance of diverse cultures in Canada is a value underwritten by the Constitution and they may be used to bolster a challenge regarding the adoption and placement of native children in non-native homes.

79. Mcleod, *supra*, n. 29, at p. 131.

80. Bala and Redfearn, *supra*, n. 14, at p. 304.

81. *Ibid.*, pp. 305-308.

82. *Ibid.*, p. 309.

83. *Ibid.*, p. 293.

84. *Ibid.*, p. 295.

85. *Ibid.*, p. 296.

86. See: Carr, *supra*, n. 44, at p. 103, for discussion of this issue in the Manitoba context.

87. Bala and Redfearn, *supra*, n. 14, at p. 297.

88. *Ibid.*, pp. 298-299.

89. For discussion of sterilization of mentally retarded persons, see: Mecredy-Williams, *supra*, n. 25, at pp. 76-79.

90. In the case of *Re: Eve* (1980) 74 A.P.R. 97 and (1981) 79 A.P.R. 359, the Prince Edward Island Court of Appeal authorized the sterilization of a 24-year-old mentally retarded woman. The sterilization is for contraceptive purposes, since the mother of Eve believes her daughter may become sexually active. The Court of Appeal decision overturned the P.E.I. Supreme Court's refusal to authorize the sterilization on the grounds that it had no jurisdiction to order sterilization for purely contraceptive reasons. This decision is presently under appeal to the Supreme Court of Canada.

In British Columbia, the parents of Infant K. sought the permission of the B.C. Supreme Court to have a hysterectomy performed on their 10-year-old mentally retarded daughter. The parents indicated that Infant K. has an intense fear of blood and they were concerned that she would react adversely when menstruation began. The Public Trustee opposed the request arguing that the parents are asking for the right to perform a hysterectomy on the basis of speculation and that every alternative method for dealing with the girl's aversion to blood should be exhausted first. The B.C. Supreme Court turned down the parents' request. On appeal, the B.C. Court of Appeal allowed the parents to proceed with the hysterectomy.

91. *Saskatchewan Discussion Paper*, *supra*, n. 27, at pp. 27-28.

92. See: Waddams, *supra*, n. 49, at pp. 174-176, 234-236, 407, and 422-424. As indicated above, Waddams argues that the injured person, whether man or woman, should be able to recover for loss of his or her own earning capacity. He suggests that in order for the damages to be calculated in a non-discriminatory manner, it will be necessary for the courts to consider that the value of the lost earning capacity is not diminished because the injured person has chosen to perform unpaid household services rather than working outside the home.

Where a death is involved, Waddams indicates that the position in Canada is that the trial judge must give consideration to the prospect of the claimant's remarriage. However, if the judge chooses to consider the prospect of remarriage a minimal factor in determining damages, the judgement will probably stand. Waddams points out that legislation was enacted in England in 1971 precluding the courts from taking account of the prospects of remarriage, or the actual remarriage of a widow, in assessing damages. As well, under the *Fatal Accidents Act* in Prince Edward Island, the marriage of any claimant is excluded from factors which can be considered in assessing damages.

93. Olsen, *supra*, n. 2, at pp. 1531-1532.

94. See: Laurie Woods, "Litigation on Behalf of Battered Women", 5 *Women's Rights Law Reporter* (1978), at 7. Woods discusses the case of *Bruno v. Codd*, 90 Misc. 2d 1047, 1048, 396 N.Y.S. 2d 974, 975 (Sup. Ct. 1977), rev'd, 64 A.D. 2d 582, 407 N.Y.S. 2d 165 (1978), aff'd, 47 N.Y. 2d 582, 393 N.E. 2d 976, 419 N.Y.S. 2d 901 (1979); a class action suit brought by twelve battered women against the New York City Police, the New York City Department of Probation, and the clerks of the Family Court. The suit alleged that the respondents engaged in a pattern and practice of denying abused wives legal protection and assistance to which they were entitled under state law. The women alleged failure or refusal by the police to respond to calls for assistance, failure to arrest abusing husbands, and denial of access to court. In 1978, the New York Police Department entered into a consent judgement with the women.

95. *Saskatchewan Discussion Paper, supra*, n. 27, at p. 10.

96. *Ibid.*, p. 16.

97. In Gibson, *Impact of Canadian Charter, supra*, n. 12, the same problems with the Manitoba *Change of Name Act* and *Vital Statistics Act* are noted at pp. 46-47 and 147.

Tax and Family Laws:
A Search for Consistency

— Louise Dulude

In principle, under Canadian income tax law a married couple has always been taxed as two separate individuals. Canada's "progressive" tax system makes the independent taxation of spouses beneficial. However, although in principle it is an independent system, a number of exceptions exist which alter and essentially jeopardize the nature of the system. Briefly, these exceptions are: transferable benefits, the attribution rules, and the spousal exemption.

The author examines the effect of taxation on the family. As economic power is one of the things women so frequently lack, she discusses various means of amending Canada's income tax laws to try to equalize the economic power between the spouses. What is needed, the author concludes, is a closer alignment between the economic provisions of the Income Tax Act and the reality of married life for women.

Why study tax issues in the context of family law? The reason is that other than laws relating to matrimonial property and family maintenance, the *Income Tax Act* is the main source of rules affecting the financial rights of spouses over their respective incomes and properties.

How does Canada's tax Act affect spousal rights over income and property? What are the basic principles that underlie the treatment of married couples in our tax laws? Are these principles consistent with the way in which family members are treated under our matrimonial property and maintenance rules? If they are not consistent, should something be done about it? These are the questions that will be explored.

Marriage Under Canada's Tax Laws

The three main decision areas regarding the tax treatment of married couples are: the choice of the tax unit, the treatment of homemakers' work, and the tax treatment of divorced spouses. In each of these areas, the choices made by Canadian legislators and the effects of these choices on women's lives will be examined.

The Choice of the Tax Unit

Visitors from the United States sometimes say that the way Canada taxes family members is "different", or "peculiar", or "interesting". The reason they are intrigued is that the American income tax system considers the spouses as a single unit instead of treating them as separate entities as is done in Canada. As a result, if both spouses in a Canadian couple have a personal income, each of them files a tax return, while almost all Americans in the same situation file only one joint return on which their two incomes are combined for the purpose of calculating their tax.

Both the Carter Commission on Taxation (1966) and the Royal Commission on the Status of Women (1970) recommended the implementation of an American-style joint taxation system in Canada. The Carter Commission justified its choice as follows:

> We believe firmly that the family is today, as it has been for many centuries, the basic economic unit in society. Although few marriages are entered into for purely financial reasons, it is the continued income and financial position of the family which is ordinarily of primary concern, not the income and financial position of the individual members. Thus, the married couple itself adopts the economic concept of the family as the income unit from the outset.[1]

The Royal Commission on the Status of Women (RCSW) did not give much of an explanation for its position, saying only that the marriage unit was "a logical basis for taxing the income of a married couple."[2] It seems that the RCSW supported joint taxation primarily because it would have solved the then-burning issue of the non-deductibility of salaries paid to people who worked with their spouses in unincorporated businesses and farms. The problem in that case was the Revenue Department's fear that if salaries paid to spouses were recognized by the tax system, millions of couples would artificially arrange their affairs to take advantage of it to reduce their income tax.

A tax saving can result from splitting a family's income between the spouses because of Canada's progressive tax rates, under which one person who makes a given amount of income will pay more tax than two people who each make half as much. This means, for example, that two spouses who each declare $25,000 of income pay considerably less tax overall than if only one of them declares the full $50,000. This problem does not exist under joint taxation, because in that system the tax is calculated on the basis of the spouses' total income, without regard to the way it is divided between them.

The decision of the RCSW to support joint taxation of the spouses was not unanimous. Elsie Gregory McGill, an RCSW member, wrote a strong dissent stating that joint taxation contradicted their report's main thrust about "the importance of the independence of the individual".[3] When the federal government responded to the Carter Commission proposals, it also rejected joint taxation because:

> . . . the commission's proposed family unit tax would have imposed a "tax on marriage" — that is, a husband and wife each having an income would together pay more tax than two people with the same incomes who were not married. This we felt to be unfair and undesirable, at least for small and medium incomes. Even then, however, a wife who goes to work would have her income added to the husband's income and in effect taxed at the rates that would apply if his income were increased by the amount of her income.[4]

Anti-joint taxation feelings grew increasingly stronger during the 1970s as more and more studies disproved the Carter Commission's contention that the higher tax rates usually produced by joint taxation would have no disincentive effect on the labour force participation of wives.[5] That, and growing feminist sentiment against joint taxation because it denies the separate existence of married women,[6] led to strong pressure on countries which had joint taxation systems to change over to individual taxation or to introduce special tax reductions for "secondary" earners.

As a result, between 1970 and 1976, six European countries switched from joint to separate taxation of the earned income of married couples.[7] In 1981, the United States introduced a new deduction for the lower income spouse.[8]

When the last official examination of Canada's tax unit was done in 1975-76 by the Interdepartmental Committee on the Taxation of Women, the federal Coordinator for the Status of Women took the following position:

> Joint returns are an idea whose time has passed. During the 1950's and 60's when most wives worked in the home, it would perhaps have been a better tax system than individual returns. In the 1970's, however, when the government is making such efforts to improve the status of women by recognizing them as individuals outside the family unit, it would seem a retrograde step . . . [9]

This was reinforced by a 1977 statement by the Canadian Advisory Council on the Status of Women which opposed the introduction of joint taxation of the spouses in Canada because it would "have the effect of reducing the independent financial security of married women who have personal sources of income."[10] The Council did not completely close the door to joint taxation, however, saying that "it might prove to be the ideal system in a society where spouses enjoyed full financial equality and were true economic partners." But, it added, "a great deal remains to be done before women can achieve equality within the institution of marriage" in Canada.[11]

In spite of all the above, the truth is that the Canadian tax system contains many features that violate the principle of "the independence of the individual". The main exceptions to the independent treatment of the spouses are: the *spousal exemption*, which is claimed by married people whose spouses have little or no personal income (this will be analysed in the next section dealing with the treatment of homemakers' work); *transferable benefits*, which can be claimed by a spouse if the other one is not in a position to do so; and *attribution rules*, which deny the validity of transfers of income and property between spouses.

■ *Transferable Benefits*

In spite of the federal government's 1969 decision to maintain individual taxation, the next few years saw the subtle erosion of this principle through the introduction of several tax provisions aimed at married couples. Introduced between 1971 and 1975, these provisions allow a spouse to claim in his or her own name a whole series of tax benefits to which only the other spouse would normally be entitled. In general, this means that a spouse can use these transferable benefits to

66

reduce his or her taxable income when the personal income of the other spouse — who is entitled to them — is too low for her or him to benefit from them. In practice, it is almost always husbands who claim the unused deductions of their homemaking wives.

The following tax benefits have thus become transferable between spouses:

■ The age exemption for people aged 65 and over: $2,480 in 1984.

■ The education exemption: $50 per month of full-time study.

■ The deduction for blind and disabled persons: $2,480.

■ The pension income deduction: maximum of $1,000.

■ The deduction for interest, dividends, and capital gains from Canadian sources: maximum of $1,000.

■ The tax credit for dividends from Canadian corporations. To claim this transferable credit, a spouse must include in his or her taxable income the dividends of the other spouse (increased to 150%).

■ Deduction of the amounts a taxpayer deposits in a Registered Retirement Savings Plan (RRSP) *in the name of the other spouse*. This does not affect the immediate tax position of the donor since his/her maximum RRSP deduction under both his/her own and the other spouse's plans remains the same.

These measures have been criticized on various counts:

■ With the exception of the spousal RRSP deduction, which depends on a real transfer of economic power between the spouses, they all assume that married couples form an economic unit so that if one spouse benefits, the other does also. In reality, in none of these cases is the wife legally entitled to a penny of the tax her husband saves because of her.

■ The first five are exemptions or deductions, which provide benefits that rise in value as taxpayers' incomes increase. This is because higher income taxpayers pay a larger percentage of their income in tax, which is why Canada's tax system is called "progressive". As a result, an exemption or deduction that reduces a rich person's taxable income is worth more than the same reduction in the taxable income of a person who makes less, and results in no savings to someone who is too poor to owe any tax.

■ The fact that the husband loses these benefits if the wife takes outside employment can have a discouraging effect on her decision to work outside the home. This is because: a) the husband will be more reticent toward her taking a paid job; and b) she will derive less value from these benefits than he does because of her lower tax rate.

- Transferable age and disability benefits are discriminatory toward people who support elderly or disabled relatives who are not their spouses. [12]

The only Canadian women's groups that made recommendations on these measures are the Quebec Status of Women Council and the Réseau d'action et d'information pour les femmes (RAIF). Both proposed that transferable tax benefits be abolished because they do more harm than good to women. [13] The only exception was the spousal RRSP deduction, which the Council believes should be retained.

■ *Attribution Rules*
The introduction in 1974 of the spousal RRSP deduction marked the first time Canadian tax laws recognized a transfer of property between husbands and wives. The only other instance was the 1980 amendment that finally allowed the deduction of salaries paid to spouses in unincorporated family businesses and farms, as well as the recognition of business partnerships between spouses.

Other than that, the general rule under our *Income Tax Act* still is to pretend that transfers of property between spouses did not take place at all. The philosophy underlying this rule is the old common law principle that the spouses are one, so that "the allocation of legal rights within the family is a trivial matter." [14] The practical reason for embedding this principle in our tax laws was the desire to prevent tax avoidance by spouses who could split their assets and income between them to minimize their tax. As previously discussed, this can happen because of Canada's progressive tax rates, under which the splitting of an amount of income between two or more taxpayers produces substantial tax savings.

The main provisions which negate transfers between spouses are the so-called "attribution" rules, which are in sections 74 and 75 of the *Income Tax Act*. Under these rules, if a rich husband gives half of his fortune outright to his penniless wife, for example, Revenue Canada will pay no attention to the gift and *he* will continue to owe tax for the rest of his life on the income she derives from it. (If he does not pay, she can be held liable.) The same principle applies to the taxation of capital gains generated by property transferred between spouses.

In practice, these attribution rules have justifiably been called "illogical, arbitrary and often unfair".[15] The main reason for these accusations is that the loopholes which various court decisions have created in sections 74 and 75 over the years are "wide enough to drive a truck through".[16] The three most glaring are: the definition of "property", which for purposes of the attribution rules does not include businesses, so that the income produced from a business which was transferred to a spouse is not affected; the transfers which give rise to the operation of attribution rules do not cover loans, even demand loans without interest (note: the May 1985 budget proposes to change this by amending the *Income Tax Act* to specify that loans are subject to attribution rules); and attribution rules that do not apply to transfers of property to corporations of which the spouse is the shareholder.

The main consequence of these enormous gaps is that anyone who can afford expensive tax-planning advice and financial manoeuvres can manage his or her tax affairs as if attribution rules did not exist. As a result, these rules prevent middle-income spouses from saving relatively modest amounts of tax by dividing their incomes between them, but are powerless to stop wealthy couples from slipping millions of dollars under the government's nose.

Again, the two women's groups that reached conclusions on these rules are the Quebec Status of Women Council and the RAIF. They both concluded that attribution rules should be repealed because they violate the individuality and autonomy of the spouses.[17] Other people also pointed out that the repeal of attribution rules would create a strong incentive for spouses to split their incomes between them to reduce their tax.[18]

In summary, Canada's tax system is mainly one of individual taxation, with a few ill-thought-out and inequitable exceptions.

The Treatment of Homemakers' Work

Two years ago, Status of Women Minister Judy Erola inadvertently stirred up a political hornets' nest when she suggested that the time may have come to abolish the spousal tax exemption. The public discussions that followed were not "ladylike", but they helped to raise women's consciousness level and interest in tax issues.[19]

The central point at stake was whether or not the tax system should take into account the value of homemakers' work, and if so how. The easiest way to understand why this is a problem is to compare two different situations.

Household A is composed of a single man who earns $30,000 a year and his full-time female housekeeper, whose salary amounts to $8,000 (including some cash and the value of her in-kind benefits such as free room and board). The man and the housekeeper both pay tax on their respective incomes. He cannot deduct his housekeeper's salary since it is a personal expense that is not related to earning his income.

Household B is composed of the same two people, but the man and his housekeeper are now married to each other. She still produces $8,000 worth of housekeeping services, but he no longer gives her a salary and she no longer pays tax. In addition, his own tax is diminished because he can now claim the spousal exemption ($3,470 in 1984 if the spouse had no personal income).

The first question this example raises is whether the extremely advantageous tax treatment enjoyed by Household B is fair to two-earner couples and other taxpayers who must either do without the services of a full-time housekeeper, or hire one without being able to deduct anything for these services. Most tax experts agree that such a state of affairs is unjust because "the taxable income of the one-earner couple is understated in that it does not include the value of services provided by the spouse who stays at home."[20]

A few people disagree with this on the grounds that two-earner families enjoy the same level of unpaid services performed by the wife at night and on weekends.[21] But this is denied by numerous time-budget studies that demonstrate that the value of unpaid household services enjoyed by families is considerably lower when the wives have outside jobs.[22] Typical data show that "employed women devote about half as much time to household tasks as unemployed women."[23]

The other problem in our example is that it is not really Household B which is getting a seemingly undue benefit, but *Husband* B, who rakes in all the advantages of the situation. He gets the same domestic services as before, but at a lesser cost, and also pays tax on a lower amount. For her part, his wife is much worse off than before. She is doing the same work, but she has lost her claim to a regular income and is no longer protected by income security programs such as unemployment insurance and the Canada (or Quebec) Pension Plan.

Has anything been proposed to come to grips with these problems? Indeed, many imaginative proposals have been made in this area, the main ones being: taxing the value of homemakers' services; granting tax reductions to those who don't enjoy untaxed homemaker services; paying a salary to homemakers and taxing them on it; abolishing the spousal exemption; and transforming the spousal exemption into a refundable credit payable to wives at home.

■ Taxing Homemakers' Services

Many tax economists and lawyers have stated that the best way of solving the problem of the untaxed value of homemaking services would be to tax the imputed (meaning "assigned") income of home-makers.[24] Having said this, they almost all add that this is unfortunately not feasible.

When Douglas Hartle designed such a system for the Royal Commission on the Status of Women, it was rejected because of the administrative problems as well as because it was:

> . . . undesirable that a married woman who stays at home keeping house for her family and having no income of her own should be liable for a tax which her husband would have to pay.[25]

These objections miss the point. There is indeed something undesirable about taxing housewives on the full value of their services, but the reason for it is hidden by the misleading language which is used to define the question. Most obscuring is the erroneous use of the term "imputed income" to refer to homemakers' services. If this were corrected, the real questions at issue would appear much more clearly and a solution might emerge.

The problem with using the term "imputed income" in this context is that it is the expression which is used to describe the services people perform *for themselves*, such as a house painter who paints his own house, or a hairdresser who fixes her own hair. When applied to housewives, this definition does not fit very well at all. True, some part of homemakers' work is devoted to their own maintenance, but since everyone must do some self-maintenance chores, that portion of their work should be ignored for present purposes. For the most part, it is not housewives who benefit from the services they provide, it is their husbands and children.

If most of the value produced by homemakers' work is not imputed income, then what is its proper characterization? An examination of household circumstances reveals two different categories: first, to the extent that housewives' work is compensated by the value of the "free" food, shelter, clothing, etc., they receive from their husbands, they are in exactly the same position as any employee who receives *income in kind*; second, above the level of the in-kind wages they receive, what housewives do is *volunteer work* of which the main beneficiaries are their husbands and children. Inasmuch as raising children is of benefit to all of society, it would also be correct to say that housewives do volunteer work for the State.

Given these facts, it is difficult to support the proposal that housewives be taxed. Their income in kind is probably not worth much more than the basic exemption ($3,960 in 1984). As for taxing husbands for the value of the volunteer services they receive from their wives, one can imagine the howls of protest if husbands were thus singled out from the ranks of all the people who benefit from volunteer work in our society!

■   *Offsetting Benefits for Non-Homemaker Households*
If the value of homemakers' services cannot be taxed, many people have said the next best way of taking it into account is to give compensating tax reductions to those who don't have access to such untaxed services.[26] One means of doing this is to allow two-earner families and single parents to claim deductions or credits for their child care costs. Another is to give an earned-income deduction or credit to the lower earning spouse.

One problem with earned-income deductions and credits, as recent U.S. experience illustrates, is that they are complicated and produce erratic benefits.[27] Other controversial aspects of "offsetting" benefits are whether tax reductions granted only to two-earner couples discriminate against other groups of taxpayers; whether the tax system is the most appropriate means by which to compensate parents for their child care expenses, and if so, whether or not these expenses should be treated as business expenditures; and to what extent such "offsetting" benefits are needed in systems where the spouses are taxed as individuals.

On the first point, the example of Households A and B above clearly shows that the failure to tax homemaker services results in *all* other households being at a disadvantage, including those made up of single parents and people who have never married. As a result, giving an offsetting benefit only to two-earner couples does discriminate against all the other non-homemaker households. The only mitigating factor in favour of such a restricted benefit, according to Yale University Professor Boris Bittker, is that the work disincentive effect is much stronger in the case of married women.[28] On the other hand, if an offsetting benefit is granted to compensate for homemakers' work in the area of child care, the more reasonable approach is to grant it to all non-homemaker households with young children (meaning two-earner couples and single parents in the labour force), since they have additional costs that are not borne by childless people.

The second area of controversy concerns the proper treatment to be accorded to child care expenditures. After reviewing the alternatives, the U.S. Citizens' Advisory Council on the Status of Women concluded in 1968 that tax deductions are "inadequate", "inequitable", and "ineffective" in helping to provide care for the children of employed mothers, and that:

> Liberalization of the deduction by extending it to higher income levels, raising the limits on the amount of the deduction and increasing the age limit for children will not improve its effectiveness . . . Such changes would simply provide tax relief to those families able to make expenditures for the care of children and disabled dependents.[29]

Instead, the Council recommended that the government intervene directly to "stimulate the development of facilities and services for provision of the needed care of children of working mothers" and give "substantial encouragement to community efforts to develop such organized facilities as day care centers . . ."[30]

This position is similar to that held by Canada's major feminist groups.[31] They are dissatisfied with the present system, under which the federal government helps pay the child care costs of poor families through the Canada Assistance Plan and those of highest income parents through tax deductions, but does practically nothing to help the majority whose earnings are closer to the average. Instead, feminist groups advocate free and universally accessible non-profit child care on a model similar to that of the school system.

Unfortunately, the implementation of such a program is hampered by two sizeable political obstacles. One is the reluctance of governments to commit the large sums necessary to set up decent systems of child care services. The other is the self-interested support of some professional women for the maintenance and even the extension of child-care deductions.

The first obstacle has resulted in the general belief that some child care tax measures should be retained in the short term. The second barrier has sparked numerous debates on the question of whether this tax recognition of child-care services should be through a deduction, which gives benefits that increase with a person's income, or through a credit, which gives the same benefit to all those who owe enough tax (because credits are deducted from the amount of tax a person owes). The credit approach was finally adopted in the United States, but the Canadian government has so far remained impervious to the pressures of women's groups in the same direction.[32]

The position of high-income professional women who prefer a deduction was explained as follows:

> Child care expenses, by their very nature, are *incurred for the purpose of earning income* (or in the case of a student, for the purpose of earning future income). Just as a business woman who has a high overhead (expensive furniture and well-paid staff) may claim the full amount of these expenditures, so ought parents who pay for child care be entitled to claim the amount actually spent. This in no way confers an "unfair advantage" on higher income families. To claim the deduction, one must first make the expenditure.[33]

The problem is that this argument has always been found invalid by the courts. The leading case for Canada is a 1891 British decision involving the deductibility of a housekeeper's wages,[34] but an American decision of 1939 made the same points even more clearly in a case involving the care of children. It held that:

> Petitioners would have us apply the "but for" test. They propose that but for the nurses the wife could not leave her child; but for the freedom so secured she could not pursue her gainful labors; and but for them there would be no income and no tax. This thought evokes an array of interesting possibilities. The fees to the doctor, but for whose healing service the earner of the family income could not leave his sickbed; the cost of the laborer's raiment, for how can the world proceed about its business unclothed; the very home which gives us shelter and rest and the food which provides energy, might all by an extension of the same proposition be construed as necessary to the operation of business and to the creation of income. Yet these are the very essence of those "personal" expenses the deductibility of which is expressly denied.[35]

American tax expert Michael McIntyre proposed another way of looking at this question. When asked whether child care expenditures should be recognized as business expenses, he answered: "Let's put it this way. What would we do if people started to raise pink elephants?"[36] This is a crude way of putting the matter, but it nonetheless makes it clear that the sole fact of having responsibilities outside the workplace is not sufficient to justify a tax deduction. If the "but for" test were adopted, caretakers' fees for a wide range of demanding pets of dubious social value would also become deductible.

This does not mean that the tax system should not take child care expenses into account, but that there is no necessary rationale to do it through a deduction or to link this tax benefit to an actual expenditure. After weighing all the arguments for and against using deductions or credits or nothing at all, Canadian Professor B.J. Arnold recommended the implementation of a credit, which he found most effective in neutralizing the work disincentive of wives, in recognizing reduced ability to pay, and in helping "lower income taxpayers whose relative ability to pay is most heavily affected."[37]

The final controversy regarding "offsetting" benefits concerns the issue of whether or not they are needed in a system of separate taxation. The discussion above answered this in the affirmative in the case of child care expenditures, but the same question arises with respect to compensating non-homemaker households for their traditional housekeeping costs. No one in Canada has expressly addressed this question, but the Interdepartmental Committee on the Taxation of Women implicitly disagreed with the idea of such compensation by finding that separate taxation already produces enough or even too much of a difference between the respective tax burdens of one- and two-earner families (because the same income spread over two people produces a lower total tax).[38] Another argument against offsetting benefits for housekeeping services is that they would make our tax system much more complicated and difficult to understand.[39]

■ *Paying Homemakers a Salary*

Some people, including Professor Jack London, have suggested that a future world might solve the problem of the untaxed value of homemakers' work by paying them a salary on which tax would be imposed.[40] Whatever the intrinsic merits of the proposals to the effect of giving housewives a salary for their services, it is difficult to see how it could solve the present problem of the undervaluation of homemakers' work, since it would make one-earner families even better off in comparison to two-earner families than they are at the present time.

■ *Abolishing the Spousal Exemption*

As pointed out by the Royal Commission on the Status of Women in 1970, it is incorrect to assume that a wife at home is a dependant:

> In most cases, the wife who works at home as a housekeeper, far from being a dependant, performs essential services worth at least as much to her husband as the cost of the food, shelter and clothing that he provides for her.[41]

As a result, the Commission found,

> In all justice the married status exemption should not be given when there is no dependant in the family. We believe that a woman does not become economically dependent by virtue of her marriage. If she is in fact dependent, it is the result of the couple's personal choice. A childless couple has the right to decide that the wife will devote all her time to homemaking but there is no reason why the State should attach an advantage to this choice by giving the husband a married status exemption. This represents a discrimination in favour of married people.[42]

Although this view has found support in many feminist circles (including endorsement by the Quebec Status of Women Council), the controversy that arose when Status of Women Minister Judy Erola expressed similar ideas shows that public opinion is far from unanimous. The main obstacle is housewives who, deprived as they are of any compensation for their work, do not see the marital exemption as a denial of their economic value, but as the only measure in the tax act that grants them some recognition.

Their position is valid since even if the exemption is given to the husband and bears no relation to the wife's work, it is nevertheless an advantage that is given to the family because of the homemaker's presence. Because of this, it is not surprising that some people see the spousal exemption as a kind of imperfect mini-salary for housewives, a minor recompense for all the unpaid services they render to society throughout their lives.

■ Transforming the Spousal Exemption into a Credit for Housewives

This proposal, put forward by the RAIF, offers an unusual interpretation of the role of the spousal exemption. According to the RAIF, all residents of Canada are entitled to a personal guaranteed income. Some receive it directly through benefits such as welfare, disability benefits, the old age pension and other payments, while the rest get it indirectly through their personal tax exemption.[43]

The only exception to this universal benefit is housewives: they are disentitled from direct income security benefits because of their husbands' incomes, and they are also bereft of their own personal tax exemption because it is given to their husbands as the spousal exemption. As a result, according to the RAIF, housewives are the only people in Canada who are not entitled to a State-provided guaranteed minimal income of their own.

The way to redress the situation, the group proposes, is to abolish the spousal exemption and divide the sums thereby recuperated among all wives or husbands at home. Instead of producing a regressive benefit to which homemakers are not legally entitled, this would give the same minimal guaranteed income to all homemaking spouses.

The least that can be said for the RAIF's recommendation is that it would be fairer than the present system. Also, if tax recognition is as important to homemakers as the reactions to Ms. Erola's suggestions seem to have demonstrated, the RAIF's proposal might be the only politically acceptable way of making some improvement to the present system at no extra cost.

The Tax Treatment of Divorced Spouses

The *Income Tax Act* provides that periodic alimony or maintenance payments for the support of an estranged spouse and/or children of the marriage can be deducted from the income of the one who pays them and must be included in the taxable income of the recipient. This rule, which is not as old as the *Income Tax Act*, dates back to 1942. Before then, no deduction was allowed for these payments and they were not included in the taxable income of their recipients.

The reason given in 1942 for introducing the present rules was "the relief of husbands in certain income tax brackets who had not enough income to pay both their maintenance obligations and the high wartime tax."[44] Not surprisingly, this change was not repealed when wartime taxes disappeared. Other rationales that were developed later to justify this tax treatment include: spousal maintenance and child support are money "gone for nought"; deductibility may be an aid to enforcement of the agreement or order to pay; deductibility permits men who are financially strapped to start anew with a new family; and this treatment allows the payment of higher amounts to wives and children by reducing the total amount of tax the payor and his ex-family have to pay.

This last effect results from this treatment of support payments for tax purposes which makes income-splitting perfectly legal between ex-spouses. This has been criticized as being inconsistent since husbands in intact families are not entitled to deduct the sums they spend on their wives and children (except for the flat-rate exemptions). Whether much, if any, of the tax saving is actually passed on to the wife has also been questioned.

When the Canadian Advisory Council on the Status of Women studied this question, it came to the following conclusions:

> Money received by an estranged wife for her own support can truly be said to be under her full control. As she can spend these sums in any way she wants . . . it is fair to add them to her own income for tax purposes.

> On the other hand, money received by an estranged wife for the maintenance of the children in her custody is not under her full control. She is in a position similar to that of a trustee holding money for the benefit of the children, and she is not free to spend this money in any way she wishes. As trustees are not expected to pay tax on the money they administer for others . . . women in this position should not have to pay tax on the money they receive for child support.[45]

Similar reasoning led to this type of tax treatment of support payments in the United States.

Comparison of Tax and Matrimonial Law Principles

Matrimonial law principles vary from province to province, but Canadian laws are similar enough to make two generalizations.

First, while spouses are living together, they are mostly separate as to property, which means each of them fully controls his or her own assets and earnings and has no power over that of the other spouse. The only important exceptions to this rule concern the squandering of the family property, transactions involving the family home, and the mutual spousal obligation of maintenance in case of need.

Second, upon divorce, assets are split between the spouses in a more or less egalitarian manner, and the maintenance obligation is or is not continued depending on the spouses' respective financial capacities and needs.[46]

Comparing these principles to our tax treatment of married couples, we find that they are basically consistent. Both matrimonial and tax laws essentially treat married people in lasting relationships as if they were financial strangers. The stress that family laws place on "maintenance" for homemakers, instead of compensation for services rendered, is a fitting counterpart to the assumption underlying the spousal exemption, that housewives are financial burdens who must be supported.

Attribution rules and transferable deductions stand out, with their incongruous assumption that spouses share everything and are full economic partners. These provisions are not consistent with our present principles of family law, and this inconsistency has harmful consequences: attribution rules discourage transfers of income and property between the spouses, and transferable deductions increase the barriers homemakers face when they decide to enter the labour force.

Complications also arise when spouses avail themselves of their rights to opt out of the legal matrimonial regime of their provinces. What happens if a couple decides that it does not want to be separate as to property during the marriage, and enters into a marriage contract that provides for the full co-ownership and joint control by the spouses of all its properties and income during their life together?

The short answer to this question is that we don't know what happens, because not a single Canadian case has been reported of spouses attempting to enforce such a marriage contract in the tax area. Although several experts have written that such a manoeuvre would not change the spouses' tax liability because it would be annulled by our attribution rules,[47] at least one expert disagrees,[48] and income-splitting on the basis of a marriage contract has apparently been found acceptable under the Quebec *Income Tax Act*.[49]

Going one step further, let us ask what would happen if a province changed its legal matrimonial regime to one of full community of property with joint ownership and control of all incomes and assets by both spouses throughout their marriage? According to the 1957 *Sura* decision[50] of the Supreme Court of Canada, which is the decisive case in that area, the effect would be that people married under such a regime would be entitled to full income-splitting for income tax purposes.

The only women's group that has given attention to these matters is the National Association of Women and the Law.[51] It recommended that the present system of individual taxation be maintained, but that spouses who actually split their incomes between them be entitled to claim a deduction for the amount transferred. This way, if a couple entered into a marriage contract providing for full sharing of all they own, each would declare half of their combined income at the end of the year.

The results of such a change would be to bring our tax and family law provisions much closer to each other and to encourage the real sharing of income and properties between spouses whose economic positions are now unequal.

While these appear to be eminently worthy goals, this proposal has been criticized by other feminists for two main reasons. First, the main beneficiaries of such income-splitting would be upper-income couples, which would make our tax system even less progressive than it is now. Second, they fear that encouraging real income-sharing between spouses might reduce some women's incentive to take outside employment.

Proponents of income-sharing answer these objections by saying that fairness to wives should have priority over progressivity. On the second point, they challenge the wisdom of trying to push all women into the work force. Instead of imposing a given lifestyle on all wives, they believe feminists should work toward maximizing women's life choices by making them financially secure whether or not they take a paid job.

Conclusion

A comparison of matrimonial and tax laws shows that both essentially treat spouses in lasting relationships as if they were financial strangers. The exceptions to this in the case of matrimonial property laws, such as the spousal obligation of maintenance and the requirement that both spouses participate in transactions involving the family home, are clearly beneficial to women and increase their financial security.

The same cannot be said in the area of tax laws. Most of the *Income Tax Act* provisions that treat spouses as a unit, including attribution rules and transferable deductions, are harmful to women and benefit only husbands or Revenue Canada. From the point of view of women's interest, these rules should be repealed.

The other conclusion to be drawn from this brief survey is that many family taxation matters require further study and discussion before solid long-term proposals can be formulated. Most important among these "unfinished" matters are the treatment of homemakers' work and the extent to which marital property agreements should be recognized by our tax laws. As women's involvement in such questions is still very recent, it will probably be some time before they are resolved.

Louise Dulude is vice-president of the National Action Committee on the Status of Women. She recently completed her Masters in Law at McGill University. Her thesis is entitled "Taxation of the Spouses in Canadian, American, British, French and Swedish Law."

Notes

1. Canada, Report of the Royal Commission on Taxation, *Taxation of Income, Part A — Taxation of Individuals and Families*, vol. 3 (Ottawa: Queen's Printer, 1966), p. 123.

2. Canada, Royal Commission on the Status of Women in Canada, *Report* (Ottawa: Information Canada, 1970), p. 304.

3. *Ibid.*, p. 429.

4. Hon. E. J. Benson, Minister of Finance, *Proposals for Tax Reform* (known as the "White Paper on Tax Reform") (Ottawa: Queen's Printer, 1969), pp. 14-15.

5. See: Michael J. Boskin, "The Effects of Government Expenditures and Taxes on Female Labor", *American Economic Review*, vol. 64, no. 2 (May 1974), p. 252; Robert E. Hall, "Wages, Income and Hours of Work in the U.S. Labor Force", in *Income Maintenance and Labor Supply*, ed. E. Cain and H. Watts (Rand McNally, 1973); Harvey S. Rosen, "Tax Illusion and the Labor Supply of Married Women", *Review of Economics and Statistics*, vol. LVIII, no. 2 (May 1976), pp. 167-172; Christine Greenhalgh, "A Labour Supply Function for Married Women in Great Britain", *Economica*, vol. 44, no. 175 (1977); Aline O. Quester, "The Effect of the Tax Structure on the Labor Market Behavior of Wives", *Journal of Economics and Business*, vol. 29, no. 3 (Spring/Summer 1977), pp. 171-180; Jane H. Leuthold, "The Effect of Taxation on the Hours Worked by Married Women", *Industrial and Labor Relations Review*, vol. 31, no. 4 (1978), pp. 520-526; Alice Nakamura and Masao Nakamura, "A Comparison of the Labor Force Behavior of Married Women in the United States and Canada, With Special Attention to the Impact of Income Taxes", *Econometrica*, vol. 49, no. 2 (1981), pp. 451-489.

6. Louise Dulude, "Joint Taxation of Spouses — A Feminist View", *Canadian Taxation*, vol. 1, no. 4 (1979); pp. 8-12.

7. Organisation for Economic Co-Operation and Development (OECD), Committee on Fiscal Affairs, *The Treatment of Family Units in OECD Member Countries Under Tax and Transfer Systems* (Paris: OECD, 1977), pp. 15-17.

8. *Economic Recovery Tax Act* of 1981, Pub. L. No. 97-34 (Aug. 3, 1981), reprinted in *U.S. Code Cong. & Ad. News*, vol. 3, no. 6 (August 1981).

9. Memo by Julie Loranger, then federal Coordinator for the Status of Women, to the Hon. Marc Lalonde, Minister Responsible for the Status of Women (and Minister of National Health and Welfare), December 21, 1976.

10. Canadian Advisory Council on the Status of Women (CACSW), *Annotated Recommendations on Women and Taxation* (Ottawa: CACSW, 1978), p. 4.

11. *Ibid.*

12. Louise Dulude, "Background Study on Women and the Personal Income Tax System", Canadian Advisory Council on the Status of Women, 1976, pp. 14-17; Louise Dulude, "Description et analyse de diverses mesures fiscales concernant les transferts entre conjoints", Conseil du statut de la femme du Québec, 1980.

13. Gisèle Audette, *Les femmes et l'impôt*, Conseil du statut de la femme du Québec, 1982, Annexe 1; *RAIF — Revue d'information pour les femmes*, no. 77/78, June 1983.

14. Boris I. Bittker, "Federal Income Taxation and the Family", 27 *Stanford Law Review* (July 1975), at 1394.

15. J.M. MacGowan, "The Tax Consequences of Marriages", *1974 Conference Report*, Canadian Tax Foundation, p. 278.

16. Jack R. London, "Taxation of the Family United", *1974 Conference Report*, Canadian Tax Foundation, p. 110.

17. *Supra*, n. 13.

18. Louise Dulude, "Taxation of the Spouses: A Comparative Study of Canadian, American, British, French and Swedish Law", Master of Laws thesis prepared for the Institute of Comparative Law, McGill University, September 1984, pp. 95-96.

19. Ann Rhodes, "How Our Income Tax Act Zaps Women", *Chatelaine* (August 1982), pp. 64, 122-128.

20. George F. Break and Joseph A. Pechman, *Federal Tax Reform: The Impossible Dream?* (Washington, D.C.: Brookings Institution, 1975), p. 35.

21. Michael J. McIntyre and Oliver Oldman, "Treatment of the Family", in *Comprehensive Income Taxation*, ed. Joseph A. Pechman (Washington, D.C.: Brookings Institution, 1977), p. 1614.

22. Oli Hawrylyshyn, "The Value of Household Services: A Survey of Empirical Estimates", *The Review of Income and Wealth*, vol. 2 (1976), pp. 101-131; Alexander Sxalai, "Women's Time: Women in the Light of Contemporary Time-Budget Research", *Futures*, vol. 7, no. 5 (1975), pp. 385-399.

23. Joann Vanek, "Time Spent in Housework", in *The Economics of Women and Work*, ed. Alice H. Amsden (New York: Penguin Books, 1980), p. 86.

24. Carl Shoup, "Married Couples Compared With Single Persons Under the Income Tax", *Bulletin of the National Tax Association*, vol. XXV, no. 5 (1940), pp. 130-135; Douglas Y. Thorson, "An Analysis of the Sources of Continued Controversy Over the Tax Treatment of Family Income", *National Tax Journal*, vol. 18, no. 2 (1965), pp. 113-132; William D. Popkin, "Household Services and Child Care in the Income Tax and Social Security Laws", 50 *Indiana Law Journal* (1975), at 241; A.F. Sheppard, "The Taxation of Imputed Income and the Rule in Sharkey v. Wernher", 51 *Canadian Bar Review* (1973), at 637-638.

25. Royal Commission on the Status of Women in Canada, p. 298.

26. Douglas Y. Thorson, p. 116; Joseph A. Pechman, "Statement Before the U.S. Congress Joint Economic Committee", in *Economic Problems of Women*, Part 2 (Washington: U.S. Congress Joint Economic Committee, 1973), p. 253; George Cooper, "Working Wives and the Tax Law", 25 *Rutgers Law Review* (1970), at 70; A.F. Sheppard, pp. 637-638.

27. Lynda Sands Moerschbaecher, "The Marriage Penalty and the Divorce Bonus: A Comparative Examination of the Current Legislative Proposals", *Review of Taxation of Individuals*, vol. 5, no. 2 (1981), pp. 133-146.

28. Boris I. Bittker, p. 1436.

29. Citizens' Advisory Council on the Status of Women, *Report of the Task Force on Social Insurance and Taxes* (Washington: U.S. Government Printing Office, 1968), pp. 96-106.

30. *Ibid.*, pp. 104-105.

31. Including the Canadian Advisory Council on the Status of Women and the National Action Committee on the Status of Women.

32. The CACSW and NAC both recommended replacing the present child care expenses deduction by a credit.

33. Christine Blain, "A Preliminary Review of the Income Tax Act, and Its Implications for An Employment Strategy for Women", Office of the Coordinator for the Status of Women, 1979, p. 15.

34. *Bowers v. Harding* [1891] 1 Q.B. 560 at 564; 3 Tax Cas. 22, at 26.

35. *Smith v. Commissioner*, 40 B.T.A. 1038 (1939), aff'd per curiam, 113 F. 2d 114 (2d Cir. 1940).

36. Said to the author in a conversation that took place on the occasion of a conference on the tax expenditure concept held at Osgoode Hall Law School in Toronto in the spring of 1979.

37. B.J. Arnold, "The Deduction for Child Care Expenses in the United States and Canada: A Comparative Analysis", 12 *Western Ontario Law Review* (1973), at 41.

38. Canada, Interdepartmental Committee on the Taxation of Women, "Report", unpublished, 1976, p. 11.

39. Louise Dulude, *Taxation of the Spouses*, pp. 126-127.

40. Jack R. London, *Tax and the Family* (Ottawa: Law Reform Commission of Canada, 1975), pp. 102-103.

41. Royal Commission on the Status of Women in Canada, pp. 293-294.

42. *Ibid.*, p. 299.

43. RAIF, pp. 15-16.

44. Michèle M. Meakes, "The Canadian Tax Treatment of Alimony and Maintenance", paper prepared for Osgoode Hall Law School, 1976, p. 21.

45. Canadian Advisory Council on the Status of Women, "Annotated Recommendations on Women and Taxation", 1978, pp. 10-11.

46. For more information on financial relations between the spouses, see: Louise Dulude, *Love, Marriage and Money: An Analysis of Financial Relations Between the Spouses* (Ottawa: Canadian Advisory Council on the Status of Women, 1984).

47. Susan Eng, "Tax Consequences of Provincial Family Law Reform Legislation", *Canadian Tax Journal*, vol. 26, no. 5 (1978), p. 562; D. Keith McNair, "The Income Tax Implications of Matrimonial Property Law Reform — The Common Law Provinces", *1979 Conference Report*, Canadian Tax Foundation, p. 268; André Lareau, "Les implications fiscales des transferts de biens effectués sous la loi sur les biens matrimoniaux du Nouveau-Brunswick", *Canadian Tax Journal*, vol. 29, no. 2 (1981), p. 157; James Ellis, "An Income Tax Perspective on British Columbia Marriage Agreements", 15:1 *U.B.C. Law Review* (1981), at 155.

48. Jack R. London, "Taxation of the Family United", *1974 Conference Report*, Canadian Tax Foundation, pp. 109-110.

49. Marc Jolin, "Aspects fiscaux des régimes matrimoniaux au Québec", *Journée d'études fiscales 1979*, p. 86.

50. *Frank Sura v. Minister of National Revenue*, 62 D.T.C. 1005.

51. Cited in Christine Blain, pp. 24-25.

The Dejudicialization of Family Law: Mediation and Assessments[*]

— *Harriet Sachs*

There is growing concern that the adversarial nature of our judicial system is ill-suited to the resolution of family law disputes, particularly the determination of custody and access. To compensate for this, there is a trend toward alternative methods of settling such disputes. Mediation, in which an independent third party works with the litigants to help them reach an amicable agreement, is one such example.

Another alternative is the use of third party assessments. The court appoints an "expert" to conduct an investigation into the family, who submits recommendations to the court.

In a review of these practices in Canada, the author discusses the problems of creating alternative means of dispute resolution. While recognizing that the role of the courts in the settlement of family disputes is inherently different than any other area of law, the author warns that without adequate research and control of standards these alternatives introduce another set of problems into family dispute settlement.

Introduction

The legal process invoked in dealing with Canadian family law (here defined as the law of marriage breakdown) is in a state of transition as a result of a number of factors. The first is the ever

---

[*]   research and interviewing done by Elizabeth Sloss

growing number of divorces; four out of every ten Canadian marriages will end in divorce.[1] This lends urgency to the proposition that our divorce laws must bring about as humane and expeditious a determination of family law disputes as possible. Second, there is the growing recognition that the legal treatment of marriage breakdown should not be an exercise in fault allocation. Third, there is increasing sensitivity to children as significant players in this process whose rights must be recognized and, most of all, protected.

All of the above have led to questioning whether or not the traditional adversarial model of dispute resolution is appropriate for marriage breakdown fights — particularly when these fights are focused on custody and access. The adversary system relies on the parties to present the evidence which will be tested through cross-examination and for an impartial decision-maker to make his or her decision based upon the evidence which the parties have chosen to call. The exercise pits one litigant against the other, increasing rather than lessening hostility. The information presented to the court is limited to that which the parties (usually the parents) have chosen to rely upon and may be incomplete. The atmosphere is artificial, designed to sort out "truth" from "falsehood". This may be less than satisfactory when there:

> . . . is little that can realistically be said to be absolutely 'true' about marital histories or children's interests. Although there must of necessity be some exploration of the past relationships between the parties, the nature of spousal and parent-child relationships is so subjective as to be incapable of translation into relevant factual evidence. Other than dates and incidents that are often peripheral to the issue before the court in a custody case, it is hard to see how a parent's attitudes towards a particular child can be assessed in a witness box as truth or dissemblance. A disputed assertion, for example, that a mother or father spends too little time with a child may have little to do with the quality of the time spent or the child's impression of the time spent.[2]

If it is accepted that children are the people whose rights we must be most anxious to protect, the question arises as to how this can be done in a system where the parties are the parents, whose interests and concerns may not be those of their children. A partial answer is to provide independent representation for children and for them to be recognized as official players in the process. This answer is less than satisfactory when the children are too young to give instructions or want nothing less than to engage in a battle which essentially involves forcing them to choose between their parents.

While nowhere in Canada have these concerns led to an abandonment of the adversarial system, certain modifications to the system which have changed its character substantially have, as a result, evolved — particularly when the issues being addressed involve children. The purpose of this paper is to examine what form these modifications have taken across Canada and to explore their implications.

The modifications to be discussed are mediation and independent assessments. Mediation involves the use of an independent third party who seeks to bring the parties to an agreement. The goal of the process is not an imposed decision, but a decision which both parties want and to which both agree. Independent assessments, on the other hand, are used almost exclusively in cases involving custody. They are examinations of the situation conducted by an "expert" who is viewed as impartial. The examination is conducted outside of the courtroom, with neither the judge nor the lawyers present. The only official record of what occurs during the assessment is kept by the assessor. The result of the examination is a report which more often than not contains a recommended disposition. This report is disclosed to the parties, filed with the court, and becomes part of the evidence which the judge considers in making his or her decision. Such assessments may occur either through the agreement of both parties or because the judge has determined that one is necessary. Similarly, the assessor is either agreed to or appointed by the court.

Both of these modifications to the adversarial system have the effect of diverting the legal process in family law from the hands of the judges. In mediation, the matter is taken out of the hands of the judiciary entirely. In assessments, someone else is basically performing the same task the judge has to perform, that is, collect the facts and reach a conclusion based on these facts. Of course, the matter still goes back to the court for a final decision, which does not have to be the same as that of the assessor. However, it is maintained that if comprehensive studies were to be done as to how often the recommendations of an assessor were embodied in the disposition of the court, the result would be "almost always". (No such comprehensive studies have been done.) As well, more often than not, parties are sufficiently aware of this that they settle after seeing the report.

Mediation

There are basically two forms mediation can take — open or closed. In open mediation, what goes on and is said is revealed to the lawyers and to the court. In closed mediation the opposite occurs: everything is confidential, allowing parties to speak freely without fear of having their words and positions used against them at a later date. Generally, in Canada, the law is developing in such a way that unless parties agree otherwise, what is said during mediation cannot be revealed during an ensuing court battle. Recognition is being given to the fact that people should be encouraged to try and settle their disputes in a free and open atmosphere without fear of reprisal for what is said.

It is important to note that mediation is not and cannot be considered an alternative to the adversarial system. If no settlement occurs through mediation, some decision-making forum must be provided.

The advantages of mediation are numerous. It is always better for people to agree on a solution to their problems, rather than having one imposed upon them. The likelihood of the resolution lasting a longer period of time is higher. It is not uncommon after a bitter court battle to find the dissatisfied party bringing the matter back to court a few years later. Through mediation, the opportunity exists to negotiate a settlement which is tailor-made to suit the needs, expectations, and lifestyles of the individual parties. It can also include a built-in monitoring system such as providing for more mediation if problems arise in the future. Court judgements, on the other hand, tend to be very blunt instruments. Litigating a family law matter is expensive, time-consuming, and divisive. At the end of the process, the relationship between the litigants is even more severely damaged. All suffer through the process, especially the children, and if some other means can be found for bringing about a *fair* resolution it should be encouraged.

The above paragraph discusses the advantages of mediation by juxtaposing it with litigation or a court battle. The fact is that over 90 per cent of the disputes which proceed in traditional ways through the legal system settle out of court after a process of bargaining between lawyers acting on behalf of their clients. Thus, what should be compared is mediation versus advocated negotiation, not mediation versus litigation. Or alternatively, what should be sought is a means of ensuring that mediation operates not only as an effective adjunct to the court process, but also as a complement to the bargaining process between lawyers.

There is no question that:

> Mediation in divorce can be an effective supplement of the legal system. The problem has arisen that, since mediation in divorce

is a currently evolving discipline, many people of varying backgrounds assume it to be a lucrative area of infringement and practice of law without any established guidelines.[3]

To effectively and *fairly* mediate a family law dispute requires a number of very sophisticated skills — an in-depth and thorough knowledge of the law so as to be able to give some accurate guidance on what is an appropriate settlement and an ability to bring people together without either becoming an advocate for one party or taking advantage of the weakness of another. Mediation conducted by someone without proper training and experience can, at best, be time-consuming and expensive and, at worst, can result in further bitterness and an unfair settlement into which one party felt effectively forced.

Across Canada, a number of people have gone into the field of mediation on a private basis. Some people are lawyers, some are social workers, psychologists or psychiatrists. Others may have no particular qualifications. There are mediation training courses available either in Toronto (mostly through Dr. Howard Irving) or in the United States. These courses are not cheap, especially if travel costs are involved. However, there is nothing to stop anyone from setting up in practice as a private mediator, whether qualified or unqualified, trained or untrained.

A cross-Canada review of the mediation facilities available through the courts shows that these facilities vary not only from province to province, but also from area to area within a province. In Manitoba, there is nothing in rural areas; in Winnipeg, the conciliation service is staffed by people who have had mediation training in Toronto.

In Saskatoon, the Unified Family Court provides mediation as one aspect of their assessment process. Steps are taken to ensure that the mediator is not the person responsible for the ultimate assessment. This prevents the assessor from beginning the assessment with preconceived notions and prejudices as a result of impressions formed during the mediation attempt. The separation of the mediation and assessment processes is also essential for the participants. If the parties know or believe that the mediator could also be the assessor, they will be on their guard not to express true feelings, concerns or attitudes for fear that these will come back to haunt them in the assessment report; the mediation would not therefore be meaningful. In Saskatoon, the mediators are social workers with either Bachelor's or Master's degrees in Social Work. No special training in mediation is provided.

British Columbia has Family Court counsellors who are appointed by the Attorney General to provide conciliation services to all levels of courts dealing with family matters in the province. These people are essentially probation officers, whose qualifications consist of a B.A. and four to five months of training in probation.

In Edmonton, the staff of the Family Conciliation Service has had formal mediation training either by Howard Irving or by the Academy of Family Mediators in the United States. They all have a Master's degree in Counselling Psychology. In Calgary, the staff of the Unified Family Court provides mediation. Their staff, all of whom have 7 to 20 years of experience, consists of four people with Master's degrees in Social Work and one with a Bachelor's degree in the same field.

In New Brunswick, mediation is made available through social workers, who have no specific training in the field. In Nova Scotia, there appear to be no government-sponsored services especially geared to mediation.

In Ontario, aside from the Unified Family Court in Hamilton, most mediation is done privately. At various times, other family courts and even the Supreme Court have had conciliation counselling available. Some still do. However, by and large many of these programs have been cancelled and have, in a sense, been replaced by an extensive pre-trial process.

The Unified Family Court in St. John's, Newfoundland, has a social arm which does provide mediation. Two of their staff have Master's degrees in Social Work.

In Quebec, family mediation is available through a Superior Court facility. The mediation is closed and deals with all family law issues — property, support, and custody. All mediators have Master's degrees in Social Work, but not necessarily any formal training in mediation *per se*. The service also has a consulting lawyer available to it.

This brief overview illustrates that even where mediation is sponsored by government, there is no consistency either in the qualifications or the training of the mediators. There are no accepted standards for the conduct of mediation and only one service, in Quebec, appears to have recognized that a lawyer might be useful. In the United States, standards of practice for family mediators have been proposed (see Appendix A).

Given this situation and the fact that mediation is such a difficult endeavour, it may be that some of the mediation conducted in Canada is being done badly. This is of particular concern to women. Women are usually the financially dependent spouse and often the victims of a sexist dynamic which has involved giving in to their spouses on a regular basis. This dynamic, combined with financial dependence, can easily leave the woman very vulnerable to pressures which may be inappropriately applied to her in mediation. As a result, she might agree to something which is not in her best interests. These concerns have led people such as Frances Olsen to conclude that:

> ... the deformalization reform strategy may have adverse effects on women. First, it fails to provide full protection for individual family members because, in encouraging agreement between the parties, it may force the weaker party to accept a resolution that gives her far less than she would be entitled to in a final adjudication . . . . Thus, although the aim of deformalization is altruism and family solidarity, the actual result is too often the perpetuation of hierarchy and domination.[4]

Janet Rifkin quarrels with this view in her article, "Mediation from a Feminist Perspective". She maintains that Olsen's view is predicated on a traditional view of law which sees the "lawsuit (as) *the* appropriate and most effective vehicle for challenging unfair social practices, for protecting individuals, and for delineating new areas of guaranteed 'rights'."[5]

The challenge Rifkin poses points out that this traditional paradigm of law is in fact patriarchal in its nature with its hierarchical, combative, and adversarial perspective. She argues that mediation challenges these notions and places the emphasis on the "female concerns of responsibility and justice. These concerns contrast with the concerns for individual rights that are characteristic of the male pedagogy dominant in law school and most other academic settings."[6]

Rifkin goes so far as to state that even where there is inequality of bargaining power she believes that mediation offers a greater possibility for a just resolution of the conflict than the traditional formal system.

> The general assumption that the lawyer can 'help' the client more meaningfully than a mediator is part of the problem . . . In many instances, although no substantive rights or legal protection are realized, patterns of domination are reinforced by the traditional lawyer-client relationship, in which the client is the passive recipient of the lawyer's expertise. This is particularly true for women clients for whom patterns of domination are at the heart of the problem.[7]

While the author does not agree with this aspect of Rifkin's thesis, since patterns of domination may also emerge in mediation which is not properly controlled by the mediator,[8] she has confronted women with the possibility that mediation may be made into a vehicle that can achieve more equality for women than the traditional legal system.

Nevertheless, it is crucial to avoid any philosophy which views mediation as the panacea for the problems of dispute resolution in family law. Furthermore, to work effectively mediation must avoid several very significant pitfalls which are summarized below.

Battered Women

In situations involving women who have been battered by their partners, mediation is effectively impossible and potentially dangerous. Such women come to the process burdened not only with an inequality of bargaining power resulting from economic disparity, but also a tremendous fear of violence. A battered woman will probably be intimidated into a settlement. For her the focus cannot and should not be on reasonable discourse, but on protection — protection which is available only through the effective use of the court process.

Child Support

Child support awards in this country are low and collection is sporadic. More work is needed to develop defined legislative and judicial standards for child support based on sound and thorough economic analyses as to the cost of raising children, combined with a tougher and more effective enforcement system. Mediation poses two threats to these developments. Lower child support may be agreed to because of the very strong pressure women feel in family disputes to give up monetary benefits to be assured of custody. Second, a mediated settlement of support may find itself removed from the enforcement powers the State does have to offer.

Property Issues

There are three prime concerns relating to the mediation of property issues. First, full financial disclosure by both sides is crucial to achieving a fair settlement of these issues. This disclosure is difficult enough to obtain through the use of lawyers with the backing of the traditional legal system. There is a very real fear that settlements achieved through the more informal process of mediation have been achieved without the necessary detailed disclosure. Second, property laws across the country are in a state of flux. If mediators are not lawyers they may not be aware of recent cases or interpretations which could affect the property dispute they are trying to settle. Finally, while mediation is proceeding, the dissipation of assets may go unnoticed and unaccounted for. The traditional legal system has safeguards against this.

Because of concerns like these, it has been suggested that mediation be restricted to custody and access issues, leaving all financial matters to the lawyers and the courts. The problem with this approach is that family law issues are not severable in this manner. One cannot deal with the welfare of the child without also assuring his or her economic well-being.

Custody

Most couples still enter the process of mediation with an unequal commitment to child-rearing. Most women are desperate to keep their children in ways that many men are not. As has already been alluded to, this can result in women bargaining away other rights in order to get custody. There is also the very real concern that in order to effect a settlement on the issue of custody a mediator may propose, and the parties may agree to, joint custody as a solution in situations where it is not appropriate.

Because of concerns like these, a number of American women have recommended that both voluntary and mandatory mediation, whether affiliated with social services or the courts, should be opposed. Canadians are just starting to seriously re-examine mediation and the appropriateness of its use in family dispute resolution. Women can focus attention on the concerns above, so that mediation models which work for, as opposed to against, women can be developed for use in appropriate circumstances.[9]

Assessments

All Canadian provinces now have provision for court-ordered assessments. Usually assessors are directly appointed by the court. In Quebec, they cannot be ordered without the parties' consent. However, if a judge wants one, he or she has appropriate methods of ensuring that consent is obtained. In Edmonton, the assessments take the form of "home studies" prepared at the request of the *amicus curiae* appointed by the court to act in the child's best interests. As of January 1985, the court can order an assessment, which will then be conducted by a psychologist or psychiatrist.

Assessments can, of course, be performed by a private assessor. There are, however, publicly funded facilities in all provinces which provide this service. In all but two provinces, these facilities are staffed by social workers who prepare the reports. Some insist that workers have a Master's degree. Others require no more than a Bachelor's degree plus experience. The exceptions are Toronto, where reports are prepared for the Family Court Clinic by psychologists or psychiatrists, and Edmonton, where, as of January 1985, the same applies. Some of these units have standard formats for assessments which their staff must follow; others do not. In almost all cases, the report concludes with a recommendation. The assessment is filed with the court, disclosed to the parties, and the assessor is available for cross-examination (although in New Brunswick the lawyers have to request cross-examination within three days of receipt of the report).

Often the release of the assessment report results in a settlement of the case. For example, in St. John's, Newfoundland, 100 per cent of the contested custody cases are referred for a court-ordered "home study". A settlement is reached in approximately 80 per cent of the cases where this home study is completed. This is because:

> Although settlement of the custody dispute is not a stated goal of the expert's evaluation, the evaluation frequently resolves the custody dispute. The litigants know that the Court has great respect for the impartial expert. They reason that the Court is likely to follow the expert's recommendation. This often leads the parties to settle the custody dispute along the lines of the expert's recommendations. [10]

Thus, while it is clear that these assessments are not binding on the judges, more often than not the recommendations contained in the reports will closely resemble the judge's disposition. This is borne out by figures collected by Ruth Parry of the Family Court Clinic in Toronto, [11] and by conversations with people at the appropriate publicly funded facilities in Saskatoon and Montreal. In the former case, we were told that "nine times out of ten" the judge follows the assessor's recommendation, while in the latter, it was pointed out that it is "*very* unusual" for the recommendations not to be accepted by the judge.

These so-called "independent" assessments are slowly becoming a necessary pre-condition to having a contested custody case decided in Canada. Under the guise of presenting a more complete and objective case, the decision making in this type of family law dispute is slowly being taken out of the hands of judges and being put into the hands of "experts". There is a dishonesty inherent in this process. Assessments are now not just another helpful piece of evidence; they are the decisive fact in the case. Assessors are not just another "opinion", they are *the* opinion. This is not being acknowledged clearly enough.

One crucial question has not been satisfactorily answered. Are the experts who perform these assessments any more qualified to make the decisions they are being called upon to make than a lay person such as a judge?

> There exists a paradox — at the same time as the demand for assessments from mental health professionals is increasing, there is a parallel growth in scepticism and criticism of the value of such expert testimony in the professional literature of both law and mental health.[12]

What kind of training and experience is needed to perform a custody and/or access assessment? Is a Bachelor's degree with four to five months training in probation work, plus a refresher course in report writing, sufficient (as in British Columbia)? Is a medical degree with a specialty in psychiatry enough? To what extent is any expert able to "objectively" make correct diagnoses concerning the personality structures of adults and children? Won't these judgements necessarily be influenced by his or her own personal biases, opinions, and experiences? How reliably can such experts predict the long-term effects on a child of a particular custody or access decision?

It must be remembered that in making assessors the decision-makers, a process is being sanctioned for which there is no transcript and from which there is no appeal. No record is generally kept as to what transpires during the examination other than the assessor's notes. If the expert says that this is what happened, he or she will be believed. The fact that this particular expert may have a horror of crying women and a tendency to view such behaviour as "hysterical" can never be established except through the protestations of the so-called "hysterical" client. No assessor is going to admit to such a prejudice. When cross-examined he or she, especially if he or she has any court experience, will be only too quick to come forth with a litany of observed behaviour to substantiate the diagnosis of "hysteria". Unlike a court hearing there is no transcript which simply records the evidence presented, yielding a document which can be examined with a view to appeal. The evidence is perceived and presented by the decision-maker, the assessor.

At the top of the assessment ladder are psychiatrists. These are the people who are assumed by the courts and the legal profession to have the most training and expertise to make the kind of judgements necessary for a custody and access assessment. What seems to have been swept under the rug by those who view assessments as a panacea for the resolution of custody disputes is the body of literature questioning both the validity (the extent to which psychiatric conclusions accurately reflect reality) and reliability (the extent to which other psychiatrists agree with these conclusions) of psychiatric opinions. This is in spite of the fact that psychiatrists such as Saul Levine and psychologists such as Robert Groves have posted warning signs for those in the legal profession.[13]

The most comprehensive overview of the reliability and validity of psychiatric testimony is contained in an article by Ennis and Litwack, "Psychiatry and the Presumption of Expertise: Flipping Coins in the Courtroom".[14] Their review of the studies concerning the reliability of psychiatric opinions shows that the chances of two psychiatrists agreeing on a specific diagnosis are barely better than 50-50, "or stated differently, there is about as much chance that a different expert would come to some different conclusions as there is that the other would agree."[15]

There are also studies which graphically illustrate that psychiatric judgements are not only unreliable with respect to the ultimate diagnosis, but also lack consistency, "even in the perception of the presence, nature and severity of symptoms."[16] Different, experienced psychiatrists observing the same interview of a particular patient will not, with any kind of significant regularity, agree on the presence or degree of a particular symptom.

Nor does the research reveal, except in the cases of the grossest kind of psychiatric behaviour, any reliable correlations between diagnoses and patterns of behaviour. Thus, there is no reason to believe that because a particular diagnosis has been made, a particular pattern of behaviour will then in fact be observed.[17] Futhermore,

> Individual psychiatrists are not given any opportunity to learn from their mistakes. Goldberg, for example, points out that clinicians rarely get feedback on the accuracy of their judgments. They may believe their judgments are reliable and valid, but they have no systematic way of testing that belief. For, "unlike other specialties, psychiatry lacks adequate statistics and follow ups, because psychiatrists have not seriously attempted to check on their methods and results the way other medical doctors regard as their scientific duty." As a result, very little of what psychiatrists think they are able to do can be adequately validated.[18]

The problem of the untrustworthiness of expert judgements is compounded in custody cases. In such cases there is a need not only to predict the behaviour of an adult given a particular diagnosis, but also to predict the likely effect of this behaviour on the emotional development of a child. Thus, we have clinical judgements of doubtful validity having to serve as the basis for predictions as to the long-term effects on a child, whose future may be full of unanticipated events. It is easy to see that the best source of data for these predictions would be follow-up studies on the effects on children of various court-ordered arrangements for custody and access. No comprehensive studies of this nature appear to exist.[19]

Okpaku, in her article on the role of psychological assessments in custody disputes, is as critical of psychological expert opinions as she is of psychiatric opinions. Aside from the question of the reliability of various psychological tests, no such test results can form the basis for a personality analysis without the intervention of a personality theory. In the area of personality theories, one is in the area of psychiatric diagnosis, with all of its weaknesses.

Okpaku assumes that a psychological assessment would be composed of both in-depth interviews and testing of the parents and the children in question. Using the personality picture of all parties which is then developed, predictions are made as to how these particular adults will continue to interact with and affect the emotional development of this particular child.

> There are two major impediments to an informed opinion resulting from this procedure. The psychologist would be making predictions about the likely future behaviour of the adults on the basis of assessments of personalities, relying presumably on one of several personality theories. And yet, in a number of rigorous, well-documented studies, the general invalidity of predictions of future behaviour based on personality theory has been established. Moreover, such predictions rely heavily upon the vague and overbroad concepts of mental disorders referred to in the foregoing discussion of the infirmities of psychological theory for decision making purposes. Equally important, even if the interviewer were sufficiently informed of past adult behaviour so that he might check assumptions concerning likely future behaviour, there is no body of relevant data indicating the likely consequences of the assumed behaviour on the child. In other words, without empirical data specifying how adult behaviour affects children, the behavioural science expert is without a scientific basis for an opinion on *any* issue in a difficult case. For example, a psychologist might decide that a father and his mother, who has offered to care for the child, would be more 'consistent' in their relations with the

child than the mother. However, without data to establish that a less than perfectly consistent mother adversely affects a child and that consistency makes up for whatever emotional trauma, if any, a child experiences when removed from its mother's custody, an opinion suggesting an award to the father would lack scientific support. The psychologist's opinion would be no better or worse than that of a lay person having strong ideas on the importance of 'consistency'.[20]

The question still remains as to whether or not psychologists and/or psychiatrists are in a position, because of their training, to be any more "objective" in their judgements of other people than a lay person, such as a judge. The answer to this question appears to be a resounding "no". Far from being objective, the expert's diagnosis seems to be influenced most by the "clinician's own personality, value system, self-image, personal preferences and attitudes."[21] Futhermore, if the data presented is complex, ill-defined, and ambiguous (which is often true in custody cases, especially difficult ones) the likelihood of intra-observer factors influencing an assessor's perception, judgement, and decision is even greater.[22] As well, unconscious conflicts of clinicians often distort their perceptions, and cause them to misunderstand a patient's true condition.[23] What implications does this have if the court-appointed assessor is going through a custody battle of his or her own?

The concerns raised by the research above are obvious. First, should any special weight be given to the evidence of experts who cannot demonstrate that the application of their expertise yields judgements and conclusions which are significantly more reliable or valid than those a lay person might reach? At a minimum, if admitted, such testimony must be in a context that affords opposing parties an opportunity for both meaningful cross-examination and the calling of evidence relating to a second assessment.

At present, much of the cross-examination of experts in custody cases is inadequate. One reason is that lawyers themselves tend to accept psychiatric judgements at face value, possibly because of their own lack of expertise in the area. However, the other reality the lawyer must face is that he or she was not present during the examination on which the assessor's judgement is based and, consequently, has little information about the circumstances that might have influenced the assessor's conclusions. One way to deal with this is to insist on the solicitor's presence at all times during an assessment. The other is to videotape all examinations and to give the counsel for all parties an opportunity to see and use these videotapes in court.

Given that assessments are likely to be influenced by who the assessor is, it is also only fair that counsel be given the right to cross-examine the assessor on his or her own personal biases, experiences, and values. At present, most judges will not allow such questions.

Finally, if even an "independent" assessment can be subject to bias and error, there should be available to both parties the opportunity for a second full assessment — where all involved people are seen by someone else who has no knowledge as to what the first assessor said.

Custody decisions are always difficult. We must be careful that, in order to avoid making them, we do not hand the matter over to a group of individuals who suffer under the illusion that their mandate is only to express an opinion, not to make a decision, and whose opinions may be no more valid than those of a judge. We must acknowledge that, at present, a custody decision, particularly in a difficult case, is "at bottom an intuitive guess for everyone."[24] There is no way of knowing whether a guess is right or wrong.

Conclusion

Family law is in a state of rapid transition which has serious implications for all involved in such disputes. Before this transition goes any further, current research and analytical thinking must be continued and intensified.[25]

Harriet Sachs, of King and Sachs in Toronto, is a specialist in family law and writes frequently on this subject.

APPENDIX A: STANDARDS OF PRACTICE FOR FAMILY MEDIATORS[26]

Preamble

For purposes of these standards, family mediation is defined as a process in which a qualified person helps family members resolve their disputes in a consensual and informed manner. It is essential to this process that the mediator be qualified and impartial; that the participants reach decisions voluntarily; that their decisions be based on sufficient factual data; and that each participant understands the information upon which decisions are reached. While family mediation may be viewed as an alternate means of conflict resolution, it shall not be a substitute for the benefit of independent legal advice.

Standards

I.   **The mediator has a duty to define and describe the process of mediation and its cost before reaching an agreement to mediate.**

Specific Considerations

A.   Before the actual mediation sessions begin, the mediator shall conduct an orientation session to give an overview of the process and to assess the appropriateness of mediation for the participants. Among the topics covered, the mediator shall discuss the following:

> (1) The mediator shall define the process in context so that the participants understand the differences between mediation and other means of conflict resolution available to them. In defining the process, the mediator shall also distinguish it from therapy or marriage counseling.

> (2) The mediator shall obtain sufficient information from the participants so they can mutually define the issues to be resolved in mediation.

> (3) The mediator and the participants shall agree upon the duties and responsibilities that each is accepting in the mediation process. The participants should understand

that either of them or the mediator has the right to suspend or terminate the process at any time.

(4) The mediator shall assess the ability and willingness of the participants to mediate. The mediator shall also assess his or her own ability and willingness to undertake mediation with these particular participants and the issues to be mediated. This is a continuing duty.

(5) The mediator shall explain the fees for mediation and reach an agreement with the participants for payment. It is inappropriate for a mediator to charge a contingency fee or to base the fee on the outcome of the mediation process.

(6) The mediator shall inform the participants that each should employ independent legal counsel for advice throughout the mediation process. In the event the mediator is a lawyer, the lawyer-mediator shall inform the participants that the lawyer-mediator cannot represent either or both of them in a marital dissolution or in any legal action.

(7) The mediator shall discuss the issue of separate sessions and shall reach an understanding with the participants as to whether and under what circumstances the mediator may meet alone with either of them or with any third party.

II. The mediator shall not voluntarily disclose any information obtained through the mediation process without the prior consent of both participants.

Specific Considerations

A. At the orientation session the parties should agree in writing not to require the mediator to disclose to any third party any statements made in the course of mediation. The mediator shall inform the participants that the mediator will not voluntarily disclose to any third party any of the information obtained through the mediation process.

B. The mediator shall inform the participants of the mediator's inability to bind third parties to an agreement not to disclose in the absence of any absolute privilege.

C. At this orientation session, the mediator must discuss with the participants the potential outcome of their disclosure of facts to each other during the mediation process.

III. The mediator has a duty to be impartial.

Specific Considerations

A.   A lawyer-mediator shall not represent either party during or after the mediation process in any legal matters. In the event the mediator has represented one of the parties beforehand, the mediator shall not undertake the mediation.

B.   A mediator who is a mental health person, shall not provide counseling or therapy to either party or both during or after the mediation process. If the mediator has provided marriage counseling to the participants, or therapy to either of them beforehand, the mediator shall not undertake the mediation.

C.   The mediator shall disclose to the participants any biases relating to the issues to be mediated both in the orientation session and also before those issues are discussed in mediation.

D.   Impartiality is not the same as neutrality. While the mediator must be impartial as between the mediation participants, the mediator should be concerned with fairness. The mediator has an obligation to avoid an unreasonable result.

E.   The mediator has a duty to promote the best interest of the children. The mediator also has a duty to assist parents to examine the separate and individual needs of their children and to consider those needs apart from their own desires for any particular parenting formula. If the mediator believes that any proposed agreement between the parents does not protect the best interests of the children, the mediator has a duty to inform them of this belief and its basis.

F.   The mediator shall not communicate with either party alone or with any third parties to discuss mediation issues without the prior consent of the mediation participants.

IV. The mediator has a duty to assure that the mediation participants make decisions based upon sufficient information and knowledge.

Specific Considerations

A.   The mediator shall assure that there is full financial disclosure, evaluation, and development of relevant factual information in the mediation process, such as each would reasonably receive in the normal discovery process.

B.   In addition to requiring this disclosure, evaluation and development of information, the mediator shall promote the equal understanding of such information before any agreement is reached. This consideration may require the mediator to recommend that either or both obtain expert consultation in the event that it appears that additional knowledge or understanding is necessary for balanced negotiation.

C.   The mediator who is a lawyer may define the legal issues. The lawyer-mediator shall not direct the decision of the mediation participants based upon the lawyer-mediator's interpretation of the law as applied to the facts of the situation. The mediator shall endeavor to assure that the participants have a sufficient understanding of appropriate statutory and case law as well as local judicial tradition, before reaching an agreement by recommending to the participants that they obtain independent legal representation during the process. This recommendation shall be made whether or not the mediator is a lawyer. If the participants or either of them choose to proceed without independent counsel the mediator shall warn them of the risk involved in not being represented, including the possibility that any agreement they submit to a court may be rejected as unreasonable in light of both parties' legal rights or may not be binding on them.

V.   The mediator has a duty to suspend or terminate mediation whenever continuation of the process would harm or prejudice one or more of the participants.

Specific Considerations

A.   If the mediator believes that the ability or willingness of either of the participants to meaningfully participate in the process is lacking the mediator has a duty to suspend or terminate the process.

B.   If the mediator believes that the agreement being approached is unreasonable, the mediator has a duty to suspend or terminate the process.

C.   The mediator should assure that each person has had the opportunity to fully understand the implications and ramifications of all options available.

D.   The mediator shall inform the participants that emotions play a part in the decision-making process. The mediator shall attempt to elicit from each of the participants a confirmation that each understands the connection between one's own emotions and the bargaining process.

E. The mediator has a duty to assure a balanced dialogue and must attempt to diffuse any manipulative or intimidating negotiation techniques utilized by either of the participants.

F. If the mediator has suspended or terminated the process, the mediator should suggest that the participants obtain additional professional services as may be appropriate.

VI. The mediator has a continuing duty to advise each of the mediation participants to obtain legal review prior to reaching any agreement.

Specific Considerations

A. Each of the mediation participants should have independent legal counsel before reaching final agreement. The mediator shall recommend that the participants obtain legal advice at the beginning of the mediation process and before the participants have reached any accord to which they have made an emotional commitment. In order to promote the integrity of the process, the mediator shall not refer either of the participants to any particular lawyers. When an attorney referral is requested, the parties should be referred to a Bar Association list if available. In the absence of such a list, the mediator may only provide a list of qualified family law attorneys in the community.

B. The mediator shall obtain an agreement from the participants in the orientation session as to whether and under what circumstances the mediator may speak directly and separately with each of their lawyers during the mediation process.

C. The mediator shall obtain an agreement from the husband and the wife that each lawyer, upon request, shall be entitled to review all the factual documentation provided by the participants in the mediation process.

D. Any agreement which is prepared in the mediation process should be separately reviewed by independent counsel for each participant before it is signed. While the mediator can not insist that each participant have separate counsel they should be discouraged from signing any agreement which has not been so reviewed.

Notes

1. Canada, Statistics Canada, *Divorce: Law and the Family in Canada* (Ottawa: Supply and Services Canada, 1983), p. 10.

2. Rosalie Silberman Abella, "Procedural Aspects of Arrangements for Children upon Divorce in Canada", 61:2 *Canadian Bar Review* (June 1983), at 447.

3. Leonard L. Loeb, "Introduction to the Standards of Practice for Family Mediators", 17:4 *Family Law Quarterly* (Winter 1984), at 452.

4. Frances E. Olsen, "The Family and the Market: A Study of Ideology and Legal Reform", 96 *Harvard Law Review* 1497 (1983), at 1542.

5. Janet Rifkin, "Mediation from a Feminist Perspective: Promise and Problems", *Law and Inequality: A Journal of Theory and Practice,* vol. II, no. 1, February 1984, p. 22.

6. *Ibid.*, p. 24.

7. *Ibid.*, p. 30.

8. The role of the mediator in equalizing power imbalances is discussed in much of the literature on mediation. See, for example: John Haynes, Ph. D., *Divorce Mediation* (New York: Springs Publishing Co., 1981). However, one must always return to the issue of ensuring that mediators are adequately trained.

9. Carole Lefcourt, "Women, Mediation and Family Law" — summary of conclusions reached at a conference on the above subject held in January 1983 and sponsored by the National Centre on Women and Family Law, New York City.

10. Victor J. Baum, "Alternatives to Litigation", in *Family Law: Dimensions of Justice,* eds. Rosalie S. Abella and Claire L'Heureux-Dubé (Toronto: Butterworths, 1983), p. 107.

11. Saul V. Levine, "The Role of the Mental Health Expert Witness in Family Law Disputes", in *Family Law: Dimensions of Justice,* p. 134.

12. Robert T. Groves, "Lawyers, Psychologists and Psychological Evidence in Child Protection Hearings", *Queen's Law Journal,* at 243.

13. *Supra,* n. 11 and 12.

14. Bruce J. Ennis and Thomas R. Litwack, "Psychiatry and the Presumption of Expertise: Flipping Coins in the Courtroom", 62 *California Law Review* (1974).

15. *Ibid.*, p. 701.

16. *Ibid.*, p. 706.

17. *Ibid.*, p. 711.

18. *Ibid.*, p. 720.

19. Sheila R. Okpaku, "Psychology: Impediment or Aid in Child Custody Cases?", 29 *Rutgers Law Review* (1976), at 1140-1141.

20. *Ibid.*, pp. 1143-1144.

21. Ennis and Litwack, p. 726.

22. *Ibid.*, p. 727.

23. *Ibid.*, p. 727.

24. Okpaku, p. 1152.

25. Work is being done in this area. See, for example: Richard A. Gardner, Ph. D., *Family Evaluation in Child Custody Litigation* (Cresgill: Creative Therapeutics, 1982).

26. Copyright 1984, American Bar Association: 17:4 *Family Law Quarterly* (Winter 1984), at 455-460.

Joint Custody[*]

— Renée Joyal-Poupart

There is a growing sentiment that it is in the best interests of children to maintain close ties with both parents after the dissolution of a marriage. In recent years, joint custody has been the focus of efforts to ensure this objective. Some of the American states have gone so far as to introduce a presumption in favour of joint custody into the law.

The author examines custody legislation and jurisprudence in a number of jurisdictions. Drawing on the American experience and on feminist literature, she argues that joint custody must not be seen as a panacea and should be granted only in cases where parents have expressly requested it.

Introduction

Joint custody of children whose parents are no longer living together is a fashionable idea. Although Canadian legislation does not make specific reference to it, for the last 12 years or so, our courts have, in some cases, sanctioned this concept. Several states in the United States have adopted legislation expressly authorizing or favouring joint custody. This issue has also given rise to heated debates among specialists and the general public alike in Canada and the United States.

---

[*] Translated from French

Is this just a passing fad or is this indeed a concept with real potential? To get a clearer idea of what has been called "the pet idea of the decade"[1] in the United States, the meaning of "joint custody" must first be clarified since this expression refers to a multifaceted phenomenon. In broad terms, it means that upon separation, the responsibility for the children will not fall to one parent alone (usually the mother), as was and still is the case in most instances today. In contrast to what happens in the case of exclusive custody, decisions concerning all aspects of the child's life may be shared: this is called *joint legal custody*. The daily physical custody of the child may be awarded to one of the parents while the other is awarded access rights to the child. In a broader context, joint custody may mean that the child lives with each of the parents alternately; this is called *joint physical custody*. This situation may give rise to very varied practical arrangements (custody alternating from week to week or month to month, or according to set periods such as the school week and the weekend, or the academic year and summer vacation).

The idea of joint custody emerged as a social and legal reality in Canada following a historical evolution. In the nineteenth century, the domination of the father in the traditional family group was a firmly established principle. This resulted in the standard common law practice of awarding custody of the children to the father in the event that the parents separated. This practice is still in effect in Nova Scotia and the Yukon; in the other English-speaking provinces, specific legislation has been enacted to eliminate this practice.[2] In Quebec, according to the *Civil Code* of 1866, custody of the children was to be entrusted to the parent who had obtained the separation from bed and board, unless the court was of the opinion that it was to "the child's advantage" to have custody awarded to the other parent or to a third party. The same presumption applied when parents who had obtained a divorce from the federal Parliament went before the Quebec courts for a decision regarding custody of their children.[3]

The "tender years" doctrine then developed which advocated awarding custody of young children to their mother. This doctrine influenced Canadian court decisions starting in the second half of the nineteenth century. It can be linked to the emergence of a "sense of family" in Western countries at that time. In a now famous work, Elisabeth Badinter clearly described the historical evolution which resulted in the mother and child holding a special place in the new "family portrait".[4] It should be noted, however, that although the mother had the dominant role in the "emotional sphere", the father retained all his economic supremacy.

Although in principle the tender years doctrine involves only children under the age of seven, case law has extended its application to minors in general. Studies conducted by Statistics Canada for the period from 1969-1979 show that 85.6 per cent of Canadian custody decisions awarded custody of the children to the mother.[5] In the majority of cases, however, custody is not contested by the husband, and the court in rendering this judgement is merely following up on an implicit or explicit agreement of the parties.

It should be noted that the custody decisions recently handed down by Canadian courts are no longer based on the "tender years" doctrine but on the concept of the "best interests of the child". This concept has been recognized in the highest courts as the main consideration in all custody decisions.[6]

Although the adjudication criteria have changed, the practical results of the process remain the same, as the studies conducted by Statistics Canada indicate. It is precisely this state of affairs which the proponents of joint custody are contesting, basing their arguments on the rights of parents and children alike. Adopting the feminist demands of shared parental responsibilities and citing the presence of women in the labour market, separated and divorced fathers — often supported by various men's associations — have begun to demand a larger share of parental responsibilities in the event of separation. This movement has met with support, as well as reservations and criticism, from many experts in the human sciences field. The arguments raised by both sides will be examined later in this paper.

Legal Aspects of Joint Custody

In this section the legal bases of the concept of joint custody, its incorporation into Canadian legal decisions and, finally, various types of formal arrangements will be examined.

Legal Bases of Joint Custody

In the Canadian constitutional context, it must first be determined whether this issue falls under federal or provincial jurisdiction. *The Constitution Act (1982)* gives the federal Parliament exclusive jurisdiction over marriage and divorce (s. 91.26), and the provincial legislatures exclusive jurisdiction over property and civil rights (s. 92.13). This general division of powers includes issues regarding custody of children.[7] It will now be determined whether the provisions of the federal *Divorce Act* are compatible with provincial legislation regarding custody of children, and to what extent they authorize legal decisions awarding joint custody.

Under the heading "corollary relief", section 10 of the *Divorce Act* provides for the awarding of custody during the proceedings:

> Where a petition for divorce has been presented, the court having jurisdiction to grant relief in respect thereof may make such interim orders as it thinks fit and just
>
> (b) for the maintenance of and the custody, care and upbringing of the children of the marriage pending the hearing and determination of the petition.

Section 11 provides for the awarding of custody at the time judgement is rendered:

> (1) Upon granting a decree nisi of divorce, the court may, if it thinks fit and just to do so having regard to the conduct of the parties and the condition and means and other circumstances of each of them, make one or more of the following orders, namely:
>
> (c) an order providing for the custody, care and upbringing of the children of the marriage.

Based on these provisions, the following observations, among others, can be made: that the *Divorce Act* considers the custody of the children as a corollary matter; that the court has very broad discretion with regard to the type of order to be handed down; that joint custody is not specifically provided for in the Act; that the rather vague and general criteria for determining custody refer more to the parents than to the children and that, in particular, the criterion relating to the child's best interests is not expressly mentioned.

Despite the silence of the *Divorce Act*, the child's best interests managed to emerge as the courts' primary criterion in child custody decisions. In a recent speech to the Vancouver Institute, Madam Justice Bertha Wilson of the Supreme Court of Canada described the evolution of this phenomenon. The concept of the child's best interests can be traced directly to the function of *parens patriae* of the Sovereign with regard to legally incapable persons, which first emerged in England during the seventeenth century. However, it was not until 200 years later that the English courts exercised this function with regard to the custody of children, and even then they intervened only in cases of extreme immorality, cruelty, and serious negligence on the part of the parents toward their children. Subsequently, the concept of the child's best interests gradually gained ground and was finally incorporated into legislation at the beginning of this century.[8]

A similar evolution occurred in Canada over the last 150 years. The concept of the child's best interests was gradually accepted as the determining criterion for awarding custody of children, first through the impetus given by the courts, then as a result of legislation introduced in several Canadian provinces.

At the end of her study of provincial legislation regarding parental authority and child custody, Anita D. Fineberg concludes that in the majority of legislative provisions, there is no legal presumption favouring one parent over the other with regard to custody of the children. Only Nova Scotia and the Yukon are exceptions to the rule since they continue to apply the old common law principle according to which custody is awarded to the father. According to the same study, the criterion of the child's best interests apparently figures in the majority of these legislative provisions, either alone or in conjuction with other criteria which are just as vague. Only Ontario, Manitoba, and British Columbia have attempted to provide a statutory indication of what is encompassed by the expression "in the child's best interests".[9]

Fineberg's paper indicates that there are no contradictions between the *Divorce Act* and provincial legislative provisions with regard to child custody. It also points out that joint custody is neither expressly authorized nor expressly forbidden by these various provisions (except in Nova Scotia and the Yukon).

Can it then be concluded that the concept of joint custody is based on relatively sound legal grounds? Could it not perhaps even be claimed that the absence of a presumption favouring one parent over the other with regard to custody would create, *de facto,* a presumption favouring joint custody? The author does not feel that this approach should be adopted since the very general terms of the relevant provisions authorize the court to render orders of all types, and the joint custody order is only one option among many.[10] In fact, care must be taken not to confuse the possession of parental authority with the exercise of that authority. Unless they are deprived of parental authority, both parents will always possess that authority, regardless of which parent is awarded legal custody of the child.[11] Moreover, a custody order can be changed and custody may pass from one parent to the other, which clearly illustrates the relevance of the above distinction. Thus, with regard to custody, the courts have great latitude for ordering either exclusive or joint custody.

However imprecise and subject to interpretation it may be, the criterion of the child's best interests was recognized by the Supreme Court of Canada, in decisions which have become leading precedents, as the primary consideration in child custody cases.[12]

Incorporation of the Concept in Case Law

In a letter addressed to the members of the Canadian Bar Association and the Jeune Barreau de Québec in 1979, Madam Justice Claire L'Heureux-Dubé of the Quebec Court of Appeal pointed out that joint custody was recognized by courts in England before it was recognized by the courts of the English-speaking provinces in Canada. In Quebec, the incorporation of this concept in case law was "much later and more timid".[13] All things considered, joint custody began to emerge in the decisions of English courts and then Canadian courts only in 1950, and it has only attained a degree of visibility in Canada since 1975.

In taking joint custody into consideration, the courts employed unfamiliar legal concepts and terms which naturally caused some confusion in the initial years of use. These concepts and terms should be examined in order to avoid any ambiguity.

"Joint custody" was the main expression which appeared in court decisions as opposed to "exclusive custody". The purpose of a joint custody order was originally to ensure the exercise of parental authority by both parents in the event of their separation. When legal custody of a child is awarded to one of the parents, with access rights to the other parent, the latter is practically excluded from decisions concerning the various aspects of the child's life, although in principle he or she continues to enjoy parental authority and even a supervisory right with regard to the child's education.[14] Joint custody orders were handed down in order to avoid this exclusion and maintain co-parenting at the decision-making level. However, joint custody did not originally include the physical custody or daily care and control of the child; this was awarded to one of the parents, and access rights were given to the other. Today, this concept has changed. In addition to legal co-parenting, many cases now include physical co-parenting. Not only are decisions made jointly, but daily responsibility for the child is also shared between the two parents.[15]

This much more concrete type of division of custody is perceived by its advocates as the only real and meaningful form of joint custody because, in their view, the formula might remain a strictly theoretical one if the sharing of everyday responsibilities is not accompanied by a sharing of decisions.

The "split order" is a type of order used primarily in England; it awards legal custody to one of the parents and physical custody to the other. This is, in fact, split custody of the child so that the parent responsible for the child on a day-to-day basis is not the parent who exercises parental authority and vice versa. Under what circumstances would this type of order seem appropriate? This is what Lord Denning had to say:

> Cases often arise in the Divorce Court where a guilty wife deserts her husband and takes the children with her, but the father has no means of bringing them up himself. In such a situation, the usual order is that the father, the innocent party, is given the custody of the child or children, but the care and control is left to the mother. That order is entirely realistic.[16]

The ingenuous sexism of this argument would make us laugh today, as does the resulting division of roles: the power to the father, the daily worries to the mother. In fact, this formula was severely criticized. It was contradictory to award physical custody of the child to a parent who was denied all means of exercising parental authority. The split order may have also caused practical problems which were very detrimental to the child, since his or her physical custodian was not authorized to make any decisions, even urgent ones, concerning, for example, the child's health. This formula has rarely been applied in Canada, except in certain cases where the custody was split between the parents, holders of parental authority, and a third party to whom the physical custody of the child was awarded.[17]

"Alternating custody" is another formula whereby the legal and physical custody of the child is awarded to one of the parents for a specific period of time and then to the other. This is not shared custody but rather a division of the custody, with each parent being the exclusive guardian for a given period. This type of order has been used in a few cases in Canada and more frequently in the United States.[18] It should be noted that this formula is similar to joint custody with regard to the physical custody of the child, but is diametrically opposed to joint custody with regard to the exercise of parental authority.

Various Types of Formal Arrangements

In a very large majority of cases, joint custody is the result of an amicable agreement between the parents, independent of any legal procedure. It is often the case that spouses decide to separate without initiating divorce or separation proceedings. It also happens that the court, even when it has a petition for divorce or separation before it, does not render a judgement concerning the custody of the children.

Depending on whether it falls under the jurisdiction of Quebec or one of the other provinces, an amicable agreement concluded between spouses has different legal status. According to common law, the separation agreement is a contract and can be enforced. The clauses regarding custody can, however, be invalidated by the court, if the court feels that they are contrary to the public policy or not in the interest of the children concerned. In civil law, the separation agreement is not executory and, as indicated by Mr. Justice Albert Mayrand of the Quebec Court of Appeal, it will be respected only as long as both parties agree to comply with it.[19]

Joint custody can also result from a court order, usually rendered following an "agreement" by the parents. Section 2 of the *Divorce Act* explicitly permits this type of agreement. It should be noted, however, that the court can refuse to sanction such an agreement if it feels that it is not in the child's best interests.[20] Even when sanctioned by the court, this agreement is still subject to review by the court, as with any other custody order.[21] In contrast to an amicable agreement which is not sanctioned by the court, the agreement which has received legal sanction has the force of law and can be enforced.

When there is no agreement between the parents regarding the joint custody of their children, the court can still hand down a joint custody order. However, judges are reluctant to do so when parents do not agree. It is in fact unlikely that the cooperation needed for this form of custody can be forced upon parents who do not wish it. This explains the small number of such orders.[22] In addition, a number of authors have come out against joint custody when the parents do not agree on this formula for sharing their responsibilities.[23]

Social Aspects of the Issue

The social aspects of joint custody will be examined first from the children's point of view, then from the perspective of women. This examination will not be exhaustive, however, since the factors involved in this issue are often related and can at times go beyond the proposed framework.

The Children's Point of View

What does joint custody mean with regard to the best interests of the child? Many authors, basing their views on research carried out on children whose parents are separated or divorced, prefer this formula because they feel it will promote the child's development.[24] The studies most frequently quoted are those of Joan Kelly and Judith Wallerstein.[25] The goal of these studies was to identify the effects of the parents' separation and divorce on their children at various stages in their development. The children who participated in the survey were in the exclusive custody of their mother. Although it is not possible within the scope of this paper to give a detailed description of the methodology used and the results of this research, it is generally agreed that:

> . . . the loss of a parent by divorce is potentially as serious as is the death of a parent. The loss of the sense of security, the fear of being vulnerable to unknown forces, the loss of a loved source of caring and of the object for role identification, results in the reaction of depression and denial, aggressivity and acting out behaviour, ranging from mild to severe neuroses and may develop into persistent character disorders.[26]

Other studies carried out by Neil Kalter; G. Awad and R. Parry; E.M. Hetherington, M. Cox, and R. Cox; and M. Roman and W. Haddad came to similar conclusions.[27] However, research conducted in Ontario on 300 families showed that the fathers who refuse or neglect to pay child support as required are those who maintain the least regular contacts with their children.[28]

In the author's opinion, all these studies indicate that the meaningful presence of both parents in the life of the child is highly desirable, from the emotional point of view as well as the social and material points of view. Is joint custody the only way to meet this objective? The studies quoted above did not demonstrate this and, moreover, many objections have been raised in various forums to the idea that joint custody is, in all cases, the best solution in the interests of the child.

The best known of the authors who have come out against joint custody are L. Goldstein, A. Freud, and A. Solnit. Citing the child's right to continuity and stability in emotional relationships, they recommend that custody of the child be given to one parent only who, moreover, would be given the power to grant or deny access rights to the other parent.[29] Although this last recommendation seems somewhat excessive and the social scientific community has come out unanimously against it,[30] we should bear in mind the reasons that prompted these authors to make this recommendation: the danger that the child would be subjected to perpetual conflict, contradictory values, and constant shuffling — physical and moral — between the father and the mother.

These arguments have frequently been advanced by judges who are reluctant to grant joint custody, especially when the parents do not agree on this formula.[31] Many also believe that it is in the best interests of the child to have a fixed residence, an actual base where she or he really feels at home. Some claim that joint custody is a catalyst for competition between parents and that the desire of the parents to win the unconditional affection of their children may make them lose sight of certain important educational objectives.[32] From a practical point of view, joint custody is feasible only when both parents live in the same neighbourhood. A child cannot really be asked to change schools, friends, and physical environment on a frequent and regular basis. Because of this very constraint, the formula is precarious and should necessarily be reviewed if one of the parents moves to another city or neighbourhood. Finally, joint physical custody is a way of life which may give the child hope — a vain hope in most cases — that his parents will get back together.[33]

The concept of joint custody is relatively new and is applied in only a few cases; conclusive research dealing with the reactions of children whose parents have been awarded joint custody has not yet been conducted. Following an intensive study, that was nevertheless limited to four families that tried this arrangement, Alice Abarbanel concludes that "there is reason to believe that joint custody is at least as good an arrangement as any other. It is neither 'good' nor 'bad': it works under certain conditions."[34]

Women's Point of View

For several years now, women and the organizations that defend their interests have been seeking the same employment opportunities that men have and a more equal division of parental responsibilities. In the search for these two objectives which are closely linked in the lives of many women, the situation has improved. However, there is still much to be done on both the individual and the collective level. Moreover, the current recession is hampering women's entry into stable and well-paying jobs.

In this general context, can joint custody be viewed as a formula compatible with the objectives sought by women? It should be noted that it is precisely in order to facilitate the division of parental responsibilities that many separated and divorced men, as well as the associations representing their point of view, are arguing in favour of joint custody.

When it is a matter of the child's best interests, the research studies quoted above tend to conclude that mothers encounter serious problems in their role as exclusive custodial parent: overwork, problems in interpersonal relationships, family tensions, isolation, confinement, and frustrations.[35]

Separation or divorce also often means poverty, misery, and stagnation for the mother as custodial parent.[36] The support payments awarded by courts are rarely sufficient to maintain the previous standard of living of the family and, in an alarming percentage of cases, the father does not fulfil his financial obligations.[37]

For all these reasons, it would seem that joint custody would be an attractive concept to women. However, without further study it should not be viewed as a miracle solution.

Joint legal custody ensures continuous control by the non-custodial parent (generally the father) over decisions to be made concerning all aspects of the children's lives. The custodial parent (usually the mother), who assumes day-to-day responsibility for the children, is therefore obliged to go through endless consultations, negotiations, and discussions which may, in many cases, become exhausting and give rise to a power model similar to that which was described earlier in connection with the split order.

Joint physical custody involves the same risk and has many other negative aspects. For example, division of physical custody often exempts the father from providing support payments for his children or considerably reduces the amount of these payments. Moreover, when the family has real estate or other property, such a division often enables the father to retain a larger share of such property than he would have if exclusive custody of the children had been awarded to the mother.

In the present state of affairs, it is therefore in the father's financial interests to obtain joint custody; for him it constitutes an advantage which inevitably corresponds to an equivalent disadvantage for the mother. Some believe that this factor comes into play fairly often in the request for joint custody by the father.[38] One fact remains. If the woman has given up the opportunity to work and earn a living in order to look after her family and at the time of separation is unemployed or employed in an unstable and poorly paid position, joint custody may aggravate the situation. With their father, the children would find comfort and material benefits; with their mother, financial difficulties and privation.

As Arthur Leonoff and Maureen O'Neil state, "It is a fact that if (women) are able to retain custody they will be awarded higher maintenance payments, either from their husband, or if they are poor by the government. As well, given the low status of most women's work in the marketplace, their role as mothers remains of highest importance to them and is the primary source of their self-esteem."[39] Unless there is an equitable division of financial responsibilities for the maintenance of the children, joint physical custody of the children should be viewed with reservations from the point of view of women.

Moreover, in each case, joint physical custody presupposes that both the mother and the father have adequate accommodation and the material means to bring up children, a requirement which is difficult without an above-average income.

Another potential source of problems is the obligation for parents who share physical custody of their child to communicate and agree on all aspects (educational, health, material, and social) of the child's development. Several authors have indicated the need for maturity on the part of both parents in this regard and the impossibility of implementing this type of division without a general framework of cooperation between the parents.[40] Of course, this constraint is as difficult to bear for the father as for the mother. But, despite the developments which have been made in this area, the situation might be a more difficult one for the mother. Even today, only a small number of fathers perform as many concrete, daily tasks as the mother in bringing up their children. When the marriage breaks down, many fathers feel deprived, disorganized, and quite overwhelmed by the task of sharing custody. The odds are that the mother will be called upon more often than she should be to do the shopping, plan outings, vacations and visits to the doctor, and so on. If not, it is the child who will suffer and the father may complain of a lack of cooperation, unless he systematically turns to other women (close relatives, a spouse or paid nannies) to assume most of the parental duties. There are numerous examples of such situations.[41]

It is not the case that fathers are incapable of assuming responsibility for their children; however, at the present time there are very few fathers who have had this experience and who are ready to perform this task fully on a day-to-day basis. In this context, the mother would be doubly penalized, if the division of physical custody led to a reduction in support payments and a less favourable division of the family assets.

Although there is no statistical data on this subject, there is evidence from many lawyers and marriage counsellors that, after a few years of joint custody, many parents want to return to exclusive custody. It would be interesting to find out what their children would have to say about the matter.

Joint custody may be a worthwhile alternative for some mothers who are financially independent, mature, and cooperative and who have ex-husbands who are equally mature and cooperative, live in close proximity, and are ready to accept concrete responsibility for the children. For the majority of mothers, however, joint custody would be only one option among many to consider with regard to the welfare of the children, and their ability to survive emotionally, economically, and socially.

Conclusion

There are unquestioning supporters of joint custody who hope that this type of custody will become the general rule and that it can be imposed by the court even when parents disagree.[42] However, a good many authors who favour joint custody are cautious in their conclusions and believe that this formula does not work in all cases.[43] Several stress the need for more detailed studies to determine the impact of this type of life on the children involved and their parents.[44]

The authors agree almost unanimously on the following general observations: that, after the parents' divorce or separation, it is beneficial for the children to maintain meaningful relationships with their father and mother to the greatest possible degree; and that the relationships between parents and children should be arranged within a general framework of cooperation.

About 30 American states have deemed it appropriate to expressly authorize joint custody through legislation.[45] The state of California has gone even further in this direction by adopting, a few years ago, a presumption *juris tantum* that joint custody is in the child's best interests when the parents agree to this type of custody. In the case of disagreement between the parents, the court must consider the possibility of joint custody at the request of one of the parents and give the grounds for its decision not to grant this type of order. By appointing an exclusive custodian, the court must, among other things, determine which of the two parents is the most likely to encourage frequent, regular contacts between the children and the non-custodial parent.[46] A few years after this legislation took effect, statistical studies showed that joint legal custody was awarded in 26 per cent of the orders (including 2 per cent in contested cases), and of those, joint physical custody was ordered in, at most, approximately 5 per cent. Despite the explicit preference of the California legislature, use of the latter option is adopted in very few cases. Moreover, 33 1/3 per cent of amicable agreements concerning custody stipulate joint legal custody.

The movement advocating a legal presumption in favour of joint custody is strenuously contested by American feminist organizations. Addressing legislative authorities in New York state on behalf of the National Organization for Women (NOW), Lillian Kosak recalled that, according to a scientific study conducted in California, a decreasing percentage of fathers (20 per cent in 1968, 13 per cent in 1972, and 7.9 per cent in 1977) are demanding exclusive or joint custody of the children, while the success rate of these requests is increasing (35 per cent in 1968, 37 per cent in 1972, and 63 per cent in 1977). This data clearly shows that fathers are not discriminated against by the courts with regard to child custody.

Arguing that joint custody can be a good solution only in a limited number of cases and only when both parents agree, NOW has come out against the establishment of any legal presumption on this matter. To date, its point of view has prevailed, since the state of New York has not introduced any legislation in favour of joint custody.

In elaborating its position on this issue, NOW stresses the negative financial consequences of this formula for women and the risks of perpetuating relationships of domination and difficult conflict situations within the family. As well, joint custody can lead to serious dangers when the father behaves violently toward his ex-wife and children.[47]

Why, then, confer a special status on this formula and place the parent who opposes it, whatever the legitimacy of his or her motives, in an eminently difficult situation, as the California legislature did a few years ago?

Given the impending legislative changes in Canada with regard to divorce, both the issue of child custody and the context in which it arises should be watched closely by interested groups, particularly women. To be more specific, what orientation is being taken in proposals with regard to child custody?

In its *Report on Family Law*, the Law Reform Commission outlines several recommendations aimed at making the divorce process less antagonistic for the parties involved, defending the interests of the children more adequately, and ensuring both parents assume as much responsibility as possible for the children after their separation. These recommendations are: retraction of grounds referring to "improper" conduct of one of the spouses, increased importance of conciliation and support services, elimination of all sexual discrimination in granting custody, explanation of the criterion relating to the child's best interests, legal representation for the child, explicit authorization of joint custody, and greater attention to the presence of both parents in the life of the child.[48]

Bill C-10, tabled in the House of Commons on January 19, 1984, follows up on many of these recommendations. In addition to instituting "no fault" divorce, this Bill granted more importance to the custody of the children than the present Act. The child's best interests are expressly mentioned, although they are not clearly defined or explained. Legal representation for the child can be ordered by the court when required to protect his or her best interests. The conduct of the spouses is not one of the criteria for awarding custody. Children should have equal access to both spouses insofar as circumstances will allow, and the financial burden for maintaining the children should be divided equitably between the parties, taking into consideration the means and needs of the parents and the children.[49]

Due to the recent change in the Canadian government, Bill C-10 introduced by the Liberal party in 1984 was never given the force of law and in the spring of 1985, Bill C-47 was introduced in the House of Commons by the Progressive Conservative government.

This new Bill maintains most of the principles as outlined above with respect to Bill C-10. However, grounds for divorce have been slightly altered: marital breakdown would be established by a separation period of one year or where proof is given of adultery or physical or mental cruelty. In the determination of custody, specific attention is paid to the best interests of the child without reference to spousal conduct. An attempt is made to distribute as equitably as possible the financial responsibility for the family, and without giving preference to one form of custody, the rights of access of both parents to the children are to be equally protected according to the circumstances.[50]

With regard to the question of the child's access to both parents, this Bill seems more flexible than Bill C-10 which, in practice, could have had some coercive and detrimental effects.

In short, more emphasis should be put on the actual, overall functioning of the process, the support services, and the adjudication criteria than on specific methods which may cause new problems rather than resolve current ones.[51] Finally, these legislative changes should encourage lawyers to adopt a consistent approach toward their clients in divorce proceedings and give rise to the development of an appropriate ethical framework.[52]

Renée Joyal-Poupart is a professor at the Faculty of Law at the Université du Québec à Montréal. She has published a number of articles on civil responsibility and on the family.

Notes

1. Aric Press, Peggy Clausen, William Burger, Pamela Abramison, John McCormick, and Sandra Cavazos, "Divorce American Style", *Newsweek* (January 10, 1983), p. 43.

2. Anita Fineberg, "Joint Custody of Infants: Breakthrough or Fad?", *Canadian Journal of Family Law* (1979), at 418.

3. Jean Pineau, *La famille* (Montreal: Les presses de l'Université de Montréal, 1982), p. 142, para. 190.

4. Elisabeth Badinter, *L'Amour en plus* (Paris: Flammarion, 1980).

5. Canada, Statistics Canada, *Law and the Family in Canada* (Ottawa: Supply and Services Canada, 1983), p. 228.

6. Bertha Wilson, "Children: The Casualties of a Failed Marriage", address to the Vancouver Institute, British Columbia, 1984, pp. 6-7.

7. *Ibid.*, p. 8.

8. *Ibid.*, pp. 2ff.

9. Anita Fineberg, p. 419.

10. *Ibid.,*, pp. 452-453.

11. Claire L'Heureux-Dubé, "La garde conjointe, concept acceptable ou non?", 39 *Revue du Barreau* (1970), at 847 and 848; Fineberg, p. 424.

12. *MacDonald v. MacDonald*, [1976] 2 S.C.R. 259; *Talsky v. Talsky*, [1976] 2 S.C.R. 292.

13. L'Heureux-Dubé, p. 838.

14. *Ibid.*, p. 848; Fineberg, p. 424.

15. L'Heureux-Dubé, p. 842; Arthur Leonoff and Maureen O'Neil, "Understanding Psychological Impediments to Joint Custody", 8 *Reports of Family Law* (2d), p. 93.

16. *Wakeham v. Wakeham*, [1954] 1 *All England Reports*, p. 436.

17. L'Heureux-Dubé, p. 838.

18. Fineberg, p. 429.

19. D. Mendes Da Costa, "Domestic Contracts in Ontario", 1 *Canadian Journal of Family Law* (1978), at 232ff.; Albert Mayrand, "La séparation de fait et ses effets principaux", 8 *Revue générale de droit*, at 11.

20. L'Heureux-Dubé, p. 838.

21. Mayrand, p. 13.

22. Fineberg, pp. 434ff.

23. *Ibid.*, pp. 438-439; Wilson, pp. 22-23; Elissa P. Benedek and Richard J. Benedek, "Joint Custody: Solution or Illusion?", *American Journal of Psychiatry* (December 1979), p. 1542.

24. Judith Brown Greif, "Access: Legal Right or Privilege at the Custodial Parent's Discretion?", 3 *Canadian Journal of Family Law* (1980), at 44ff; Julien D. Payne, "Co-Parenting

Revisited", 2 *Family Law Review* (1979), at 243ff.; Julien D. Payne and Patrick J. Boyle, "Divided Opinions on Joint Custody", 2 *Family Law Review* (1979), at 163ff.; Mel Roman and William Haddad, "The Case for Joint Custody", *Psychology Today* (September 1978), pp. 98ff.; Edward J. Rosen, "Joint Custody: In the Best Interests of the Child and Parents", 1 *Reports of Family Law* (2d), at 116ff.

25. Joan B. Kelly and Judith Wallerstein, "The Effects of Parental Divorce; Experiences of the Child in Early Latency", *American Journal of Orthopsychiatry* (1976), vol. 46, no. 1, pp. 20ff.; "The Effects of Parental Divorce; Experiences of the Pre-school Child", *Journal of the American Academy of Child-Psychiatry* (1975), vol. 14, no. 4, pp. 600ff.; "The Effects of Parental Divorce: Experiences of the Child in Later Latency", *American Journal of Orthopsychiatry* (1976), vol. 46, no. 20, pp. 256ff.

26. Rosen, p. 120.

27. Neil Kalter, "Children of Divorce in an Out-Patient Population", *American Journal of Orthopsychiatry* (1977), vol. 47, no. 1, pp. 40ff.; G. Awad and R. Parry, "Access Following Marital Separation", *Canadian Journal of Psychiatry* (1980), vol. 25, pp. 357-358; E.M. Hetherington, M. Cox, and R. Cox, "Divorced Fathers", *The Family Coordinator* (October 1976), pp. 47ff.; M. Roman and W. Haddad, *The Disposable Parent: The Case for Joint Custody* (Penguin ed., 1979), p. 23.

28. M. O'Neil and A. Leonoff, "Joint Custody: An Option Worth Examining", *Perception* (November-December 1977), p. 30.

29. J. Goldstein, A. Freud, and A. Solnit, *Beyond the Best Interests of the Child*, 2nd ed. (New York: Free Press, 1979), pp. 12,13, and 17.

30. Wilson, p. 19.

31. Fineberg, p. 430.

32. *Ibid.*

33. *Ibid.*, p. 448.

34. Alice Abarbanel, "Shared Parenting after Separation and Divorce, A Study of Joint Custody", *American Journal of Ortho Psychiatry* (1979), vol. 49, p. 328.

35. Greif, p. 47; Sally E. Palmer, "Custody and Access Decisions, Minimizing the Damage to Families", 12 *Reports of Family Law* (2d), at 235.

36. *Newsweek*, pp. 46-47; Canada, Statistics Canada, *Canada's Lone-Parent Families* (Ottawa: Supply and Services Canada, 1984), cat. no. 99-933; L. Weitzman, "The Economics of Divorce; Social and Economic Consequences of Property, Alimony and Child Support Awards", 28:6 *U.C.L.A. Law Review* (1981), at 1240.

37. Law Reform Commission of Canada, *Family Law: Enforcement of Maintenance Obligations* (Ottawa: Information Canada, 1976), pp. 23ff.; Institute of Law Research and Reform, *Matrimonial Support Failures: Reasons, Profiles and Perceptions of Individuals Involved* (Edmonton: University of Alberta Law Center, 1981), vol. 1, p. 25.

38. *Newsweek*, p. 44; Shulman and Pitt, "Second Thoughts on Joint Child Custody: Analysis of Legislation and Its Implications for Women and Children", 12 *Golden Gate Law Review*, at 538.

39. Leonoff and O'Neil, "Understanding Psychological Impediments to Joint Custody", pp. 95-96.

40. *Ibid.*, p. 94; Fineberg, p. 442; Benedek and Benedek, p. 1542.

41. Micheline La France, "La paternité, cuvée 1984", *Châtelaine* (November 1984), pp. 193 ff.; Mireille Lamy and Paul Boudreau, "Un témoin particulier", *Hom-Info* (December-January-February 1984), p. 21.

42. Payne and Boyle, p. 170; Holly L. Robinson, "Joint Custody: An Idea whose Time Has Come", 21 *Journal of Family Law* (1982-83), at 673ff.

43. Abarbanel, p. 328; Fineberg, p. 454; Roman and Haddad, "The Case for Joint Custody", p. 105; Rosen, p. 122.

44. Benedek and Benedek, p. 1543; *Newsweek,* p. 44; Palmer, p. 244.

45. Jay Folberg, "Joint Custody", in *Family Law: Dimensions of Justice*, eds. Rosalie S. Abella and Claire L'Heureux-Dubé (Toronto: Butterworths, 1983), p. 190.

46. *Ibid.*, p. 188; Robinson, p. 675.

47. Lillian Kosak, presentation to New York State legislators on "Lobby Day", March 24, 1981, concerning legislation providing for joint custody presumption/preference.

48. Law Reform Commission of Canada. *Report on Family Law* (Ottawa: Information Canada, 1976), pp. 13ff. and pp. 49ff.

49. Canada, House of Commons, Bill C-10, *An Act to amend the Divorce Act*, 2nd session, 32nd legislature, 32 Elisabeth II, 1983-84, arts., 2, 8, 9, and 10.

50. Canada, House of Commons, Bill C-47, *Divorce and Corollary Relief Act*, 1st session, 33rd legislature, 33-34 Elizabeth II, 1984-85, arts. 8, 15, and 16.

51. Folberg, p. 191; Greif, p. 46; Rosen, p. 123; Wilson, pp. 35ff.

52. Leonoff and O'Neil, "Understanding Psychological Impediments to Joint Custody", p. 96; Palmer, pp. 232 and 244; Wilson, p. 40.

The Ideal Marital Property Regime — What Would It Be?*

— *Freda M. Steel*

If marriage is truly a partnership, the economic interdependence of the spouses must be reflected in matrimonial property laws. In recent years, there has been strong pressure from feminists for the implementation of a system of "full and immediate" community of property. The theory behind this is that only where both spouses have equal rights to all the property will the true partnership nature of the marriage be recognized.

Community of property takes a number of forms — "traditional", "deferred", and "full and immediate" — each of which is examined here. The author argues for a combination of the latter two as the ideal matrimonial property regime.

Introduction

The decade of the seventies witnessed a massive revolution in our concepts of marriage and the family.[1] It was inevitable, despite initial reluctance,[2] that the law relating to family relationships would change accordingly. In particular, many systems of marital property were radically transformed, and Canada's was no exception.[3]

This paper examines the reasons behind the recent reform of marital property law in Canada, the present legislation, and the need for further

---

* The author would like to thank her research assistant, Sherri Walsh, L.L.B., for her assistance with this project.

change. The extraordinary breadth of the topic and the variety of regimes and legislation make generalizations inescapable. Thus, the themes developed and conclusions reached represent a canvas painted with broad strokes.

Property-holding within a marriage is a complex and emotional issue.[4] For more than a decade before the reforms were actually introduced, law reform commissions across Canada studied the problem of marital property reform.[5] The reports gave birth to a cornucopia of surveys, briefs, and law review articles which discussed the advantages and disadvantages of the various proposals.[6] Finally, in every province in Canada, these recommendations were translated into legislation.[7]

Although the reports and surveys considered a variety of marital property regimes,[8] in the end, for the common law provinces in Canada, the regime of separate property was replaced by legislative schemes of deferred community property,[9] although the scheme in each province was slightly different. Under the civil law of Quebec, a regime of community property was also replaced by a combined system of co-management during marriage and deferred sharing of property upon dissolution of marriage.[10]

These various legislative schemes represent a fundamental change in Canada's marital property law. They have been in operation in the various common law provinces from four to six years and in Quebec since 1970. Aside from the natural confusion inherent in the introduction of a new scheme, questions are beginning to arise concerning the effectiveness of the property law reform. Marriage is now perceived as an economic partnership where the contributions of both spouses are of equal weight. The objective of these legal reforms was to develop a marital property scheme that reflected this new vision. Are these new property-sharing schemes achieving that objective?

Before answering that question, it is helpful to explore the history behind the present legislation.

The Regime of Separate Property

A system of marital property division reflects the prevailing ideologies in society. Early English matrimonial law treated the husband and wife as a single person,[11] usually to the detriment of the wife. As a married woman, the wife lost most of her personal property,[12] and her husband became the owner or, at least, had the use and benefit of her real property.[13] The law denied a married woman's legal existence.[14]

The onset of the Industrial Revolution saw the introduction of increasing numbers of women into the ranks of wage-earners and professionals. While single women retained complete control over their assets, the wages brought home by their married sisters became the property of their husbands. The medieval common law took no account of the needs of married women who were gainfully employed outside the house and who, through their own earnings, contributed to the maintenance of the family.[15]

The regime of separate property was first introduced as a reform measure in the cause of women's equality, as an attempt to eliminate the inequality of early English matrimonial law. Reformers claimed that if men owned their property unfettered by the claims of spouses then women should have the same right.[16] In England, such reform was achieved by the passage of the *Married Women's Property Act* in 1882.[17] Similar Acts were passed in most of the common law jurisdictions in Canada[18] and the United States.[19] The Acts gave married women the right to manage and dispose of their own property and earnings in the same way as could their husbands or a single woman.[20] By providing that both her pre-marital and post-marital property was to remain the wife's separate property, the statutes put her on equal legal footing with her husband and treated the spouses as if they were strangers.[21]

Although the regime of separate property was first introduced as a reform measure, its retention for such a long period in the twentieth century resulted in hardship.

The regime of separate property did safeguard the freedom and independence of the spouses and it did facilitate business transactions. However, it did not have any means of measuring, in terms of property rights, the value of the spouse's work in child care and housekeeping. Thus, especially with respect to the spouses who stayed at home and whose contributions were in terms of physical labour, the law of separate property was first and foremost the law of the double standard.[22]

By the mid-seventies it had become more than clear that the law of separate property was ill-suited to the modern concept of marriage. However, the case that acted as the public catalyst for legislative reform was that of Mrs. Murdoch,[23] the Alberta farm wife who was told that her 15 years of labour on the family farm was no more than that of an ordinary farm wife, and therefore she was not entitled to any proprietary interest in the farm property. This was not the first time that Canadian farm wives had been denied any interest in lands they had helped cultivate,[24] yet perhaps because *Murdoch v. Murdoch*[25] was decided at a time when agitation for women's rights was receiving considerable publicity, it soon became a symbol across Canada for the necessity of far-reaching marital property law reform.[26]

It was apparent to all those concerned that a new marital property regime was necessary. It was also apparent that any new marital regime must establish an economic partnership between husband and wife[27] without depriving either of equal status or unduly hampering their independence.[28]

The co-existence of these two concepts — the independence and equality of each spouse with the idea of marriage as a joint venture — must of necessity be an uneasy one. The two concepts can never really be completely reconciled. All jurisdictions face the same basic difficulty and have resolved it in different ways.

The majority of jurisdictions have a variant of one of the following regimes: community of property, deferred community property (with or without judicial discretion), and separate property subject to judicial discretion. None of the countries applying these regimes actually apply them in their pure form but rather they combine features of several systems to offer spouses alternatives so that there are virtually as many systems as there are countries.

Generally speaking, the phrase "community of property" has been used to refer to three types of matrimonial property regimes:

- Traditional community of property: one in which all property owned and acquired by either husband or wife during marriage is the common property of both although the husband has sole control and management of it. Often the regime is modified, for example, to exclude gifts or inheritances from a third party.

- "Full and immediate" community of property: also a regime in which matrimonial assets are shared immediately upon marriage (entitlement arises at the time of the marriage rather than the time of the dissolution). However, the administration of those assets is shared jointly by the spouses.

- Deferred community property: based on a general theory that all marital property (again the definition of marital property depends upon the jurisdiction) is to be shared equally when the marriage partnership is dissolved. Separate property rights continue to exist during marriage although some restrictions are placed on those rights to protect the eventual deferred distribution between the spouses. Deferred sharing regimes currently exist in countries such as Denmark, Sweden, Norway, and Finland.[29] In Sweden, there was a regime of deferred sharing in operation as early as 1920.[30] This type of regime was also the choice of the Royal Commission on the Status of Women.[31]

Although there are significant differences in the legislation, the provinces of Canada have all opted for the regime of deferred community of property as a cure for the ills of separate property,[32] and traditional community of property which was the regime in Quebec before 1970.

The Present System

Generally the various deferred community property regimes are similar in that: they apply only to legal as opposed to common-law spouses; they are tempered to some measure by judicial discretion; and no proprietary interest vests until court order. All of the schemes recognize that contributions to the family through homemaking and child care are as worthy of recognition to the accumulation of assets as are financial contributions.[33] With respect to the manner of holding marital property (that is, deferred community), the regimes are similar.

However, there are significant differences among them which are fundamental.[34] The major differences lie in the nature of the matrimonial property caught in the regime, the event triggering the regime, the kind and degree of judicial discretion (if any), the treatment of the matrimonial home, and the restraints on disposition during the existence of the regime.

In a deferred community regime, a spouse is not entitled to an interest in the property of the other until the making of a court order.[35] Most of the Acts require that the marriage have broken down before an application to the court for division of property may take place. The typical events accepted as evidence of marital breakdown are: decree of divorce, declaration of nullity,[36] an order for judicial separation,[37] the completion by the parties of a separation agreement,[38] spousal separation for a specific period of time[39] or, in one province, dissipating property to the detriment of the other spouse.[40] Only Saskatchewan and Manitoba allow spouses to apply to the court at any time during the marriage even though marital breakdown has *not* occurred.[41]

In most of the provinces, if marriage breakdown occurred while both parties were alive, the surviving spouse may commence an application against the estate of the deceased spouse.[42] However, where no marriage breakdown occurred before death, only four provinces allow an order to be made in favour of a surviving spouse,[43] and only two of those four provinces accord that spouse full rights under both matrimonial property law and the law of succession.[44]

Upon the occurrence of a "triggering" event and an application being made to the court, the marital property is then presumed to be equally divisible between the spouses regardless of which spouse has legal title to it.[45]

The difficult question arises when a definition of marital property is sought. Initially, the provinces define marital property by reference either to its use (for example, property ordinarily used for family purposes such as shelter, transportation, and recreation)[46] or by reference to the nature of its acquisition (that is, property acquired during marriage).[47] Interest can also arise where there has been a contribution to the property by the other spouse.[48] Exclusions and additions are then grafted on to the initial definition.

The province of Ontario was the first *common law* province to inaugurate a matrimonial property regime and the legislation is considered seminal.[49] The Ontario legislation defines a family asset as a matrimonial home and property owned by either or both spouses and ordinarily used by both spouses, or the children, for family purposes while the spouses are residing together (referred to as the user formula).[50] How the property is used and not how it was acquired is the determining factor. This is contrary to most full community property regimes where pre-marital assets and assets acquired by gift or inheritance are automatically excluded.

The court does have the discretion to divide the family assets unequally where a strictly equal division would be inequitable. Among the six enumerated factors which must be taken into account are the length of the co-habitation and separation, the date the property was acquired (for example, before marriage), and the extent to which it was acquired by inheritance or gift.[51]

Commercial assets may be intruded upon only where the spouse has impoverished the family assets[52] or where a division of family assets would be inequitable having regard to the enumerated factors or where a division of family assets alone would be inequitable. The latter situation takes into account the effect of the assumption by one spouse of household management duties on the ability of the other spouse to enhance his or her business assets.[53] It is not always clear which assets are business assets and which are related to the family. The courts have also found it difficult to determine to what extent indirect, non-financial contribution can create an interest in the other spouse's business assets.[54]

Since the Ontario legislation was seminal and was the first of its kind passed in Canada, many provinces have modelled their legislation upon it. *The Family Law Reform Act* of Prince Edward Island[55] is one example. The nature of the property included in the matrimonial regime in Prince Edward Island is identical to that of Ontario except with regard to the determination of the value of a family asset which was acquired pre-maritally. With respect to that type of asset, only the appreciation which has accrued over the life of the marriage becomes a family asset.[56] This is more in line with the ordinary rule followed in full community property regimes where pre-marital assets are excluded. In the Ontario family asset regime, the fact that the family asset was acquired pre-maritally may be taken into account, but neither it nor its unappreciated value is automatically excluded.[57] The rest of the Prince Edward Island Act is basically similar to that of Ontario.

The British Columbia Matrimonial Property regime[58] employs the user formula definition for family assets along the lines of the Ontario Act. Specifically excluded from the definition of a family asset is business property owned by one spouse to which the other spouse has made no direct or indirect contribution.[59] An indirect contribution includes savings through effective household management; as a result, there would be very few business assets excluded from this family asset definition.[60] In Ontario, the assumption of household management duties can lead to the division of non-family assets,[61] whereas in British Columbia, this changes the actual character or nature of the assets.

One interesting specific inclusion in the British Columbia family asset definition is the right of the spouse under a pension, home ownership or retirement savings plan, whether or not these are used for family purposes.[62]

Notwithstanding the *prima facie* equal division rule for family assets in the B.C. legislation, the court may divide the family assets in unequal shares where an equal division would be unfair, having regard to several enumerated factors, including the length of the marriage, the length of the separation, the date of acquisition of the property, and the extent to which it was acquired through inheritance or gift.[63] The court may likewise, where it would be unfair having regard to the same enumerated factors, make a division of non-family assets.[64]

The Newfoundland,[65] Nova Scotia,[66] and New Brunswick[67] Acts also closely resemble the Ontario legislation in general form. Although Newfoundland and Nova Scotia seem to use a definition based on the method of acquisition, both provinces exclude commercial assets[68] so that in actual practice their legislation is most similar to Ontario in that property used for a family purpose may form most of what is available for division. New Brunswick defines marital property as property used for a family purpose or, even if not so used, property acquired during marriage.[69] However, it also excludes business assets.[70]

Since the "user" provinces limit divisible property to family assets, they also have some sort of provision to provide relief in situations where a non-titled spouse has made a contribution to an excluded asset belonging to the other spouse.[71] The definition of "contribution" varies from province to province.

The Manitoba,[72] Alberta,[73] and Saskatchewan[74] Acts are similar in that they allow for a much greater possibility of sharing of commercial assets than the Acts modelled upon the Ontario legislation. Their definition of marital property concentrates on the method of acquisition[75] and therefore, for the most part, marital property is property acquired by either spouse during marriage, subject to the exclusion of a number of types of property which initially fell within that definition.

The Manitoba regime, subject to certain specific exceptions,[76] applies to every asset, family or commercial, of each spouse, acquired during the marriage while the spouses are cohabiting and also acquired before and in contemplation of the marriage.[77] This is different than the Ontario position where the regime applies to all assets acquired before the marriage which are used for family purposes. The definition of commercial asset is simply every asset that is not a family asset as subsequently defined.[78] Insurance policies and pension plans are family assets, whether or not they are used for a family purpose, according to a recent amendment.[79]

At any time during the marriage or after marital breakup each spouse is *prima facie* entitled to an equal division of both family and commercial assets which are caught in the matrimonial property regime.[80] The court may divide assets unequally if, in the case of family assets, the court is satisfied that division of those assets in equal shares would be grossly unfair or unconscionable, having regard to any extraordinary financial or other circumstances of the spouses or the extraordinary nature or value of any of their assets.[81] In the case of commercial assets, if the court is satisfied that an equal division of these assets would be clearly inequitable having regard to any circumstances the court deems relevant, the court may change the equal division. These circumstances include a variety of enumerated factors such as the unreasonable impoverishment of the family asset by either spouse, length of cohabitation, and nature of the assets, amongst others.[82]

The Alberta Act[83] contains no definition of asset and no classification of assets into family assets and commercial assets. However, a source base rather than a user base is used to determine whether or not a particular asset is caught within the matrimonial property regime.[84] The regime covers all assets of either or both spouses, except the market value as of the date of marriage, or the date of acquisition of property acquired pre-maritally or by gift or inheritance.[85] Accordingly, only the appreciation is caught within the marital property regime. This provision is rather like that in the Manitoba Act.[86]

Upon a triggering event occurring, each spouse is entitled to a distribution of the matrimonial property which may or may not be in equal shares depending on the nature of the property.[87] The division of the *appreciation* of property acquired pre-maritally or by gift or inheritance which falls within the regime takes place in such shares as the court considers just and equitable having regard to a variety of enumerated factors.[88] The division of all other marital property takes place in equal shares unless it appears that it would not be just and equitable to do so having regard to the same enumerated factors.[89]

The Saskatchewan Act[90] exempts property owned by an individual at the time of marriage, while retaining a discretion to override the exemption in appropriate cases.[91] Other than exempt property, the Act contains a presumption of equal sharing.[92] However, the court retains a very broad discretion to order an unequal division or to refuse any division at all, having regard to 17 enumerated factors or to "any relevant fact or circumstance".[93]

The legal regime in Quebec is currently the Partnership of Acquests.[94] It was introduced in 1970 and applies to spouses married subsequent to July 1970. The regime employs the standard "source" definition so that only assets acquired by either spouse during the marriage fall within the property regime and, as is traditional, gifts and inheritances are automatically excluded.[95] Triggering events include a separation or a divorce[96] and the legal regime only applies in the absence of a spousal agreement opting out of the legal regime.[97] As the regime is one of deferred community property, the spouses are separate as to their property during their marriage, with the exception that substantial gifts cannot be made without the other spouse's consent.[98]

There were some significant reforms introduced to the regime in 1980,[99] specifically the concept of a compensatory allowance.[100] The court, in its discretion, may award one spouse a compensatory allowance where that spouse has enriched the share of the other spouse during marriage. A right of ownership or possession in the marital home may be granted as part of a compensatory allowance. The effect of this reform is to allow the exercise of considerable judicial discretion with respect to property settlements at the dissolution of marriage.[101]

These new amendments apply to all married couples regardless of their matrimonial regime or marriage contract. They also apply to couples married before the legislation came into effect.

From this short summary of the legislation currently in force, it would appear that while the provinces have all agreed on how the property is to be held (that is, deferred discretionary community property regime), there are a number of different answers to the questions relating to the nature of the property to be brought into the regime, the triggering mechanism, and the degree of judicial discretion allowed in the scheme.

In order to properly evaluate the Canadian legislative schemes, it would be useful to compare them to the answers found by other jurisdictions, specifically full community property regimes.

Alternative Marital Property Regimes — Community Property

In contrast with the regime of separate property which emphasized individuality at the expense of sharing, the *traditional* regime of community property[102] emphasized the concept of sharing at the expense of individuality. In a traditional community property regime, similar to early English matrimonial law, the husband was considered head of the family and was given the power of possession, income management, and disposal.[103] Traditional community property law maintained a dichotomy between ownership and control.

At the beginning of the twentieth century, traditional community property was a prevalent matrimonial property regime in most West European countries.[104] Yet, the same economic and social conditions that required reform in separate property jurisdictions also affected the traditional community property regimes. They also had to deal with the tension between sharing and equality experienced in the separate property jurisdictions. While in the common law world this meant greater emphasis on participation in assets, in a civil law world the direction of reform was toward the autonomy and legal equality of the spouses. Although seen from a different perspective, the essential problem remained the same. An equilibrium had to be achieved between the concept of sharing within a marriage and that other postulate of modern times, equality of the husband and wife.

The traditional community property jurisdictions found three alternative solutions. Some expanded the role of the wife while retaining ultimate control in the hands of the husband. France[105] and South Africa[106] are examples of this type of solution.

In France, for example, after the matrimonial property reform of 1965,[107] the husband remained legal head of the family and consequently manager of the community property, even though the wife's participation in management was increased, because there were fears of deadlock between the spouses as to property decisions.[108]

The author believes, and does not think it controversial, that, for Canadians, any matrimonial regime that offered either spouse anything less than equal management power would be unacceptable. Every law reform commission report studying the issue rejected the concept of introducing any regime that offered anything less than equal management.

The more relevant category of community property regimes, for the purposes of this paper, is a full and immediate community of property regime in which matrimonial assets are shared immediately upon marriage and both spouses have joint management rights.

Italy has had a scheme of full and immediate community property since 1975.[109] Similar regimes exist in the Soviet Republic and most East European countries.[110] In the United States, of the eight traditional community property jurisdictions,[111] Washington,[112] California,[113] Arizona,[114] Texas,[115] New Mexico,[116] Idaho,[117] and Louisiana[118] now have provisions for joint management.

Each community property state has its own statute, constitution, and history of judicial interpretation. Thus, as with Canadian legislation, although there is a thematic uniformity there are also significant differences.

Generally, under the American community system, property is classified as either separate or community property.[119] Separate property generally consists of property owned by a spouse before marriage and property received by gift or inheritance during marriage. In five states, the income from separate property received during marriage remains separate property[120] while in Louisiana, Texas, and Idaho such income is included in the community.[121] In all of the eight community property states, however, there is a presumption that all the property owned by the spouses is community property and the spouse who claims that certain property is his or her separate property has the burden of establishing that claim.

During the marriage, each spouse retains the ownership of his or her separate property and the corresponding right to control, manage, and dispose of such property. The community property, consisting of all other property acquired by the spouses during the marriage, is jointly managed.[122] What this generally means is that either spouse alone may manage and control the community property but certain important transactions, usually involving real estate or substantial assets, require their joint participation.[123] For example, in California, either spouse has the right to manage and control the community personal property. A spouse who operates or manages a business or an interest in a business that is community property has the sole management and control of that business or interest. However, both spouses must consent to a transfer or encumbrance of community real property.[124]

The feature which especially distinguishes a full community of property regime is that each spouse owns a present, vested, undivided one-half interest in all the community property of the spouses. In a deferred community of property regime, on the other hand, a proprietary interest only vests upon court order.

Upon divorce, a spouse generally retains ownership of his or her separate property. It is only the community property that is divisible.[125] California, Louisiana, and New Mexico provide that, with certain minor exceptions, the community property is to be divided equally.[126] The statutes of the remaining community states provide that the court has discretionary power with respect to the division of the marital property.[127]

138

The British Columbia Royal Commission on Family and Children's Law is the only commission report in Canada which recommended the adoption of a regime of community property with joint management.[128] The regime would have provided for the immediate co-ownership of all assets by the spouses as soon as they were acquired, with the exception of gifts and inheritances. Both spouses would have had equal rights of management over their common assets, subject to some exceptions designed to make the regime more flexible.

The Commission felt that full and immediate community property with joint management by the spouses was the only matrimonial regime that would truly recognize the equality of the spouses in the marriage partnership. Since each partner owned a one-half interest in the community during marriage, upon dissolution each party would have a right to a one-half interest without regard to conduct and with no allowance for judicial discretion to change the 50/50 distribution.[129]

The only Canadian legislation which initially proposed a variant of community property was Manitoba's *Marital Property Act*.[130] The Act, which was passed by the New Democratic government in June 1977, and was to have come into force on January 1, 1978, proposed a regime of full community property with joint management for all family assets. The sharing of commercial assets would have been deferred until the dissolution of the marriage. However, a new provincial government was elected in November 1977, and the new Progressive Conservative government passed a bill suspending the Act and replacing it with the present Act. The *Marital Property Act* currently in force in Manitoba sets up a deferred sharing regime for both family and commercial assets.[131]

Conclusion — Where Should We Be Going?

There are two essential questions to be answered when structuring a marital property regime that harmoniously blends the independence of the individual, the equality of the spouses, and the concept of marriage as an economic partnership. The first question is how property in a marriage shall be held. The second question is which property shall be shared.

An answer to the first question involves a consideration of the three marital property regimes mentioned previously: traditional community of property, full and immediate community of property with equal management rights, and deferred community of property.

A system of full and immediate community property with equal management rights for both husband and wife has many advantages. It gives greater weight to the concept of marriage as a cooperative venture than does any other marital property regime. It gives a greater assurance of equality and certainty. It also prevents the possibility of dissipation of assets by one spouse alone. Not only does common ownership make reality out of the theory of partnership but it also carries with it the emotional and psychological benefits derived from the reality of present ownership for the spouse who is not gainfully employed outside the home.[132] Perhaps most importantly it re-adjusts uneven economic power during marriage.

However, questions arose in most minds when a jurisdiction contemplated a move to a regime of full community property. These included uncertainties over how to cope with the complexities introduced when two individuals manage one piece of property and neither one has veto power over the other, and how to adequately protect third parties.

It is difficult, if not impossible, to accept the British Columbia Commission's proposition that one of the advantages of community property is its simplicity. On the contrary, the rules and formula are very complex.[133]

> Of the three major approaches . . . community of property would involve the most wide-ranging and radical changes in the economic and social fabric of a jurisdiction in which it was adopted. Community of property creates a whole new context and a whole new set of problems, not only for spouses, but also for anyone entering into transactions with a married person.[134]

For example, since the spouses may own three or more distinct kinds of property (that is, separate property, community property and, depending on the state, quasi-community or conflicts of law property) and since present interests vest upon marriage, complexities of identification, tracing, and commingling are immediately apparent.[135] Additional problems of tracing and commingling are encountered in those jurisdictions which treat the income or accruals on separate property as separate property.[136]

Another problem arises where community funds are used to pay off debts or liabilities on separate property or to improve separate property. For example, one spouse may have purchased a home before the marriage but may have discharged mortgage or tax liabilities out of money earned during the marriage. In these circumstances, the house is separate property but the community is entitled to compensation for the use of its funds in the discharge of liabilities on the home. Similar types of problems arise where separate property has been used to improve, or discharge debts on, community property. "Rules have been developed to resolve these issues but litigation remains quite common not only between the spouses themselves and their respective successors in interest, such as heirs and beneficiaries, but also between the spouses and third parties, such as creditors or taxing authorities."[137]

Many of the most serious questions in a community property system arise in the context of protection granted third parties. It is the requirement of adequate mechanisms to protect third parties which more than anything else necessitates a more complex legislative structure than is necessary in other regimes.[138] For example, the question of responsibility for the payments of debts arises. The community property is liable in various degrees, depending on the state, for the antenuptial debts of the spouses. The situation with respect to contractual obligations assumed during the marriage is more varied and "is, at best, confusing".[139]

The concurrent and joint management of community property is also not without its potential problems. For example, there can be a problem with respect to a spouse who operates a community property business should the other spouse use the power to manage and control in a way which interferes with the operation of the business.[140] Also, in some community property states, the spouse with the power to manage certain community property can, acting alone, make a gift of that property and thereby eliminate the other spouse's one-half interest.[141]

Furthermore, since these regimes are state based, a number of conflict of laws problems arise when spouses move from a state with a community property regime to one with a separate property regime, or vice versa. In some states, an additional property classification referred to as quasi-community property has been devised which is used in dealing with this problem. The high mobility rate and conflicts rules add to the complexity of the system.[142]

Thus, the basic fairness in a community property regime must be purchased at the cost of a fairly elaborate structure of legal rules affecting the spouses and all persons with whom they deal.

Of course, none of these problems are by any means insurmountable. However, careful thought must be given to the tradeoffs received for the adoption of additional complexity in an area of law where simplicity and ease of application are important considerations.

> The policy decision to be made is whether the added complexities are balanced with the additional social benefits that would be brought by the creation of present property interests in both married partners. [143]

In making this policy decision, it is relevant to refer to the decisions of other jurisdictions. Most of the present community property jurisdictions with joint management rights were previously traditional community property regimes and have had a history of community property. [144]

The complexities and difficulties of readjustment are perceived to be even more acute when the jurisdiction has a history of traditional separate property. [145] Thus, it is interesting to note that very few jurisdictions with a separate property regime have implemented a full community property regime for more than a few years. [146]

On the other hand, many traditional community property jurisdictions have chosen to adopt a regime of deferred community property, rather than community property with equal management. A partial list of these jurisdictions includes Argentina, Colombia, Denmark, Finland, Iceland, Norway, Sweden, Uruguay, and West Germany. [147]

Of particular interest to Canadians is the experience of the province of Quebec. Its legal regime before 1970 was one of community property during marriage but it now operates under a system of deferred sharing of property upon dissolution of marriage. The Quebec Commission's report stated that the traditional community of movables and acquests had been falling out of favour and in the last five years (before 1970) more than 70 per cent of married persons in Quebec preferred to contract out of the standard regime. [148]

Why have so many jurisdictions chosen a deferred system as opposed to a full community property regime? A deferred community regime is less complex, less restrictive of the freedom of spouses to act independently, and seems to best approximate a harmonious balance among the objectives of all three possible regimes. [149]

What is lost by the adoption of a deferred as opposed to a full community scheme? Simplicity and independence should not be bought at the expense of equity. Aside from the significant psychological benefits already mentioned, the fundamental difference between the two regimes is the lack of a present vested interest in the deferred community regime.

The absence of this present vested interest is of special significance in two kinds of situations: those dealing with the marital home and those where one of the spouses is dissipating assets. The absence of the present vested interest would not be of particular significance in the case of the management of business assets, for example, since the management provisions (as opposed to the transfer provisions) of many community property jurisdictions approximate that of a deferred sharing scheme.[150]

Under a system of deferred sharing, each spouse is largely free to control and dispose of his or her own property during the marriage. A spouse could take advantage of this freedom by reducing his or her assets thereby depriving the other spouse of a fair share. This dissipation of assets might take several forms: excessive gifts, sales to third parties at less than market value, and hiding assets or squandering money.

The present statutes attempt to deal with these potential problems in a number of ways. In Alberta, the actual or threatened dissipation of assets by a spouse serves as a basis for an application to the court for immediate sharing.[151] Upon an application being brought, a court is empowered to take into account excessive gifts or improper real estate transactions when assessing the value of the asset.[152] The same approach is taken where one spouse dissipated, destroyed or concealed assets during the marriage.[153] All the statutes give the courts the power to prohibit certain types of disposition.[154]

With respect to the marital home, most provinces have recognized the special nature of this asset by creating unique provisions surrounding it. The general nature of these provisions grant both spouses *immediate* rights of enjoyment and possession in the matrimonial home and prevent its being sold without the consent of both spouses.[155] In general, the legislation does not affect title to the home,[156] so much as the right to occupy it[157] and prevent its disposition.[158]

For example, in Ontario, the matrimonial home is accorded a special status and has a regime of its own.[159] During the life of the marriage, two types of rights, with corresponding obligations, are dealt with: the right to possession of the matrimonial home and the right to deal with (sale, mortgage or lease) the matrimonial home. Whatever right to possession one spouse has, the other automatically acquires by virtue of the marriage. Neither spouse may deal with his or her interest in the matrimonial home without the consent of the other or a court order.[160]

The matrimonial home is also accorded special status in the Alberta Act so far as possession is concerned.[161] While the right to possession of one party is not automatically acquired by the other by virtue of the marriage (as in the Ontario Act), the court may order exclusive possession to either spouse and this order will take precedence over any order for division of matrimonial property.[162] Once the order for exclusive possession is registered, the owner spouse may only deal with the matrimonial home if he or she has the consent in writing of the spouse in possession or by court order.[163]

In Manitoba, there is no special marital home regime comparable to the special matrimonial home regime in the Ontario Act. Nevertheless, by virtue of the Manitoba Act, whichever right to possession one spouse has, the other automatically acquires by virtue of the marriage.[164] The right is expressly subordinated to the possibility of an order of sole occupancy under the *Family Maintenance Act*.[165] The *Dower Act* grants a spouse's protection against dealing with the marital home without the consent of the other spouse.[166]

In addition, two provinces allow an application for division of assets at any time *during* the marriage[167] and one stipulates a spouse's right to a reasonable living allowance during the marriage,[168] in addition to the common law right of the wife to pledge her husband's credit for the purchase of necessaries.

The effect of the best of these various provisions taken together is to offer the non-titled spouse significant legal protection and some psychological reassurance. However, having gone so far there seems little reason not to go the final step. The special nature and importance of this asset requires more than what is presently in place. Since there are already restrictions on the disposition of the marital home, immediate vesting would not add great complexity to real property transactions. A system of co-ownership of the marital home could co-exist with a deferred sharing regime without causing unduly complicated problems.[169]

Co-ownership of the marital home was recommended by the Law Reform Commission of Saskatchewan in 1976[170] and by the Ontario Law Reform Commission in 1974.[171] It was also the recommendation of the English Law Commission which focused on providing vested ownership rights in the matrimonial home because in most cases the home was the spouse's principal asset.[172]

Co-ownership of the marital home should include leasehold interests in rented accommodation[173] and contain an allowance for judicial discretion upon termination of the regime to vary the *prima facie* equal sharing in extraordinary circumstances. It should also include co-ownership of the household contents of the marital home acquired during marriage and not acquired by gift or inheritance to one spouse alone.[174]

Yet going even further, even if it were felt that a full community regime with respect to *all* assets were the most appropriate scheme in Canada, this would still not solve the most important questions that remain in *any* marital property regime.

Economic power-sharing during marriage is not as important as economic power-sharing after marriage breakdown or death. Even though Manitoba does have provisions for property division during marriage and court-ordered living allowances during marriage, indications are that these provisions are not used.[175] Most property disputes that require State intervention arise after marriage breakdown.

The suggestion of an immediate community regime is not a solution in itself, since important questions remain in respect of the property to be included. Economic power-sharing during marriage is hollow if the only assets shared by the wife are the home and car while the husband retains ownership and control over the business assets. The most restrictive pool of property eligible for division is found in those community property states which treat income from separate property as separate property and allow only the community property of the spouses to be divided on divorce.[176] The nature of the assets to be divided are at least as important as the manner of ownership.

Those statutes that do not have a presumption of equal sharing of commercial assets do not go far enough. If marriage is a partnership then it is a partnership which relates to both the family and the commercial assets. Thus, all assets acquired by the spouses during the marriage with the exception of gifts and inheritances, but including income and appreciation from assets acquired before marriage, should be divisible.[177]

The concept of marital assets should be broadened and redefined to keep pace with the changing nature of wealth in our society. For example, it should include the valuation of "goodwill" attached to the business or profession of one of the spouses[178] and the spouse's professional degree and licence itself if acquired after the marriage and acquired by virtue of the work of both spouses.[179] It should include such important intangible "new property" assets as pensions, annuities, and life insurance policies.[180]

Most of the jurisdictions discussed, whether full or deferred community property, have provided for a *prima facie* equal division of sharing. "A presumption of equal sharing of assets acquired during marriage is an essential cornerstone of matrimonial property law."[181]

Yet almost all have allowed for judicial discretion to vary that equal sharing in appropriate circumstances.[182] Some judicial discretion is essential to accommodate the infinite variety of circumstances. However, experience has shown that broad judicial discretion may defeat the legislative intention of equal sharing. Where an Act has an especially wide discretion granted to the courts it sometimes occurs that 50/50 splits are not the norm but rather the exception.[183] Thus, judicial discretion should be limited to unusual situations.[184]

Another serious problem with respect to the present schemes relates to the event that must occur before a spouse may make an application to the courts for a division of the value of the property or, as it is sometimes called, the triggering event. For most provinces this event must relate to marital breakdown.[185] This is inappropriate for two reasons. First, it may be that, during marriage, a spouse wishes to obtain an accounting and division because of fears of dissolution by the other spouse. Giving a spouse that right gives him or her the psychological reassurance present in a full and immediate community regime without requiring a marital breakdown.

Second, allowing the non-income-producing spouse a greater share upon divorce than upon the death of the other spouse seems not only inconsistent but can only encourage death-bed divorces. "One consequence of the marriage breakdown focus is that a spouse in a weaker asset position who forbears rather than separates may be penalized for sticking with the marriage."[186] The widow or widower should receive at least the same protection and benefits under the property regime as the divorced person.

Even in the provinces where a marital property order may be made upon death, it may only be made in favour of the surviving spouse. The estate of a deceased spouse has no right to a division of property. If the principle underlying the equal division of marital assets is that marriage is a partnership then that principle is equally applicable to those assets after the death of one of the spouses.[187]

This is, in effect, what occurs in the full community property American states. On both divorce and death, a spouse or the deceased spouse's personal representative is entitled to his or her separate property and one half of the community property.[188]

Moreover, equal division of assets upon death under a marital property act should not affect the rights of a surviving spouse under the law of succession.[189] Property obtained under a marital regime is property obtained as of right based upon contribution. Property acquired by the surviving spouse by will, or on an intestacy, or as a result of an award under family relief legislation, is obtained because of different considerations whether those considerations be gift, need, or by virtue of the marriage relationship itself.

Summary and Suggestions

In conclusion, it is this author's opinion that an ideal marital property regime would contain the following elements:

■ During marriage, the matrimonial home and the household goods acquired during marriage would be jointly owned by the spouses. Upon termination of the regime, whether by death or divorce, the court would have the discretion to vary that equal division in appropriate circumstances, along with the total property division of the spouses.

■ During marriage, each spouse would be entitled to a "reasonable living allowance" from the other with the freedom to spend it as he or she sees fit (see *Family Maintenance Act* S.M. 1978, c.25, s.3).

■ Other than the marital home and household goods, spouses should hold marital assets by means of a system of deferred community property.

■ All assets (with the exception of gifts and inheritances) acquired by either spouse during the marriage, and the appreciation and income from pre-marital assets, should be subject to a presumption of equal sharing. This definition would include commercial assets.

■ The court would have the discretion to depart from the presumption of equal sharing only in circumstances where an equal sharing would be grossly unfair or unconscionable.

■ An application could be made to the court for a division of assets at any time during the marriage or upon termination of the marriage whether by divorce, separation or death.

Freda Steel, a professor at the faculty of law at the University of Manitoba, writes frequently on family law and women's issues.

Notes

1. See, for example, the discussion of changing attitudes towards marriage in: Canada, Royal Commission on The Status of Women in Canada, *Report* (Ottawa: Information Canada, 1970), pp. 225-230; Mary Ann Glendon, "Modern Marriage Laws and Its Underlying Assumptions: The New Marriage and the New Property", 13:4 *Family Law Quarterly* (1980), at 441.

2. A gap has always existed between social opinion and the law. As Sir Henry Maine wrote in 1861:

   > With respect to them (i.e., progressive societies) . . . social necessities and social opinion are always more or less in advance of Law. We may come indefinitely near to the closing of the gap between them, but it has a perpetual tendency to reopen. Law is stable: the societies we are speaking of are progressive. The greater or lesser happiness of a people depends on the degree of promptitude with which the gulf is narrowed. (Sir Henry Sumner Maine, *Ancient Law*, London: John Murray, 1930, p. 31.)

3. Marital property is an area under provincial jurisdiction. The division of powers between federal Canada and the various provinces and territories is still as laid down by the *Canada Act* and especially in sections 91 and 92 of that Act, which allocate legislative powers. As far as matrimonial property is concerned, the relevant provisions are s.91(26), s.92(12), and s.92(13).

4. One author characterized the area of property division upon divorce as "currently the most controversial area of family law and one to which no satisfactory solution has yet been found", Deech, "Book Review", 94 *L.Q. Rev.* 474 (1978).

5. In Canada, reports have been issued by law reform agencies in seven provinces including Quebec. These are: Quebec Civil Code Revision Office, *Report on Matrimonial Regimes* (Montreal: 1968); Newfoundland Family Law Study Project VIII, *Property Rights in the Family, Final Report* (St. John's: 1970); Ontario Law Reform Commission Family Law Project, *Report on Family Law, Part IV, Family Property Law* (Toronto: Ministry of the Attorney-General, 1974); British Columbia Royal Commission on Family and Children's Law, *Report on Matrimonial Property, 6th report* (Vancouver: 1975); Alberta Institute of Law Research and Reform, *Report No. 18 Matrimonial Property* (Edmonton: 1975); Manitoba Law Reform Commission, *Reports on Family Law Part II, Property Disposition* (Winnipeg: 1976); Saskatchewan Law Reform Commission, *Proposals for a Saskatchewan Matrimonial Homes Act*, Report to the Attorney General (Saskatoon: 1976). In addition, the Nova Scotia Law Reform Advisory Commission has published a study entitled *The Development of Matrimonial Property Law in England and Nova Scotia, an Historic Perspective* (Halifax: 1975).

   The Law Reform Commission of Canada has also made recommendations in its *Report on Family Law* (Ottawa: Information Canada, 1976). The report was published with a view to promoting uniformity in marital property law across Canada.

   Elsewhere, the English Law Commission has issued a series of three reports on family property: *Family Law, First Report on Family Property: A New Approach*, Law Com. No. 86 (London: H.M.S.O., 1978); *Family Provision on Death*, Law Com. No. 61 (London: H.M.S.O., 1974); and *Family Law, Third Report on Family Property and the Matrimonial Home*, Law Com. No. 86 (London: H.M.S.O., 1978).

   In the United States, the National Conference of Commissioners on Uniform State Laws has dealt with the topic in s.307 of the *Uniform Marriage and Divorce Act*, Uniform Laws Annotated (St. Paul, Minnesota: West Publishing Co., 1979), vol. 9, Matrimonial, Family and Health Laws, Supplementary Pamphlet 1974 to 1977.

6. See, for example: M. Rheinstein, "Division of Marital Property", 12 *Willamete L.J.* 413 (1976); H.H. Foster and D.J. Freed, "Marital Property Reform in New York: Partnership

of Co-Equals?", 8 *Family Law Quarterly* 169 (1974), at 173; F.F. Freedman, "The Juridical Capacity of the Married Woman in Quebec: In relation to partnership of acquests and recent amendments to the Civil Code", 21 *McGill L.J.* 518 (1975); P. Jacobson, "Comment on Law Reform Commission of Canada, Family Property, Working Paper 8 (1975)", 8 *Ottawa Law Rev.* 290 (1976), at 292; J. Neville Turner, "Confusion in English Family Property Law — Enlightenment from Australia?", 38 *Mod. L. Rev.* 397 (1975); A. Angelo and W. Atkin, "A Conceptual and Structural Overview of the Matrimonial Property Act 1976", 7 *New Zealand Universities Law Review* 237 (1976-77), at 248.

7. *Matrimonial Property Act*, R.S.A. 1980, c. M-9; *The Family Relations Act*, R.S.B.C. 1979, c.121; *The Marital Property Act*, R.S.M. 1970, c. M45 (also C.C.S.M., c. M45); *Marital Property Act*, S.N.B. 1980, c. M-1.1; *The Matrimonial Property Act*, S. Nfld. 1979, c.32; *Matrimonial Property Act*, S.N.S. 1980, c.9; *Family Law Reform Act*, R.S.O., 1980, c.152; *Family Law Reform Act*, S.P.E.I. 1978, c.6; *Civil Code of Quebec*, art. 464 and arts. 480 to 517; *The Matrimonial Property Act*, S.S. 1979, c. M-6.1.

8. The majority of reports considered three marital property regimes: separate property with judicial discretion, deferred community property, and full and immediate community property.

9. *Supra*, n. 7.

10. *Ibid.*

11. E.G. Strong, "Joseph M. Shoate", New York 22 (1917): "Upon marriage the husband and wife are one and the husband is the one." For general reference, see: E. Jenks, *A Short History of English Law* (London: Methuen & Co. Ltd., 1920), pp. 225-229; P.M. Bromley and P.R.H. Webb, *Family Law* (Wellington: Butterworths, 1974), p. 758; and Sir William Blackstone, *Commentaries on the Laws of England* (Oxford: Clarendon Press, 1765), vol. 1, ch. 15.

12. Sir William Blackstone, *Commentaries on the Laws of England* (Oxford: Clarendon Press, 1765), vol. 1, ch. 15, p. 430.

13. Sir William Blackstone, *Commentaries on the Laws of England*, 2nd ed. (Oxford: Clarendon Press, 1766), vol. 1, p. 433.

14. "By marriage, the husband and wife are one person in law: that is, the very being or legal existence of the woman is suspended during the marriage, or at least is incorporated and consolidated into that of the husband: under whose wing, protection and cover, she performs everything. . .", Sir William Blackstone, *Commentaries on the Laws of England*, 15th ed. (London: Strahan, 1809), vol. 1, p. 442.

15. O. Kahn-Freund, "Recent Legislation on Matrimonial Property", 33 *Modern L. Rev.* 601 (1970), at 605. See also: M. Glendon, "Matrimonial Property: A Comparative Study of Law and Social Change", 49 *Tulane L. Rev.* 21 (1974-75), at 29.

16. H. Sargisson, "Matrimonial Property Legislation — Its History and a Critique of the Present New Zealand Law", 3 *Auckland University L. Rev.* 82 (1976-79), at 83. The reform movement was supported and lobbied for by influential individuals, such as John Stuart Mill, who was devoted to the principle of equal and political civil rights for men and women.

17. 45 and 46 Vict., c.75 (U.K.). See also: the *Matrimonial Causes Act* 1857 (U.K.) and the *Married Women's Property Act* 1870 (U.K.).

18. Every province in Canada, except Quebec, had a statute similar to the English one. See, for example: *The Married Women's Property Act*, S.O. 1884, c.19.

19. In the United States, state legislatures began enacting laws designed to remove or reduce the disabilities of married women as early as 1839 (in Mississippi). By the end of the century all states had such legislation. See: M. Glendon, *supra*, n. 15, at p. 31, and "Married Woman Acts", 14 *Amer. L. Rev.* 788 (1880).

20. E.A. Cheadle, "The Development of Sharing Principles in Common Law Marital Property States", 28 *U.C.L.A. Law Rev.* 1269 (1980-81), at 1275.

21. L.N. Brown, "English Law in Search of a Matrimonial Regime", 4 *Ottawa L. Rev.* 331 (1970-71), at 332.

22. Law Reform Commission of Canada, *supra*, n. 5. For a general description of the disadvantages of the law of separate property, see: J. Temkin, "Property Relations During Marriage in England and Ontario", 30 *International and Comparative Law Quarterly* 190 (1981), at 191.

23. (1974), 13 R.F.L. 185 (S.C.C.); [1975« 1 S.C.R. 423; 41 D.L.R. (3d) 367. The work performed by Mrs. Murdoch was described as "haying, raking, swathing, mowing, driving trucks and tractors and teams, quietening horses, taking cattle back and forth to the reserve, deboning, vaccinating, branding, anything that was to be done" (1974), 41 D.L.R. (3d) 367, at 380.

24. See, for example: *Weisgerber v. Weisgerber* (1969), 71 W.W.R. 461 (Sask. Q.B.); *Rooney v. Rooney* (1969), 68 W.W.R. 641 (Sask. Q.B.); *Klutz v. Klutz* (1968), 2 D.L.R. (3d) 332 (Sask. Q.B.).

25. *Supra*, n. 23.

26. "The conscience of Canadians was shocked by the application of the present law in a recent Supreme Court of Canada decision in *Murdoch*. When the law requires such results, then nothing could be more apparent than the fact that such law is no longer tolerable in a society that professes its laws to be both humane and just", Law Reform Commission of Canada, *supra*, n. 5, at pp. 2-3.

27. See, for example: *Report of the Royal Commission on Marriage and Divorce* (England), 1951-55 CMD 9678, para. 644 (1956):

> Marriage should be regarded as a partnership in which husband and wife work together as equals, and the wife's contribution to the joint undertaking in running the home and looking after the children is just as valuable as that of the husband in providing the home and supporting the family.

See also: Law Reform Commission of Canada, *supra*, n. 5, at p. 3: "marriage is an economic, emotional and cultural partnership"; British Columbia Royal Commission on Family and Children's Law, *supra*, n. 5, at p. 2: "marriage is a partnership of shared responsibilities"; and Law Reform Commission of Saskatchewan, *supra*, n. 5, at p. 2: ". . . most people in Saskatchewan today view marriage as a partnership of equals based on both status and the differing contributions of the spouses."

In addition, the surveys indicate that the public's conception is that of a marriage partnership. A survey of English attitudes towards matrimonial property indicated that a very substantial majority of those interviewed favoured the joint ownership of at least some property by the spouses regardless of how title had been taken or who had actually paid for the property. Of the 1,877 married couples interviewed, 91% of the husbands and 94% of the wives felt that the matrimonial home and its contents should legally be jointly owned irrespective of who paid for it. See: J.E. Todd and L.M. Jones, "Matrimonial Property" (London: Office of Population Censuses and Survey, Her Majesty's Stationery Office, 1972).

In a Canadian survey conducted in 1975, 63% of 1,044 people interviewed felt that where a man has been the chief wage earner in the family, he should have to share equally with his wife any assets accumulated during their marriage if the two decided to separate. Also, 23%

felt that whether or not sharing occurred depended on the circumstances. Only 10% indicated that they did not favor an equal sharing. Answers did not vary greatly from region to region across Canada nor were there great differences between the attitudes of men and women. See: Law Reform Commission of Canada, *supra*, n. 5, at pp. 271-272.

The Alberta Commission also conducted a survey with similar results and concluded:

> If the law does not now recognize the wife's claim to an equitable share in matrimonial property, there seems to be a basic incongruity between the law and the attitudes of Albertans. See: L.W. Downey Research Association Ltd., "Matrimonial Property in Alberta: Facts and Attitudes", in Institute of Law Research and Reform, University of Alberta, *Working Paper on Matrimonial Property*, 1974. The chief conclusion drawn from the results of the survey "is that the majority of Albertans view marriage as a joint venture — a partnership where each spouse contributes to the domestic economy, where property brought into the marriage and property acquired during the marriage is considered to belong to both spouses, and where upon dissolution of the marriage, property should be equally divided. (p. 79).

28. M.D. Freeman, "Towards a Rational Reconstruction of Family Property Law", 25 *Current Legal Problems* 84 (1972), at 88. See also: H. Hahlo, "Matrimonial Property Regimes: Yesterday, Today and Tomorrow", 11 *Osgoode Hall Law Journal* 455 (1973), at 466.

29. See: *infra*, n. 148.

30. Marriage Law of June 11, 1920, No. 415. For a general discussion of the Swedish system, see: M. Rheinstein, *supra*, n. 6, at p. 42l; and H. Sussman, "Spouses and Their Property Under Swedish Law", 12 *Am. J. Comp. L.* 553 (1963).

31. September 28, 1970, Information Canada, Ottawa. Chapter 4, paragraph 89 reads: ". . . (W)e recommend that those provinces and territories, which have not already done so, amend their law in order to recognize the concept of equal partnership in marriage so that the contribution of each spouse to the marriage partnership may be acknowledged and that, upon the dissolution of the marriage, each will have a right to an equal share in the assets accumulated during marriage otherwise than by gift or inheritance received by either spouse from outside sources." See also: M.A. Shone, "Principles of Matrimonial Property Sharing: Alberta's New Act", 17 *Alta. L. Rev.* 143 (1979), at 148.

32. "Separation of property has been tried and found wanting; its simplicity proved too stern and rugged and will never return." O.M. Stone, "Matrimonial Property Law: the Movement towards Equality — Separation or Community? Canadian (especially Albertan) and English Experience", 16 *Alta. L. Rev.* 375 (1978), at 384.

33. See, for example: Man. preamble, N.B. s.2; Nfld. s.17; N.S. preamble; Ontario s.4(5); P.E.I. s.5(7); Sask. s.20. For a detailed discussion of the Acts, see: A.J. McClean, "Matrimonial Property Canadian Common Law Style", 31 *U. of T.L.J.* 363 (1981).

34. "Starting with essentially the same basic premises the provinces have managed to enact legislation of at times bewildering diversity. That clearly has its disadvantages, and if changes are contemplated in the legislation the desirability of some degree of uniformity is a consideration which should be taken into account", McClean, *supra*, n. 33, at p. 435.

35. It is only in British Columbia that spouses automatically become tenants in common in matrimonial property on marriage breakdown. See: *The Family Relations Act*, R.S.B.C. 1979, c.121, s.43(2). See also: *Marital Property Act*, S.N.B. 1980, C.M.-1.1, 2.20 and *The Matrimonial Property Act*, S. Nfld. 1979, c.32, 2.6.

36. *Matrimonial Property Act*, R.S.A. 1980, c.M-9, s.5(1)(a); *The Family Relations Act*, R.S.B.C. 1979, c.121, s.43(1)(c)(d); *Marital Property Act*, S.N.B. 1980, c.M-1.1, s.3(1)(a), (b); *The Matrimonial Property Act*, S. Nfld. 1979, c.32, s.19; *Matrimonial Property Act*,

S.N.S. 1980, c.9, s.12(1)(a), (b); *Family Law Reform Act*, R.S.O. 1980, c.152, s.4(1); *Family Law Reform Act*, S.P.E.I. 1978, c.6, s.5(1).

37. *Matrimonial Property Act*, R.S.A. 1980, c.M-9, s.5(1)(b); *Family Relations Act*, R.S.B.C. 1979, c.121, s.43(1)(c).

38. *The Family Relations Act*, R.S.B.C. 1979, c.121, s.43(1)(a).

39. Where spouses are separated and there is no reasonable prospect of reconciliation or resumption of cohabitation — *The Family Relations Act*, R.S.B.C. 1979, c.121, s.43(a)(b), 44; *Marital Property Act*, S.N.B. 1980, c.M-1.1, s.3(1)(c), (d); *The Matrimonial Property Act*, S. Nfld. 1979, c.32, s.19(1)(c); *Matrimonial Property Act*, S.N.S. 1980, c.9, s.12(1)(c); *Family Law Reform Act*, R.S.O. 1980, c.152, s.4(1); *Family Law Reform Act*, S.P.E.I. 1978, c.6, s.5(1). In Alberta, an order may be made if a court is satisfied that they have been living separate and apart for at least one year immediately before the application, or, if for a period of less than one year, that there is no possibility of their being reconciled — *Matrimonial Property Act*, R.S.A. 1980, c.M-9, s.5(1)(c).

40. *Matrimonial Property Act*, R.S.A. 1980, c.M-9, ss.5(1)(a), (e); 12(e), (1)(c).

41. *The Marital Property Act*, S.M. 1978, c.24/M45 and *The Matrimonial Property Act*, S.S. 1979, c.M-61, s.21(1).

42. In New Brunswick (*Marital Property Act*, S.N.B. 1980, c.M-1.1, s.5), Ontario (*Family Law Reform Act*, R.S.O. 1980, c.152, s.4(3)), and Prince Edward Island (*Family Law Reform Act*, S.P.E.I. 1978, c.6, s.5(3)), a surviving spouse may only continue an application already started before the death of the other spouse. In all the provinces, the estate of the deceased spouse may not initiate an application but in New Brunswick, Ontario, Prince Edward Island, and Saskatchewan the application of the deceased spouse may be continued if initiated before death. See: McClean, *supra*, n. 33, at p. 365.

43. *Marital Property Act*, S.N.B. 1980, c.M-1.1, ss.4,5; *The Matrimonial Property Act*, S. Nfld. 1979, c.32, s.19(1)(d); *Matrimonial Property Act*, S.N.S. 1980, c.9, s.12(1)(d); *The Matrimonial Property Act*, S.S. 1979, c.M-6.1.

44. *The Matrimonial Property Act*, S. Nfld. 1979, c.32, s.19(2); *Matrimonial Property Act*, S.N.S. 1980, c.9, s.12(4).

45. The courts have the discretion to vary the equal division. See: *infra* in text, at pp. 915.

46. See: Ontario, Prince Edward Island and, in part, British Columbia. See generally with respect to this categorization: McClean, *supra*, n. 33.

47. See: Alberta, Manitoba, Saskatchewan, Newfoundland, Nova Scotia, and New Brunswick (in part).

48. British Columbia, New Brunswick, Newfoundland, Nova Scotia, and Prince Edward Island.

49. *Family Law Reform Act*, R.S.O. 1980, c.152, in effect March 31, 1978.

50. *Family Law Reform Act*, R.S.O. 1980, c.152, s.3(b).

51. *Family Law Reform Act*, R.S.O. 1980, c.152, s.4(4).

52. *Family Law Reform Act*, R.S.O. 1980, c.152, s.6(a).

53. *Family Law Reform Act*, R.S.O. 1980, c.152, s.6(b)(i) and s.6(b)(ii).

54. The case of *Leatherdale v. Leatherdale* (1983), 142 D.L.R. (3d) 193 is a prominent example of these difficulties. After studying the reported cases in jurisdictions which used a family assets/business assets distinction, the Saskatchewan Law Reform Commission, *infra*, note 182, concluded that "the approach does not work well and . . . is not founded on any rational examination of the reasons why matrimonial property is shareable" (p. 51-52).

The Attorney-General for the Province of Ontario has suggested that the Ontario legislation may be amended to move away from the family assets/business assets distinction. See: Robert Stephens, "New split of family assets sought", *The Globe and Mail*, national edition, March 22, 1984, p. 4.

55. *Family Law Reform Act*, S.P.E.I. 1978, c.60, in effect December 31, 1978.

Both Ontario and Prince Edward Island have sections which address situations where family assets should not be equally divided because it would be inequitable due to contributions made by spouses, *financial or otherwise*. Whereas section 4(5) of the Ontario legislation specifically includes child care and household management as a factor in unequal contribution, Prince Edward Island legislation does not. However, the jurisprudence on this point in Prince Edward Island has held that the legislation does contemplate household and child care being taken into consideration.

56. *Family Law Reform Act*, S.P.E.I. 1978, c.6, s.5(4).

57. *Family Law Reform Act*, R.S.O. 1980, c.152, s.3(b).

58. *The Family Relations Act*, R.S.B.C. 1979, c.121 (Part 3), in effect March 31, 1979. Partial reform of the separate property regime was first initiated in 1972 when the British Columbia legislature enacted section 8 of *The Family Relations Act*, S.B.C. 1972, c.20, repealed by *The Family Relations Act*, S.B.C. 1978, c.20, s.89. Section 8 allowed a court to award an interest in property to a non-titled spouse where that spouse could prove that "contribution" to it had been made. See generally: K.B. Farguhar, "Section 8 of *The Family Relations Act* — An Experiment in the Exercise of Judicial Discretion and the Distribution of Matrimonial Property", 13 *U.B.C.L. Rev.* 169 (1979).

59. *The Family Relations Act*, R.S.B.C. 1979, c.121, s.46.

60. McClean, *supra*, n. 33, at pp. 402-405.

61. The case of *Leatherdale v. Leatherdale* (1982), 30 R.F.L. (2d) 225 (S.C.C.) emphasized the limited ability of the court to intrude into commercial assets.

62. *The Family Relations Act*, R.S.B.C. 1979, c.121, s.43(a). See also: a similar inclusion in *The Marital Property Act*, R.S.M. 1970, c.M-45, s.1(2).

63. *The Family Relations Act*, R.S.B.C. 1979, c.121, s.51.

64. *Ibid.*

65. *The Matrimonial Property Act*, S. Nfld. 1979, c.32, in effect July 1, 1980.

66. *Matrimonial Property Act*, S.N.S. 1980, c.9, in effect October 1, 1980.

67. *Marital Property Act*, S.N.B. 1980, c.M-1.1, as amended by S.N.B. 1980, c.24, s.11.

68. *The Matrimonial Property Act*, S. Nfld. 1979, c.32, s.16(b)(iv); *Matrimonial Property Act*, S.N.S. 1980, c.9, s.4(1)(e).

69. *Marital Property Act*, S.N.B. 1980, c.M-1.1, s.1.

70. *Ibid.*

71. British Columbia, New Brunswick, Newfoundland, Nova Scotia, Ontario, and Prince Edward Island.

72. *The Marital Property Act*, S.M. 1978, c.24 (also C.C.S.M., c.M45), in effect October 15, 1978.

73. *Matrimonial Property Act*, R.S.A. 1980, c. M-9, in effect January 1, 1979.

74. *The Matrimonial Property Act*, S.S. 1979, c.M-6.1, in effect January 1, 1980.

75. As was stated previously, although New Brunswick, Newfoundland, and Nova Scotia use the definition based on acquisition, their legislation is closer to that of Ontario in practice.

76. Specifically excluded from the matrimonial property regime are assets acquired by gift, assets acquired by inheritance, and amounts received by one spouse as an award of damages for personal injuries. See: *The Marital Property Act*, S.M. 1978, c.24/M-45, ss. 7,8.

77. *The Marital Property Act*, S.M. 1978, c.24/M45, s.4 as amended by S.M. 1983, c.53, ss. 2,3.

78. *The Marital Property Act*, S.M. 1978, c.24/M45, s.1(1)(b) as amended by S.M. 1980-81, c.26, s.21; S.M. 1982, c.17, ss. 1,3; S.M. 1983, c.53, s.1.

79. *The Marital Property Act*, S.M. 1978, c.24/M45, s.1(2), as amended by S.M. 1982, c.17, s.2.

80. *Family Law Reform Act*, R.S.O. 1980, c.152, s.4(1).

81. *Family Law Reform Act*, R.S.O. 1980, c.152, s.4(4).

82. *Family Law Reform Act*, R.S.O. 1980, c.152, s.4(6).

83. *Matrimonial Property Act*, R.S.A. 1980, c.M-9.

84. *Marital Property Act*, R.S.A. 1980, c.M-9., s.7(1).

85. *Marital Property Act*, R.S.A. 1980, c.M-9., s.7(2).

86. *The Marital Property Act*, R.S.M. 1983, c.53, s.3.

87. *Matrimonial Property Act*, R.S.A. 1980, c.M-9., s.7(4).

88. *Matrimonial Property Act*, R.S.A. 1980, c.M-9., s.7(3).

89. *Matrimonial Property Act*, R.S.A. 1980, c.M-9., s.7(4).

90. *The Matrimonial Property Act*, S.S. 1979, c.M-6.1, in effect January 1, 1980. This act replaced section 22 of *The Married Women's Property Act*, S.S. 1974-75, c.29 which was amended in 1975 to permit the court to take into consideration the indirect contributions of both spouses on a division of marital property. The amendment was only intended as a stopgap measure, pending a comprehensive examination of marital property law. See: *Tentative Proposals for Reform of the Matrimonial Property Act*, Law Reform Commission of Saskatchewan, September 1984, p. 4.

91. *The Matrimonial Property Act*, S.S. 1979, c.M-6.1, s.23(1).

92. *The Matrimonial Property Act*, S.S. 1979, c.M-6.1, s.21(1).

93. *The Matrimonial Property Act*, S.S. 1979, c.M-6.1, s.21(2).

94. *Civil Code of Lower Canada*, arts. 1266C-1267D.

95. *Civil Code of Quebec,* arts. 481, 482.

96. *Civil Code of Quebec,* art. 497.

97. *Civil Code of Quebec,* art. 464.

98. *Civil Code of Quebec,* art. 494.

99. Book II of the *Civil Code of Quebec* entitled "The Family" was enacted by virtue of *An Act to Establish a New Civil Code and to Reform Family Law,* L.Q. 1980, c.39; G.Q. 1981, 1087; G.Q. 1982, 3299, parts of which were proclaimed in force on April 2, 1981 and December 1, 1982.

100. *C.C.Q.,* arts. 439, 459, 533, 559; *C.C.B.C.,* art. 735.1. This award, termed the "compensatory allowance", may be granted by a court in the absence of a satisfactory agreement between the parties with respect to reimbursement at the dissolution of the marriage for any cause including the death of one of the parties. For a general discussion of the 1980 amendments and the compensatory allowance, see: K. Connell-Thouez, "Matrimonial Property Regimes in Quebec Before and After the Reform of 1981: Adapting Traditional Institutions to Modern Reality", *Contemporary Trends in Family Law: A National Perspective* (Toronto: Carswell, 1984), p. 27.

101. *Ibid.,* p. 28.

102. Community property, with its *prima facie* equal division of the community fund upon termination of a marriage, is often misleadingly referred to as a system of civil law. Actually, the concept of joint ownership of marital property did not exist in Roman law. It originally descended from the customs of Germanic tribes, primarily but not exclusively, the Visigoths.

The Germanic tribes' concept of the wife's sharing in the accumulations of a marriage was evoked by economic and social realities. Nomadic life was hard, requiring the direct participation of wives with their husbands in the protection and acquisition of property, which consisted chiefly of the spoils of war. Tribal councils recognized the contribution of the wives by granting them a right to share in the booty. See: R. Bartke, "Community Property Law Reform in the United States and in Canada — A Comparison and Critique", 50 *Tulane L. Rev.* 213 (1976), at 260.

For a general discussion of community property regimes, see the following:

W. deFuniak and M. Vaughn, "Why Community Property is so Misunderstood — Knowing its Origins is the Key", 1 *Comm. Prop. J.* 97 (1974) discusses the differences between the common law and community property systems.

W. deFuniak and M. Vaughn, *Principles of Community Property,* 2nd ed. (Tucson: University of Arizona Press, 1971).

S. Greene, "Comparison of the Property Aspects of the Community Property and Common-Law Marital Property Systems and Their Relative Compatibility with the Current View of the Marriage Relationship and The Rights of Women", 13 *Creighton Law Rev.* 71 (1979-80), at 73.

103. The same attempts of the English upper classes to obtain some independence for their women in early English matrimonial law were duplicated in community property jurisdictions. In France, for example, where a community of movables and acquests had been introduced as the standard system by the Code Napoleon in 1804, the wealthy developed the "contrat de mariage" to secure extensive powers to women to deal with their property. (See: Sargisson, *supra,* n. 16, at p. 88.)

104. At the beginning of the twentieth century, the following jurisdictions had some kind of community property regime (that is, traditional, full or deferred) as the legal regime of marital property:

1) Universal community (all assets of both spouses are placed into a common fund) —Brazil, Denmark, Finland, Iceland, Netherlands, Norway, Portugal, South Africa, and Sweden.

2) Community of movables and acquests (all immovables owned by either spouse at the time of marriage remains the separate property of the owner spouse. The movable property of the spouses, no matter when acquired, and the immovables acquired during the marriage are jointly shared) — Belgium, France, Haiti, Luxembourg, and Quebec.

3) Community of acquests (only assets acquired during marriage by gainful activity are shared) — Argentina, Arizona, Bolivia, California, Chile, Colombia, Cuba, Ecuador, Idaho, Louisiana, Nevada, New Mexico, Paraguay, Peru, Puerto Rico, Spain, Texas, Uruguay, and Washington.

(See: Rheinstein, *supra*, n. 6, at p. 416; Hahlo, *supra*, n. 28, at p. 459).

105. In France, for example, reforms were first introduced in 1907 which gave the wife powers of management over her "biens réservés", that is, the earnings she obtained through working outside the home. Unfortunately, this law was not formulated so that third parties could easily ascertain whether or not an asset was one that a married woman could dispose of on her own. Therefore the French law, like its Belgian counterpart of July 20, 1932, remained virtually impossible to apply until it was amended in the 1940s. (See: Rheinstein, *supra*, n. 6, at p. 421). Further reforms up until the 1940s abolished the legal incapacities of the married woman. This movement toward autonomy was significant but in practice hardly far-reaching because the community, and thus the husband as manager of the community, still had the right to enjoy the separate property of the wife and consequently, the wife had only the absolute right to transfer the bare reversion of her separate estate. (See: Sargisson, *supra*, n. 16, at p. 86.)

106. See: F. Viljoen and E. duToit, "The Matrimonial Property Regime of the Transkeian Marriage Act of 1978", 13 *Comparative and International Law Journal of South Africa* 86 (1980).

107. The *Code Napoleon* was replaced with a new community of acquests, which entitled the spouses to share in all property acquired since the marriage except gifts and inheritances. Loi No. 65-570 of July 13, 1965. The Act came into force on February 1, 1966.

108. The law passed in 1965 also gave the wife veto power over important property transactions and separate management over her reserved portion of the community. In addition, both spouses separately administer their own separate property. See: Hahlo, *supra*, n. 28, at p. 468. In 1970, the husband was finally deposed as head of the family but he retained his position as head of the community because of anticipated practical difficulties in joint administration. They can, however, agree on joint administration and, outside of management of the community, the wife has full legal capacity and no longer needs her husband's consent to carry on a trade or profession. See: Glendon, *supra*, n. 15, at p. 37, and D.G. MacDonald Allen, "Community of Property in France", 128 *Solicitor's Journal* 26 (January 13, 1984). This law was amended in May 1985 to the effect that it now gives each spouse the same rights of management over community property.

109. *Italian Civil Code* as amended by *New Family Law* of May 5, 1975, art. 180.

110. For example, current Czechoslovakian law suscribes to the law of community property of the type applied in the Soviet Union, which it adopted due to the Soviet influence. The change to community property occurred in the Soviet Union in 1926. Community property of the spouses comprised all property acquired by them during marriage from their work.

The provisions were further developed by the new RSFSR *Family Code* of 1969 and the regime of community property was made mandatory with no allowance for contracting out. See: G. Glos, "Community Property in Czechoslovakia and the Soviet Union as Compared with Other Community Property States", 7 *Review of Socialist Law* 169 (1981), who criticizes the present regime and the reasons behind its introduction. "The Soviet brand of community property was not so much introduced in the Soviet orbit in order to protect the wife but rather to expand collectivist ideas into the sphere of marital property" (p. 188). See also: Gorecki, "Matrimonial Property in Poland", 26 *Modern L. Rev.* 156 (1963), and Lasok, "Matrimonial Property — Polish Style", 16 *International and Comparative Law Quarterly* 230 (1967).

111. Most of the other states have modified their separate property regimes to allow for distribution of marital property upon marriage dissolution by a court according to what the court considers to be fit and just. For example, the Massachusetts alimony and equitable distribution statute (Mass. Gen. Laws Ann. ch. 208, Section 34 (West. Supp. 1982)) provides as follows:

> Upon divorce or upon motion in an action brought at any time after a divorce, the court may make a judgment for either of the parties to pay alimony to the other. In addition to or in lieu of a judgment to pay alimony, the court may assign to either husband or wife all or any part of the estate of the other. In determining the amount of alimony, if any, to be paid, or in fixing the nature and value of the property, if any, to be so assigned, the court, after hearing the witnesses, if any, of each party, shall consider the length of the marriage, the conduct of the parties during marriage, the age, health, station, occupation, amount and sources of income, vocational skills, employability, estate, liabilities and needs of each of the parties and the opportunity of each for future acquisition of capital assets and income. The court may also consider the contribution of each of the parties in the acquisition, preservation or appreciation in value of their respective estates and the contribution of each of the parties as a homemaker to the family unit.

See, generally: L. Monroe Inker and Margot Ames Clower, "Towards a New Justice in Marital Dissolution: The Massachusetts Statutory Scheme and Due Process Analysis", 16 *Suffolk University Law Review* 907 (1982). See also: S. Greene, *supra*, n. 102, at pp. 71 and 99.

112. Wash. Rev. Code, s.26.16.030 (1974).

113. Cal. Civ. Code, ss. 4800-4811; 85100-85138 (1972 Supp.). For a discussion of the California system, see: S.W. Prager, "The Persistence of Separate Property Concepts in California's Community Property System, 1849-1975", 24 *U.C.L.A. L. Rev.* 1 (1976-77); N.M. Sabban and P.G. Hoffman, "California's Community Property Laws: Planning for a Move to California", 121 *Tr. & Est.* 10-12 (June 1982).

114. Arizona Rev. Stat. Ann., ss. 25-213-214 (Supp. 1973). See: Keddie, "Equal Management and Control of Arizona Community Property", 2 *Comm. Prop. J.* 9 (1975).

115. Texas community property is a mixture of deferred community and community with joint management. During the marriage, each spouse is the sole manager of community property "that he or she would have owned if single." If community property subject to the sole management of one spouse is "mixed" with community property subject to the sole management of the other spouse, the "mixed" community property is subject to joint management. See: Tex. Civ. Stat., s4621, now V.T.C.A. Family Code, s5.22. See also: F. Schroeder, "Matrimonial Property Law Reform: Evaluating the Alternatives", 11 *U. of B.C. L. Rev.* 24 (1977), at 27, and J. McKnight, "Texas Community Property Law — Its Course of Development and Reform", 8 *Cal. W.L. Rev.* 117 (1971-72).

116. *Community Property Act* of 1973 N.M. Stat. Ann. Art. 56-4A (Supp. 1973) s1.1. See: G. Quijano, "Matrimonial Property Law Reform in Canada: From Separate Property to Community Property with Joint Management — Principle v. Pragmatism", 13 *Osgoode Hall L.J.* 381 (1975), at 393, and A.K. Bingaman, "The Community Property Act of 1973: A Commentary and Quasi-Legislative History", 5 *N.M.L. Rev.* 1 (1975).

117. Idaho Code Article 32-912 (Supp. 1979) Rev. 1. The legislation gives both spouses concurrent and equal rights to manage the community property.

118. *The Louisiana Civil Code* was modified in January 1980 to provide for equal management of community by both spouses. See: K. Connell-Thouez, "The New Community of Acquests and Gains in Louisiana", 26 *McGill L.J.* 320 (1980-81), and J.M. Riley, "Analysis of the 1980 Revision of the Matrimonial Regimes Law of Louisiana", 26 *Loyola Law Review* 453 (1980). It was the last among the community property states in the United States to adopt some form of equal management between spouses.

Each spouse acting alone may manage, control or dispose of community property, with specific exceptions. Certain transactions involving community property, such as immovable (real) property, furniture or furnishings located in the family home, and a community business, require the consent of both husband and wife . . . . In other instances, that is, managing a community enterprise and disposing of individual items of an inventory, one spouse alone is given exclusive managerial power in the interest of commerce. Movables that are issued or registered, such as automobiles, shares of stock, or certificates of deposit, may be sold by the spouse or spouses in whose name the property is registered.

119. California law classifies property held by a married couple as community property, separate property or quasi-community property. The definition of quasi-community property varies depending on whether the reference point is dissolution or death. Upon dissolution, the definition refers to property acquired by a spouse while domiciled elsewhere, which would have been community property had the acquiring spouse been domiciled in California at the time of acquisition. See: N.M. Sabban and P.G. Hoffman, "California's Community Property Laws: Planning for a Move to California", 121 *Tr. & Est.* 10 (June 1982).

120. *George v. Ransom*, 15 Cal. 322, at 324-325 (1860); Ariz. Rev. Stat. s25-213 (1976); Nev. Rev. Stat. s123.130 (1973); N.M. Stat. Ann. s57-4A-2-A,-C (Supp. 1975); Wash. Rev. Code Ann. s26.16.010 and 26.16.020 (1961).

121. *Clafin & Co. v. Pfeifer*, 76 Tex. 469, 473, 13 S.W. 483, 485 (1890); *Epperson v. Jones*, 65 Tex. 425, 428 (1886); *De Blane v. Lynch,* 23 Tex. 25, at 29 (1859). The Idaho Code also provides that if the instrument by which the wife acquires separate property provides that the rents and profits therefore be applied to her sole and separate use, then the management and disposal of such rents and profits belong to the wife. *Idaho Code, s*32-906 (1963). The *Louisiana Code* allows the wife, by written instrument, to reserve the income of her property for her own separate use and benefit. La. Civ. Code Ann., arts. 2386, 2402 (1972).

The California courts and Texas courts reached different results on the question of whether income from separate property is community property or separate property. The California court which held that the income of the wife's separate property was also her separate property sought to protect that income from the husband's creditors. See: *George v. Ransom*, 15 Cal. 322 (1860). The ruling applied reciprocally to the husband's separate property so that income therefrom increased his separate property rather than becoming community property in which the wife was entitled to share. Thus, the rule which resulted from the desire to protect the wife could be used to her detriment if the husband had large separate holdings and the wife had none. See: *Beam v. Bank of America*, 6 Cal. 3d 12, 490 p. 2d 137, 98 Cal. Rptr. 137 (1971).

It was precisely this disadvantage to the wife that the Texas court relied on to support its rule that income from separate property is community property. See: *De Blane v. Lynch*, 23 Tex. 25, at 28-29 (1859). The Texas court, of course, thereby left the income of the wife's separate property to the husband's creditors. See: J. Younger, "Community Property, Women and the Law School Curriculum", 48 *N.Y.U.L. Rev.* 211 (1973), at 220-222. See also: Greene, *supra*, n. 102, at p. 72.

122. Ariz. Rev. Stat. s25-211 (1976); Cal. Civ. Code s5110 (West. Supp. 1979); Idaho Code s32-906 (1963); La. Civ. Code Ann. art. 2324 (1971); Nev. Rev. Stat. s123.220 (1973); N.M. Stat. Ann. s57-4A-2-B (Supp. 1975); Tex. Fam. Code s5.01(b) (1975); Wash. Rev. Code Ann. s26.16.030 (1961).

123. Except for Texas:

. . . In Texas each spouse is now entitled to manage and control the community property that he or she would have owned if single. Generally, this would place under a spouse's management and control that spouse's earnings, income from his or her separate property, recoveries for personal injuries, and the income from assets in these categories. Other community property, including property subject to the sole management and control of the spouses which has become commingled, is subject to the joint management and control of both spouses.

See: Greene, *supra*, n. 102, at p. 88.

124. See: Sabban and Hoffman, *supra*, n. 119, at p. 11.

125. Except for Washington, where both separate and community property are subject to division by the court; Wash. Rev. Code Ann. Art. 26.08.110 (1961).

126. See: C. Bruch, "The Definition and Division of Marital Property in California: Towards Parity and Simplicity", 33 *Hastings Law J.* 771 (1981-82), at 777, fn. 38.

> 38. Only California, New Mexico, and Louisiana mandate equal distribution of the community property at divorce and do not authorize any property awards from separate property. Compare Cal. Civ. Code s4800 (West Suppl. 1981), La. Civ. Code Ann. arts. 1290, 1308, 2336, 2341 (West 1952 and Supp. 1981), La. Code Civ. Pro. Ann. art. 82 (West 1960), and N.M. Stat. Ann. s40-4-7 (1978). Equal division of community property is provided by case law: *Michelson v. Michelson*, 86 N.M. 107, 520 P. 2d 263 (1974) with Ariz. Rev. Stat. Ann. s25-318 (Supp. 1980): "(T)he court shall assign each spouse's . . . separate property to such spouse. It shall also divide the community, joint tenancy and other property held in common equitably . . . without regard to marital misconduct."; Idaho Code s32-712 (Supp. 1980): "The community property must be assigned . . . as the court . . . deems just . . . Unless there are compelling reasons otherwise, there shall be a substantially equal division . . . (A) homestead . . . from the separate property of either . . . must be assigned to the former owner . . . subject to the power of the court to assign it for a limited period to the other spouse."; Nev. Rev. Stat. s125.150 (1979): "(T)he court . . . (s)hall make such disposition of . . . (t)he community property . . . and . . . (a)ny . . . joint tenancy (property) . . . as appears just and equitable . . . ." The court may also set aside property or place burdens on it for the benefit or support of the children. And Tex. Fam. Code Ann. tit. 1, s3.63 (Vernon 1975): "(T)he court shall order a division of the estate of the parties (as) the court deems just and right . . . ." An award may be made from separate property under case law: *Campbell v. Campbell*, 586 S.W.2d 162 (Tex. Civ. App. 1979); Wash. Rev. Code Ann. s26.09.080 (Supp. 1980): "(T)he court shall . . . make such disposition of the property and the liabilities of the parties, either community or separate, as shall appear just and equitable . . . ." Among the factors to be considered are "(t)he economic circumstances of each spouse . . . including the desirability of awarding the family home or the right to live therein for reasonable periods to a spouse having custody of any children.

127. See, for example: Ariz. Rev. Stat. s.25-318 (1976), Tex. Fam. Code Ann. tit. 1., s.3.63 (Vernon 1975); Wash. Rev. Stat. Ann. s.26.08.110 (1961); Idaho Code s.32.712 (1963). The criteria referred to by the courts in determining an equitable division of property are similar to those contained in Canadian legislation. See: Greene, *supra*, n. 102, at p. 98.

128. British Columbia Royal Commission on Family and Children's Law, *Report*, First Working Paper of the Working Group on Matrimonial Property (1974).

129. *Ibid.*, p. 14: "We have taken a policy choice that assumes equality of contribution . . . . We happily adopt the rigid system of fixed property rights the English Commission was so concerned to avoid."

The British Columbia government did not agree with its commission's recommendations. It enacted a regime of deferred sharing of family assets with judicial discretion.

160

130. *The Marital Property Act*, S.M. 1977, c.48.

131. *The Marital Property Act*, S.M. 1978, c.24/M45.

132. Royal Commission on Family and Children's Law, *supra*, n. 5, at p. 16.

133. See, for example: Carol Bruch, *supra*, n. 126, at p. 775-776 where she states:

> Home ownership is but one example of the increasing complexity of property division under current California law. Special problems also have developed with regard to pensions: the supremacy clause of the United States Constitution sometimes divests a non-employee spouse of any interest in a federal pension, the division of other pensions is frequently troublesome, and there is confusion concerning payments that involve recompense for disabilities. Other changes in the law have raised questions about the rules controlling tort recoveries, the valuation of good will, post-separation income, assets acquired with mixed separate and community components (including questions of title and the relevance of borrowed moneys), the divorce court's jurisdiction over separate property, and over claims arising out of a couple's cohabitation before marriage, the treatment at death or divorce of property brought to California, and distribution by a probate court of some forms of property and debts.

> An examination of the issues posed in typical divorce and probate cases over the past decade, and of the relative financial postures of divorced men and women, indicates that the system stands in need of reform. Marriage should entail neither convoluted doctrines, exorbitant litigation costs, impoverishment of widows and widowers, nor strikingly disparate post-divorce wealth.

Also see: H. Verrall and A. Sammis, *Cases and Materials on California Community Property* 7 (2nd ed.; 1971) as quoted by Bruch in 1982, at p. 778.

> The (California community property) system is one which can be tolerated but which is in need of a comprehensive review to make it meet the minimum conditions of an acceptable marital property system. These conditions should at least be a system simple enough to be generally understood by the people, a system coordinated with the business and the governmental orders of the day, and a system quick and cheap of administration. No one of these conditions can be said to characterize the California system.

134. Law Reform Commission of Canada, Working Paper on Family Property Law, *supra*, n. 5, at p. 26.

135. For an example of the problems that arise with respect to tracing and commingling of funds, see: S.D. Rosenson, "Divorce California Style", 4 *L.A. Lawyer* 29 (April 1981).

136. See: *supra* in text, at pp. 17-18.

137. Law Reform Commission of Canada, *supra*, n. 5, at p. 323.

138. G. Quijano, "Matrimonial Property Law Reform in Canada: From Separate Property to Community Property with Joint Management — Principle v. Pragmatism", 13 *Osgoode Hall L.J.* 381 (1975), at 387.

139. Greene, *supra*, n. 102, at p. 94.

140. *Ibid.*, p. 90. See also: J.S. MacDonald, "The Impact of Equal Management Upon Community Property Businesses", 13 *Idaho L. Rev.* 191 (1976-1977).

141. Arizona, Idaho, and New Mexico exempt real property from gratuitous transfer by the managing spouse. In California, Texas, and Washington a gift of community property cannot be made by one spouse alone unless the transfer is a "mere trifle". Greene, *ibid.*

142. For a discussion of the special problems that may arise as a result of moving to or from a community property jurisdiction, see: J.M. Kinnebrew, "Texas Community Property", 121 *Tr. & Est.* 15 (June 1982). See: P.W. Buchschacher, "Rights of a Surviving Spouse in Texas in Marital Property Acquired While Domiciled Elsewhere", 45 *Tex. L. Rev.* 321 (1966-67); N.L. Lay, "Marital Property Rights of the Non-Native in a Community Property State", 18 *Hastings L.J.* 295 (1966-67); A.N. Polasky, J.S. Mullin, and P.O.H. Pigman, "Estate Planning for Migrating Clients", 101 *Tr. & Est.* 876 (1962); T.M. Sheehan, "Selected Community Property Problems of the Migrant Spouse", 7 *Fam. L. Q.* 433 (1973). The *Uniform Disposition of Community Property Rights at Death Act* S S13 has sought to alleviate some of these problems.

143. Law Reform Commission of Canada, *supra*, n. 5, at p. 23.

144. The only exceptions are the East European countries. See: *supra*, n. 110 and *infra*, n. 146.

145. Such a change in the context of a jurisdiction that has always had separation of property would involve changes in many areas of the laws. In addition to further amendment to provincial family law, changes would have to be made to the laws dealing with tax, intestate succession, gifts, pensions, commercial law, insurance law, and ownership and rental of property. For example, given the present nature of our income tax system, some difficulties would arise with respect to the question of attribution of property income and capital gains. However, the fundamental question that would arise would be whether couples operating under a joint management community property scheme would be allowed to split incomes with respect to earned income, resulting in lower rates of tax payable for the couple but a massive loss of revenue for the federal government. Such a loss of revenue would inevitably have to be made up from other sources. See: *Sura v. MNR* (S.C.C.), but see: *Poe v. Seburn* (USSC). It should be noted that the benefit of income-splitting is higher for high-income couples than it is for lower income couples. Within the context of the family, treating the couple as a unit and therefore allowing their income to be split jointly between them, may be equitable. However, the net result may be inequitable in terms of tax policy.

146. Between 1939-1948, several of the current common law property states (Michigan, Nebraska, Oklahoma, Oregon, Pennsylvania, and the territory of Hawaii) passed community property laws to gain tax advantages for married couples similar to those enjoyed by couples in the (approximately) eight community property states. See: ch. 273, 1945 Hawaii Sess. Laws (repealed 1949); Act 317, 1947 Mich. Pub. Act (repealed 1948); L.B. 410, 1947 Neb. Laws 426 (repealed 1949); S s1-15, 1939 Okla. Sess. Laws, at 356-360 (repealed 1945); S s1-15, 17-18, 1945 Okla. Sess. Laws (repealed 1949); ch. 440, 1943 Or. Laws (repealed 1945); ch. 525, 1947 Or. Laws (repealed 1949); Act 550, 1947 Pa. Law.

In 1948, the Internal Revenue Code extended the advantages of income-splitting to all married taxpayers. The new community property laws were all immediately repealed except for Pennsylvania's which had been declared unconstitutional *(Willicox v. Pennsylvania Mut. Life Ins. Co.,* 55 A.2d 521 (Pa. 1947)).

In addition, both Czechoslovakia and Russia subscribed to the system of separation of property prior to the introduction of the Soviet community property system.

147. Argentina — Law of April 22, 1968; Columbia — Law No. 28 of 1932; Denmark — Law No. 56 of March 18, 1925; Finland — Law No. 234 of June 13, 1929; Iceland — Law of June 20, 1923; Norway — Ch. 3, para. 16, Law No. 1 of May 20, 1927; Sweden — Marriage Law of June 11, 1920, No. 415; Uruguay — Law No. 783 of September 18, 1946. See generally: Rheinstein, *supra*, n. 6, and I.M. Pedersen, "Matrimonial Property Law in Denmark", 28 *M.L.R.* 137 (1965).

Many of the disadvantages of a traditional regime of community property were eliminated in the system elaborated in Federal (West) Germany under the *Equal Rights Law* of July 1957. Under Gleichberechtigungsgesetz, each party manages and controls his/her property as if it were separate, but on dissolution of the marriage there is an accounting procedure to calculate and equalize their gains during the marriage. This has come to be known as a system of 'deferred community' although there is at no time any community. See: *supra*, n. 32, at p. 384.

Also see generally: E.D. Grave, "German Law", in *Comparative Law of Matrimonial Property*, ed. by A. Keralfy (London, 1972), at 114.

148. Roger Comtois, *Traité théorique et pratique de la communauté de biens* (Montreal : Recueils de droit et de jurisprudence, 1964), p. 317, para. 37ff.

149. See, for example: Stone, *supra*, n. 32, at p. 387, where she states, "Separate administration by both spouses during the marriage of property held and income received, from whatever source, seems both socially desirable, practical and simple."

150. In Texas, for example, each spouse has the sole management and control of the community property that he or she would own if single, including personal earnings, income from separate property and any profits arising from the business. "Thus, in most instances the management of property in Texas closely parallels management in the common law states." Kinnebrew, *supra*, n. 143, at p. 16.

151. *Matrimonial Property Act*, R.S.A. 1980, c.M-9, s.5(1)(e).

152. *Matrimonial Property Act*, R.S.A. 1980, c.M-9, s.8(h). See also: *The Marital Property Act*, S.M. 1978, c.24/M45, s.6(8)(9).

153. *Matrimonial Property Act*, R.S.A. 1980, c.M-9, s.8(1). See also: *The Marital Property Act*, S.M. 1978, c.24/M45, s.6(7).

154. McClean, *supra*, n. 33, at p. 372-373. For example, in Alberta, British Columbia, and Saskatchewan, the court may prohibit a transfer to a donee, or to a person who is not a *bona fide* purchaser for value. Quebec "controls" the problem of dissipation by requiring the consent of both spouses to the making of substantial gifts (art. 494).

155. While many jurisdictions grant special rights to spouses during the marriage with respect to the marital home, some provinces extend this special treatment to the contents of the marital home. For example, the new Quebec legislation extends this protection to household goods and furniture (C.C.Q., arts. 449-450).

The new *Civil Code of Quebec* also limits the right of a spouse to alienate the family home (C.C.Q., arts. 452-456) and requires the agreement of both spouses with respect to disposition of a lease of the family home during the marriage (C.C.Q., art. 451). See: Connell-Thouez, *supra*, n. 100, at p. 35. The author notes at p. 36 that:

> . . . this scheme for preserving the milieu of the family intact at the dissolution of the marriage does not adequately address those cases where the family residence is owned by one spouse either as an acquest or at his separate property.

For a general discussion of the special treatment of the matrimonial home, see: McClean, *ibid.*, p. 373.

156. The one exception is the Newfoundland legislation where spouses automatically become co-owners in joint-tenancy (s.6).

157. In seven provinces, both spouses have an automatic equal right to possession of the matrimonial home, and in all provinces the courts have a discretion of conferring an exclusive right to possession on one spouse. Equal right to possession: *The Marital Property Act*, S.M. 1978, c.24/M45, s.6(2); *Marital Property Act*, S.N.B. 1980, c.M1-1, s.18(1); *The Matrimonial Property Act*, S. Nfld. 1979, c.32, s.6(1); *Matrimonial Property Act*, S.N.S. 1980, c.9, s.6(1); *Family Law Reform Act*, R.S.O. 1980, c.152, s.40(1); *Family Law Reform Act*, S.P.E.I. 1978, c.6, s.40(1); *The Matrimonial Property Act*, S.S. 1979, c.M-6.1, s.4.

Exclusive right to possession: *Matrimonial Property Act*, R.S.A. 1980, c.M-9, ss. 19, 20; *The Family Relations Act*, R.S.B.C. 1979, c.121, s.77; *The Marital Property Act*, R.S.M.

1970, c.M-45, s.6(2); *Marital Property* S.N.B. 1980, c.M-1.1, s.23(1)(a); *The Matrimonial Property Act*, S. Nfld. 1979, c.32, s.13(1); *Matrimonial Property Act*, S.N.S. 1980, c.9, s.11(1); *Family Law Reform Act*, R.S.O. 1980, c.152, s.45(1)(a); as amended by R.S.O. (1984), c.32, s.18(2); *Family Law Reform Act*, S.P.E.I. 1978, c.6, s.45(1)(a); *The Matrimonial Property Act*, S.S. 1979, c.M-6.1, s.5.

158. All the provinces impose restrictions on a titled spouse's power to disposition of the matrimonial home. See: McClean, *supra*, n. 33, at p. 379. Seven of the Acts make provision for special treatment of property other than the matrimonial home, property such as "the contents of the matrimonial home" (British Columbia, Ontario, and Prince Edward Island); "family assets" (Manitoba); "household goods" (Alberta, New Brunswick, and Saskatchewan). See: McClean, *supra*, n. 33, at pp. 382-383.

159. *Family Law Reform Act*, R.S.O. 1980, c.152, Part III.

160. *Family Law Reform Act*, R.S.O. 1980, c.152, s.42. Similar treatment of the matrimonial home is found in Saskatchewan. Part I of the *Matrimonial Property Act*, S.S. 1979, c.M-6.1 recognizes the right of each spouse to possession of the matrimonial home and household contents. These rights exist regardless of which spouse has legal title to the home. They exist during the course of the marriage and are not dependent on a court order. Such rights were recognized by law before the enactment of marital property legislation, and the *Matrimonial Property Act*, S.S. 1979, c.M-6.1 merely codified and extended these rights.

In addition, the *Homesteads Act*, R.S.S. 1978, C. H-5 requires that the wife consent to any transfer or encumbrances of the homestead. Thus a husband could not unilaterally put his wife out of possession of the family home by transferring it to a third party. Nor could a third party foreclose upon a mortgage or take possession of the home unless the wife had consented to the mortgage. The recent report of the Saskatchewan Law Reform Commission, *infra*, n. 171, suggests an amendment so that the effects of non-compliance with the consent or requirement are explicitly set out. If one spouse purports to transfer or encumber the matrimonial home without the consent of the other spouse, the transaction will not be registrable in the Land Titles office.

161. *Matrimonial Property Act*, R.S.A. 1980, c.M-9, Part II.

162. *Matrimonial Property Act*, R.S.A. 1980, c.M-9, ss. 19, 21.

163. *Matrimonial Property Act*, R.S.A. 1980, c.M-9, s.22(3).

164. *The Matrimonial Property Act*, S.M. 1978, c.24/M45, s.6(2).

165. *The Family Maintenance Act*, S.M. 1978, c.25, as amended; see s.10(1).

166. *The Dower Act*, S.M. 1964, c.16, s.1, as amended; see s.3(1).

167. *Supra* in text, at p. 7; *supra*, n. 41.

168. The right of a spouse to support and maintenance includes the right, while living with the other spouse, to periodic reasonable amounts for clothing and other personal expenses and the right to sole discretion free of all interference from the other spouse in the use of those amounts. *The Family Maintenance Act*, S.M. 1978, c.25, s.3.

169. Law Reform Commission of Canada, Working Paper on Family Property Law, *supra*, n. 5, at p. 317.

170. Law Reform Commission of Saskatchewan, *Proposals for a Saskatchewan Matrimonial Homes Act* (May 1976) — which recommended legislation that would provide for co-ownership of the matrimonial home.

164

171. In 1974, the Ontario Law Reform Commission proposed that:

> . . . the principle of co-ownership in the matrimonial home should be adopted: a principle that would entitle the husband and wife to equal shares in the home secured by their joint control and rights of occupation, retained for their joint enjoyment and capable of being disposed of or otherwise dealt with only with the consent of both spouses or by order of the court.

Ontario Law Reform Commission, *Report on Family Law, Part IV: Family Property Law* (Toronto: 1974), p. 135.

172. The Law Commission No. 86, Family Law, *Third Report on Family Property: The Matrimonial Home (Co-Ownership and Occupation Rights) and Household Goods* (London: Her Majesty's Stationery Office, 1978), Part I. See also: Law Commission, Published Working Paper No. 42, *Family Property Law*, at para. 1.86 (1971). For a detailed examination of all the proposals contained in the Law Commission's third report on family property, see: O. Stone, "Reports of the Law Commission", 42 *Mod. L. Rev.* 192 (1979).

The report proposed certain exceptions; for example:

1) a person who acquires a separate interest in a property before or on marriage may, by written declaration signed by him and attested by a witness before the marriage, exclude statutory co-ownership of that property.

2) a similar exclusion is recommended in respect of the matrimonial home acquired by gift or inheritance during marriage or by gift in contemplation of marriage.

3) the third major exception "which casts great doubt on the acceptability of the whole scheme as presented, is that statutory co-ownership will not apply when the marriage ends in divorce, or a decree of nullity or when a decree of judicial separation is made. (Report, paras. 1.179-1.182). In such circumstances the court will have the discretion to make orders in respect of all other types of property owned by both spouses. In this connection the suggested scheme of statutory co-ownership of the matrimonial home should be considered in the perspective of the total property relations between the spouses." Stone, *ibid.*, p. 196.

173. Temkin, *supra*, n. 22, at p. 200. Quebec law requires the consent of both spouses to sublet, transfer or terminate a lease after the owner of the building has been advised that the apartment is a matrimonial residence (arts. 451-453).

174. The English Law Reform Commission did *not* also propose joint ownership with regard to household goods, an issue also considered in their report. Instead the report proposed that, upon the application of a spouse, a court may order that a spouse be given the right to use and enjoy the household items actually belonging to the other (para. 3.31). Quebec law protects the household furniture from being pledged, removed or sold without the consent of both spouses (art. 449).

This proposal was criticized by one author who stated, "Nonetheless, household goods are by their very nature shared as much by the spouses as the home itself. Thus a strong argument can be made for extending the Law Commission's proposals for co-ownership of the matrimonial home to household goods." See: A. M. Bradstreet, "Marital Property Law in England and California: A Comparative Study and Critique", 4 *Hastings Int'l and Comparative Law Review* 143, at 157.

The term "household goods" may be taken to include all things that are used in or are reasonably necessary for the running of the home, except clothing, jewellery, personal items, and things used by a spouse primarily for business purposes. See: Law Reform Commission of Canada, *Studies on Family Property Law* (Ottawa: Information Canada, 1975), and *supra*, n. 5, at p. 351.

175. There have been no reported cases on the sections and my discussions with lawyers and judges have failed to turn up one instance of an application under either section.

176. For example, in *Re Estate of Crichton*, 20 N.Y. 2d 124, 281 NY 2d 811, 228 N.E. 2d 799, at p. 807 (Ct. App. NY 1967) deciding the question whether the community property laws of

Louisiana or the separate property laws of New York should be applied, Judge Keating remarked that depending upon the nature of the property in the estate, a surviving spouse under New York law might well be entitled to receive a greater portion of the overall estate than under the community property system. See: Glos, *supra*, n. 110, at p. 169, ft. 3, and Greene, *supra*, n. 102, at p. 101.

177. At present, the Saskatchewan *Matrimonial Property Act* includes the appreciation and income from pre-marital assets. In a recent report from the Saskatchewan Law Reform Commission, *infra*, n. 181, this was seen as a particular problem because of the rapid inflationary increase of farmland values in the province in the last few decades. After studying the operation of the present Act, the Commission concluded that:

> Property brought into marriage by a spouse should ordinarily be exempt from division *including any increase in value unrelated to the efforts of the spouses* (p. 12) (emphasis added)

This proposal would place the onus on the non-titled spouse to prove contribution. It would bring to Saskatchewan all the problems associated with the definition of a "contribution". If one accepts the basic premise that marriage is a partnership with each spouse contributing equally, then the spouses should share "for better or worse" — for appreciation or depreciation. Profits from businesses often result from market forces yet they are considered legitimate profits nonetheless.

The proposal provides a special rule for the matrimonial home. The appreciation of the matrimonial home after marriage would be shareable in all cases. This is done by fixing the exemption at the equity in the property at the time it became the matrimonial home.

The proposals of the commission would place into legislation a judicial development in the Saskatchewan courts referred to as the "capital base theory". The capital base theory was based on the concept that if a spouse brought property into the marriage that served as the base from which other matrimonial property was built up, this special form of contribution should entitle that spouse to a greater than equal share of the non-exempt matrimonial property.

The judicial development of this theory was stopped recently by the Supreme Court of Canada in the case of *Farr v. Farr* (1984), 39 R.F.L. (2d) 1. In that case, the Supreme Court concluded that:

> (T)he Capital Base Theory seems to me to be wholly incompatible with the statutory presumption of equal distribution subject to a finite set of exemptions which characterized the legislation.

For a discussion of other cases highlighting some of the problems of the Saskatchewan Act, see: The Saskatchewan Law Reform Commission of Canada, *infra*, n. 181, at pp. 48-50.

178. See: Raggio, "Professional Goodwill and Professional Licenses as Property Subject to Distribution upon Dissolution of Marriage", 16 *Family Law Quarterly* 147 (1982-83).

The question of whether a professional practice has goodwill distributable as part of marital property arises in situations where one spouse has established a private medical, dental, legal, accounting or other professional practice and it appears that the spouse's earnings from the practice are in part attributable to goodwill that has accumulated to the practice during the marriage.

See also: Connell-Thouez, *supra*, n. 100, at p. 49; Adams, "Is Professional Goodwill Divisible Community Property", 6 *Comm. Prop. J.* 61 (1979).

179. Connell-Thouez, *ibid.*, at p. 51. See also: Bruch, *supra*, n. 126, at p. 773 where the author points out that:

> . . . until 1982, California courts were consistently unwilling to classify a spouse's enhanced earning capacity as community property. Although this rule may now be changing, the transformation is still far from complete. This asset, the most valuable in many marriages, therefore goes to a spouse without mention in the property division.

180. See: M.A. Glendon, *The New Family and the New Property*. The author points out that for increasingly large numbers of people, the principal type of wealth is "new property", consisting of a profession or employment and such work-related benefits as pensions and insurance. This is seen as a change from the holding of "old property" such as real estate, financial assets, stocks, and other traditional forms of wealth.

The term "new property" was popularized by Charles Reich, "The New Property", 73 *Yale L.J.* 733 (1964), and *The Greening of America* (1970). Glendon, *supra*, states at p. 3:

> Reich suggested . . . that, for most people, their employment or profession, and work-related benefits such as pensions, have come to be the principal forms of wealth, and that, for many others, claims against government are the main source of subsistence. Reich argued that these new forms of property, such as jobs or entitlements, are not only our chief forms of wealth, but are also the bases of various statutes in our society and that, as such, they should be accorded legal protection analogous to that which our legal system has offered more traditional forms of wealth.

181. Saskatchewan Law Reform Commission, *Tentative Proposals for Reform of the Matrimonial Property Act* (September 1984), p. 25.

182. In community property states where courts are to make an equitable division, the factors considered by the courts are similar to those considered in the common law states. Greene, *supra*, n. 102, at p. 102. For a discussion of the factors considered in the common law American states, see: *supra*, n. 112. For a discussion of the factors considered by the Canadian statutes, see: *supra* in text, pp. 6-15.

183. See: Shone, *supra*, n. 31, at p. 163 where she states:

> Assessments of the actual experience under legislation granting a judicial discretion to distribute property in unspecified proportions vary. The "Statement on Matrimonial Property Laws in Canada" published by the federal Advisory Council on the Status of Women in January 1978 expresses dissatisfaction with the value which the courts are placing on this work relative to work outside the home in the provinces of British Columbia and Saskatchewan where, as has been seen, a judicial discretion to adjust property interests has been introduced by statute. The observations of a Saskatchewan writer stand in contrast. Ron W. Hewitt saw a tendency in the Court of Queen's Bench judgments which he reviewed for judges to divide property equally: "the amount of an award under s.22 varies considerably but an even division is fairly common."

See also: F.M. Steel, "Canadian Legislative Reform in the Law of Matrimonial Property and the Role of Judicial Discretion" (M.A. thesis — May 1978), where the author discussed the experience of several jurisdictions with the use of judicial discretion in the division of marital property (including British Columbia, Saskatchewan, the United States, England, and New Zealand). The author reached the conclusion (see p. 118, "Judicial Discretion v. Fixed Rights") that "judicial variation should only be available in those situations where an equal sharing would be grossly inequitable" (p. 133).

184. Speaking of the court's discretion to deviate from equal sharing with respect to marital property-sharing, Stone, *supra*, n. 32, at pp. 385-386, wrote: "In the light of history, and of recent experience in England and New Zealand, my personal view . . . is that women should not hand over to an overwhelmingly male judiciary crucial questions about who provides the next meal and how." In the United States, efforts have been made to structure and control the discretion of trial judges, "whose freedom to make subjectively based decisions is viewed as a real, albeit, lesser danger." Bruch, *supra*, n. 126, at p. 777.

See, for example: *Uniform Marriage and Divorce Act* s307 (Alternatives (a) and (b)); Foster, "Equitable Distribution", *N.Y.L.J.*, July 24, 1980, at 1, col. 2: "The court, in its decision (under New York's new equitable distribution law), must set forth the factors it considered and the reasons for its decision and such may not be waived by either party or counsel. This provision is mandated to guard against an abuse of discretion and to facilitate appeals."

185. See: *supra* in text, at pp. 7-8.

186. Shone, *supra*, n. 31, at p. 153.

187. The Ontario Law Reform Commission recommended a deferred sharing system that would operate upon death. See: J. Bankier, "An Act to Reform the Law Respecting Property Rights and Support Obligations Between Married Persons and in Other Family Relationships: A Critique", 1 *Fam. L. Rev.* 33 (1978).

188. Greene, *supra*, n. 102, at p. 110.

189. McLean, *supra*, n. 33, at pp. 365-368.

To Marry or Not to Marry?
A Study of the Legal Situation
of Common-Law Spouses
in Canadian Law*

— *Suzanne P. Boivin*

"Common-law" relationships, in which couples live together without the sanction of marriage, are becoming a frequent social phenomenon. In recent years the law has begun to recognize these relationships as de facto marriages and hence give them the same treatment.

The author examines the legal treatment of common-law spouses and argues that while there is growing legal recognition of this new form of family unit, the law does not provide adequate protection for it. In order to alleviate major problems which arise on the dissolution of these relationships, the author proposes a new legislative approach to the "common-law" marriage.

Introduction

Nowadays, it is common for two people to live together as a couple in a relationship that may have all the characteristics of marriage, but none of the legal framework. It is difficult to define this type of relationship or to find appropriate words to describe the persons involved. Indeed, the terms used to refer to such individuals are many. Ethel Groffier[1] interprets this diversity as a manifestation of

---

* Translated from French

concern that this relationship, referred to in this paper as a common-law relationship,[2] should not be equated with marriage.

Until very recently, common-law relationships were given no legal status whatsoever in Canada, for fear of legitimizing behaviour that would deviate from the moral order imposed by Church and State in order to uphold the patriarchal system of right to property ownership. The existence of a monogamous family unit that is easy to classify and control by legislation facilitates the acknowledgement of paternity, which is the key to the transfer of a man's wealth to his heirs.[3] Nevertheless, the recognition of common-law spouses who observe the same rules of conjugal fidelity and who, frequently, conform to the same stereotypes as do their married counterparts, does not constitute a threat to the established order, as long as the State has access to certain information, on filiation in particular. This explains the growing trend towards integrating common-law relationships, that resemble those of married couples, into social law. Under these circumstances, the State has nothing to lose and everything to gain, since by imposing a legislated structure on a private relationship, the State may free itself of certain obligations to provide economic support. Even in cases where legislation makes common-law spouses eligible for public benefits, the situation most often involves a transfer from one envelope to another — for example, from social assistance to worker's compensation.

In spite of this, common-law relationships do not carry all the same rights and obligations as marriage. Rather than re-think the institution of marriage — an institution which still meets the expectations of many of our citizens — from the ground up, Canada's provinces have opted for a compromise solution. Consequently, the legislation refers to the common-law relationship but does not equate it with marriage.

The purpose of this paper is to provide an overview of the present status of Canadian law with respect to common-law relationships, by analysing the rights and obligations of spouses and the parent-child relationship. While it is recognized that other family models exist in Canadian society,[4] the relationship of the heterosexual couple that has not gone through the marriage ceremony will be the focus.[5] Subsequently, the arguments for and against a broader legal framework for common-law relationships will be examined.

Present Status of Canadian Law

Rights and Obligations of Spouses

In general, attitudes toward common-law relationships have changed quite dramatically in Canadian society. There was a time when a union that was not "consecrated" by Church or State was frowned upon. Disapproval manifested itself in the rules of law, which prevented legal force being given to transactions between common-law spouses. For example, they could not benefit from domestic contracts, gifts *inter vivos*, or testamentary dispositions.[6]

Today, public policy no longer prohibits common-law relationships, and all Canadian jurisdictions have adopted measures which deal expressly with common-law spouses. Thus, provided they satisfy the criteria stipulated in the legislation, common-law spouses have the same rights and obligations as married spouses under certain laws.

■ *Criteria for Application and Interpretation*

Under what circumstances will a common-law relationship be recognized by law? It should be noted that the criteria vary from one jurisdiction to the next and, even within the same jurisdiction, from one piece of legislation to the next. In order for a union to have legal recognition as a common-law relationship, the man and woman must live together and there must be a degree of stability and permanence ranging from one to seven years, or they must have produced one or more children. In some cases, it is necessary for the parties to have lived together as husband and wife or for a person to have been represented publicly as the spouse of the other person.[7]

When legislation uses such terms as "spouses", "wife", or "widow", without defining them, it is not clear whether these terms apply only to married spouses. In these cases, it is necessary to rely on the rules of interpretation. The context must be examined, that is, the other provisions of the same law, or the more general context, namely, the customary practices of society. In principle, the courts are reluctant to give a broad interpretation which includes common-law spouses.[8]

There are three areas of law in which special rules applying to married persons exist: social law, matrimonial law, and tax law. The treatment of common-law relationships in these areas will now be examined.

■ *Social Law*

"Social law" refers to a broad range of laws providing for entitlement to public benefits. All the jurisdictions have adopted legislation, for example, to award benefits to victims of occupational injuries. Other circumstances under which a person may claim public benefits can vary slightly from one jurisdiction to another. As a rule, entitlement extends to the victims of a crime or a disaster, persons injured during an act of good citizenship and, in Quebec, victims of an automobile accident. "Social law" also includes entitlement to social assistance and insurance or retirement benefits under public and private plans.

In theory, benefits under both private and public plans are payable to the beneficiaries and their "dependants", including the "surviving spouse". As a rule, a definition of "surviving spouse" which incorporates common-law spouses is included. Earlier, the criteria which are most often applied to determine when a common-law spouse is recognized by law were outlined.

It is impossible, in this study, to review all the social laws which may apply in the various jurisdictions. The provisions of private insurance and retirement plans also vary. In theory, a brief check with the government agencies concerned or with the benefits clerks of private companies should be sufficient to determine whether common-law spouses are also eligible. It is important that the common-law spouse be expressly mentioned because, as discussed earlier, if the word "spouse" is not defined, the courts will tend to limit its meaning to "legal" spouses only.

Professor Winnifred H. Holland's recent study on the applicable legislation in common law jurisdictions shows that the common-law spouse has been fairly well integrated into social legislation.[9] This is also true in Quebec.[10]

There are two problems which may prevent a common-law spouse from receiving benefits. First, a conflict may arise between a legal spouse and a common-law spouse, for example, where a husband who is separated but not divorced from his wife has a common-law relationship with another woman. Second, depending on the proof required, a claimant may have difficulty establishing that she meets the legal criteria — particularly, that she has been publicly represented as the spouse of the beneficiary. However, this type of problem should not arise in the majority of cases.

Social law therefore treats common-law relationships more or less as marriages. This makes it possible for common-law spouses to receive benefits; however, it can also prevent them from receiving those benefits. This is the case when eligibility for benefits is based on income earned, for example, in the case of social or legal aid.[11] If the person is involved in a common-law relationship, the authorities will take into account the income of the couple rather than just the income of the person applying for assistance.

Nevertheless, there are still some distinctions between legal spouses and common-law spouses. Only legal spouses have the right, on dissolution of the marriage, to share in the pension credits accumulated by each of the spouses during the marriage.[12] In addition, it is not certain that Canadian insurance laws allow a person to insure the life of his or her common-law spouse, whereas there is no doubt that this possibility exists for married persons.[13]

■ *Matrimonial Law*[14]

Theoretically, matrimonial law creates special rules for married persons. These rules govern the right to habitation and ownership of the family residence, the obligation to provide support, and the division of assets upon the dissolution of the marriage. As the result of either legislative amendments or judicial interpretation, common-law spouses are increasingly being brought within the scope of these special rules.

Domestic Contracts. One method of ensuring a more comprehensive integration of common-law spouses is by allowing them to enter into domestic contracts. This solution, which will be discussed later, is provided for in matrimonial legislation in Ontario, Newfoundland, Prince Edward Island, New Brunswick, British Columbia, the Yukon, and to a lesser degree in Manitoba.

In other jurisdictions, there is no reason to question the validity of a domestic contract,[15] provided that it is not perceived strictly as an arrangement for sexual services.[16]

Principal Residence. In theory, the owner of a house has the right both to decide who can live there and to sell the house at will. One exception to this principle is when a house is used as the principal residence of a married couple. In this case, common law recognizes that the spouse has the right to live in the residence, even if the other spouse is the sole owner.[17] Some jurisdictions have adopted legislative provisions specifying the rights of spouses with respect to the principal residence.[18] The provisions are intended to prevent one of the spouses from deciding to sell, rent or even mortgage the residence without the consent of the other spouse. In the case of separation or divorce, one of the spouses could obtain the right to live in the residence to the exclusion of the other. Some legislation allows the spouse whose name does not appear on the title deed to claim a proprietary interest in the principal residence. The primary goal of these provisions is to prevent family life from being disrupted by the unilateral action of one of the spouses. They also serve to acknowledge the fact that both spouses contribute, either through money or through their labour, to the acquisition of the residence. The residence is often the only significant asset acquired during the couple's life together.

Some jurisdictions stipulate that common-law spouses can benefit from provisions regarding the principal residence. The procedure varies: common-law spouses must either include the provisions in a domestic contract or request an order from the court.[19]

Support. The law states that certain persons have an obligation to provide for the other members of their family. Spouses are bound to do so for the duration of their marriage, in accordance with the means of each party and, after the dissolution of the union, in accordance with need and ability to pay. When a marriage is ended by the death of one party, the law may provide for a portion of the estate to be set aside[20] for the surviving spouse and children, the will notwithstanding. More often, the laws provide for a petition for support which, rather than being charged against the spouse, is charged against the estate.

Common-law spouses may include support provisions in a domestic contract. Support obligations between common-law spouses are also partially recognized by family law. Throughout the relationship, common-law spouses are also obliged to provide support in most jurisdictions, either by legislation or jurisprudence.

On dissolution of the union, the status of common-law spouses differs from that of married spouses. Only Ontario, Manitoba, and British Columbia recognize the right to support payments after a period of cohabitation.[21] An order may be requested in Ontario and Manitoba if cohabitation has been continuous for a period of not less than five years or involves a relationship of some permanence (one year in Manitoba) where a child has been born.[22] In British Columbia, the provisions applicable to married spouses also apply to common-law spouses, provided that the parties have lived as husband and wife for at least two years. However, it is important to recognize that the support awarded to the beneficiary spouse is not very substantial.

What happens if a spouse dies? As a rule, common-law spouses do not inherit *ab intestat*. The only protection offered is in legislation providing for relief for the dependants of a deceased person, but most jurisdictions do not include common-law spouses.[23]

Division of Assets. As in the case of a marriage, the dissolution of a common-law relationship may involve litigation concerning owner-ship of the couple's assets.

An example is a woman who cohabited with a man for ten years. At some point, they decided to move to a farm. They found a suitable farm and bought it, but in the man's name only, despite the fact that the woman contributed either directly or indirectly to the purchase. On occasion, they worked off the farm; the man's income was higher than that of the woman. On the other hand, the woman did all the house-work, looked after the garden, prepared meals for the part-time workers, and did farm chores. In addition, she participated in the purchase of furniture and the costs of maintaining the home. One day, the man announced that he wanted to marry someone else, and the woman was thrown out or left the farm. Who owns the farm?

The example given is a farm, but it could be a house, land, a trailer, shares in a company, a cottage or furniture. The case could pertain to a married couple or a couple involved in a common-law relationship. Many couples have common-law relationships which last a number of years and they accumulate assets during that time.

A similar scenario was analysed by the Supreme Court of Canada in *Murdoch v Murdoch*.[24] In this well-known case, the farm was in the husband's name. The wife had contributed financially to the purchase of the house and had taken care of the household chores. She asked the court to disregard the title deed and to award her half the farm. The judges refused on the grounds that her contribution did not exceed that of any normal wife under the circumstances.

Mrs. Murdoch is only one of many married or common-law spouses who have claimed, before the courts, a proprietary interest in the assets acquired during their relationship. In the majority of cases, it is the woman who must demand her rights since, generally, assets of value are registered in the man's name.

The outcry of indignation raised by the *Murdoch* decision led to the adoption, in all jurisdictions, of special legislative provisions with respect to the division of assets of a married couple. These provisions do not provide a total solution. However, it would be superfluous to provide a detailed analysis of these provisions in this study, since they do not apply to common-law spouses.[25]

Common-law spouses must satisfy the criteria for division of assets established in case law. It must be borne in mind that, generally, the right of ownership depends on a contract or title. How will the courts respond to a woman who has neither of these documents but who claims that the assets of her former spouse belong partially to her?

Courts presented with such actions have tended to apply the theories of right of ownership which apply in other circumstances.[26] Each of the theories applied in the common law jurisdictions and in the province of Quebec (a civil law jurisdiction) will be examined.

In common law jurisdictions, two theories have been invoked by the courts: "resulting trust" and "constructive trust". The basis of the trust theories is that the party who would appear to own the property does not own it on his or her own behalf but holds it for the benefit of someone else.

To establish the existence of a resulting trust, evidence must be adduced of the common intent of the parties to share the assets registered in the name of one of the parties. How can such an intent be established? The courts have acknowledged that it is difficult, if not impossible, to provide direct evidence of intent. They have therefore agreed to analyse each case presented in order to try to discern implicit intent. However, this solution has had its problems since the judges do not always agree among themselves. Confronted with a given situation, some have decided that intent was established, whereas others have decided the opposite.

In view of the problems involved in providing and analysing evidence, some judges have gradually abandoned the concept of resulting trust in favour of the theory of constructive trust. For constructive trust, proof of common intent is no longer required. The following must be proved: the enrichment of one party, the corresponding impoverishment of the other, and the lack of any legal basis for this situation.[27] In *Pettkus v. Becker*,[28] the Supreme Court decided that the man, who had benefitted from the efforts of his common-law spouse for more than 19 years, should have realized that she was entitled to expect to share in the fruits of her labour eventually. The court therefore studied the case in relation to the criterion of "reasonable expectations". However, the decision was not unanimous. The dissenting judges approved awarding a right of ownership to the woman but based their decision on resulting trust. Common law litigants now often plead both resulting trust and constructive trust, in the hope of winning the case under one of the theories.

The criteria outlined in *Pettkus* nevertheless pose problems with respect to evidence. How can the impoverishment of the woman be established, especially if her contribution was primarily through her work in the home and not through a financial contribution? How can it be established that it was through the woman's efforts that the man acquired a particular asset?

Evidence relating to these issues is difficult to prove. Most couples live from day to day without bothering to save this or that receipt, or to keep track of each party's contribution. Moreover, the woman's financial contribution is often less than that of the man. The courts take into account the difference in contributions, although the situation is often the result of wage discrimination, inability to find a full-time job, time spent raising a family, and numerous other factors. A contribution in the form of services is often difficult to establish and is particularly open to the subjective evaluation of judges.[29] In addition to these problems, it is difficult to establish a link between the woman's contribution and the estate acquired by the man. The Supreme Court of Canada recently agreed to hear the case of *Sorochan v. Sorochan*,[30] involving a man and a woman who had had a common-law relationship lasting 40 years. The Supreme Court will have to decide if a resulting trust based on unjust enrichment was created, even in the absence of a direct link between the assets acquired and the work done by the litigant.

In Quebec, two theories are pleaded for the division of assets, particularly for married spouses but also increasingly for common-law spouses: the theory of *de facto* partnership and the theory of unjust enrichment.[31] The common law concepts of trust do not apply in Quebec since, in civil law, a trust can only be created if certain formalities are respected.

To prove the existence of a *de facto* partnership, it must be established that the parties intended to form a partnership in a venture. As a "partner", the woman will be able to claim her fair share of the partnership, even if the title deed is in the man's name. Note, however, that in Quebec the criterion of "reasonable expectations" has not yet been readily accepted and proof of intent will be required by some judges. Moreover, the woman will be required to establish that she made a direct or indirect contribution to the financing and management of the venture. The contribution can be in the form of money, goods or services. However, it must exceed that of mere participation in the relationship (providing furniture or running the household). In the recent case of *Beaudoin-Daigneault v. Richard*, the Supreme Court confirmed the existence of a *de facto* partnership between the common-law couple, who had operated a farm. It remains to be seen if the principles will be applied in the same way in actions involving a house purchased by the man during the relationship rather than a farm. The concept of venture does not fit in with this scenario.

The civil law theory of unjust enrichment is similar to resulting trust, as described in *Pettkus*. To date, the theory has not been applied by the courts with respect to the division of the assets of a couple. In view of its conclusion based on the *de facto* partnership, the Supreme Court did not see fit to rule on unjust enrichment in *Beaudoin-Daigneault*. Moreover, two judges of the Court of Appeal had rejected the application of this theory. Their opinion was that the impoverishment of the woman to the man's benefit did in fact have a legal basis since the woman had counted on the advantages of the relationship and on the hope of a more comfortable life with the man she loved.[32]

Whether under the applicable legislation in the common law jurisdictions or under Quebec civil law, the chances of obtaining a fair share of the assets on dissolution of the common-law relationship remain slim.[33] To date, common-law spouses have won their cases when the relationship was a long one and when it showed all the characteristics of a conventional marriage.[34] In most cases, the couples operated a small family business, such as a farm.

Finally, even if the woman succeeds in adducing all the evidence required, she will not necessarily be entitled to half the assets. She may be awarded the estimated value of her contribution.[35]

■ *Tax Law*

Finally, the last aspect of law which attaches specific consequences to married spouses is tax law. In theory, any person, married or unmarried, is treated as an individual for tax purposes. Nevertheless, certain rules treat a married couple as a single unit.

It is not within the scope of this paper to undertake a detailed review of the tax system, nor to approve or disapprove of the rules which apply to married persons. However, it is interesting to compare the situation of married and common-law spouses in terms of the tax system.

Recent amendments to tax legislation, both at the federal level[36] and in Quebec,[37] address common-law spouses. Nevertheless, the vast majority of the provisions which apply to married persons do not apply to common-law spouses, because the definitions of the terms used — "spouse", "married taxpayer", "married person", and "widow" — have not been broadened.[38] Consequently, common-law spouses cannot take advantage of certain deductions for which married persons are eligible, particularly the married persons' exemption, the transfer of unused deductions, and the spouse's contribution to an RRSP. On the other hand, common-law spouses are not subject to the rules which treat married persons as a single economic unit, such as the attribution rules. Consequently, their incomes are considered on an individual not a couple basis.

A few years ago, common-law spouses became eligible, in principle, for two rights which previously applied only to married persons: the right to transfer assets from one spouse to the other without tax consequences[39] and the right to claim deductions for support payments.[40]

In practice, however, the amendments benefit few people in common-law relationships. In order to be eligible for the special provisions regarding the transfer of assets, common-law partners must satisfy the very strict conditions set out by the legislation, namely:

- that provincial legislation authorizes the transaction between the common-law spouses;

- that the taxpayer satisfies the conditions set forth in the provincial legislation or that there is a written agreement complying with the said legislation;

- that a decree, decision or order has been handed down by a competent tribunal; and finally,

- that the law in question is one prescribed under the regulations adopted pursuant to the *Income Tax Act*.

These requirements are more demanding than those applicable to married spouses who, all things considered, simply have to follow the civil rules of their jurisdiction. Furthermore, legislation making specific provision for common-law spouses to conclude this type of transaction exists in only a few provinces. According to the relevant regulation, the only "prescribed" law to date is the *Family Law Reform Act* of Ontario. Thus, for the time being, only common-law spouses living in Ontario can take advantage of these new provisions.

With respect to support payments, the Act requires that an order be handed down by a competent tribunal in accordance with the laws of the province, and that the taxpayer belong to a "prescribed category" of persons set forth in provincial legislation. This provision therefore excludes any possibility of an amicable agreement and is limited in its scope to jurisdictions which expressly recognize an obligation on the part of former common-law spouses to pay support. No regulations have been adopted to define the "prescribed category" required by the section; as a result, no one is eligible at this time.

The amendments introduced to Quebec's *Taxation Act* reflect almost exactly the federal legislation. One author[41] concluded that the amendments currently apply only to common-law spouses who live in Quebec but who previously resided in Ontario and transferred assets pursuant to Ontario provincial laws.

For all practical purposes, current tax legislation ignores common-law relationships. Nevertheless, the mere fact that new provisions have been introduced, despite the difficulties involved in their application, indicates that Revenue Canada has begun to recognize common-law spouses.

Following this brief overview of the situation of the spouses themselves, it is useful to compare the legal aspects of common-law relationships with those of marriage in terms of the parent-child relationship.

Rights and Obligations of Spouses with Respect to Children of the Union

Little by little, the distinction between legitimate and illegitimate children is disappearing. In the United States, the evolution has been the result, in part, of claims based on constitutional guarantees.[42] In Canada, some jurisdictions[43] have abolished all distinctions, and others have adopted measures to this effect.

Theoretically, a child is legitimate if the parents were legally married at the time of the birth or conception, if they were married after the birth, or if the marriage, albeit void, had putative effects. These situations carry a presumption of paternity which applies to the husband of the child's mother.

In addition, the law creates a presumption of paternity in the case of children born within a certain period following the dissolution of the marriage.[44] When a legally married woman cohabits with a man other than her husband, problems may arise in establishing paternity in the face of the legal presumptions of paternity, or in obtaining a decision on conflicting presumptions.[45]

Certain laws create various presumptions, for example in the case where the mother is cohabiting with a man at the time of the child's birth, or where the mother has cohabited with a man and a child is born within a certain period after cohabitation has ended. In the case of conflicting presumptions, provincial legislation in New Brunswick provides that no presumption of paternity may be made, except where a declaration by the natural father overrides the husband's presumption of paternity if the mother was not cohabiting with the husband at the time of the child's birth.[46]

■ *Support in respect of the parents*
Owing to the abolition of the distinction between legitimate and illegitimate children in Ontario, New Brunswick, Quebec, the Yukon, and Manitoba,[47] illegitimate children are now covered by legislation governing the right to support. In Prince Edward Island and Nova Scotia,[48] illegitimate children still have special status but they have the same right to support.

In British Columbia, Saskatchewan, and Newfoundland, illegitimate children of parents who cohabited for a certain period of time are also entitled to support.[49]

In certain cases, the obligation to provide support is imposed not only on the parents of the child but also on persons who treated the child as their own or who cohabited with the natural parent for a certain period of time.[50]

An illegitimate child's right to support may be contingent on the natural father's voluntary acknowledgement of the child, or judicial recognition of paternity.[51] It should be noted that this path is not open to all mothers. Theoretically, the mother must be living alone, or if she is married, must be separated from her husband. Moreover, any action must be initiated within the prescribed delay.

Ontario legislation is among the most progressive, since it no longer requires a declaration of paternity before an order for support can be issued.[52] The Ontario law is also breaking new ground in that it authorizes contracts between common-law spouses concerning the support of a child, contracts which may be the subject of a court order. These contracts may deal with the payment of the expenses for pre-natal care and birth, child support, and burial expenses of the child or mother.[53]

■ *Support in Respect of the State*
In terms of benefits under social legislation, illegitimate children are given more recognition than common-law spouses. Several pieces of legislation expressly state that the provisions apply to illegitimate

children. When legislation awards benefits to the "child", a problem of interpretation may arise, since the rule of interpretation under common law excludes illegitimate children. Recent decisions allow that the word "child" refers *prima facie* to all children, legitimate or illegitimate.[54] Nevertheless, this position is not unanimously held and some judges will require a clearer statement from the legislator before setting aside the traditional rule.[55]

Family allowance benefits[56] are payable regardless of the marital status of the parents.

■ *Custody and Access Rights*

Disputes may arise between the parents themselves or between parents and third parties, particularly foster families or adoptive parents. Under common law, the mother retained custody of illegitimate children. This practice has been maintained in some jurisdictions.[57]

More and more, however, legislation is decreeing that the best interests of the child should come first, a criterion which is already recognized in case law.[58] Thus, there is no longer any reason to think that the mere fact of living with someone in a common-law relationship would have negative consequences on custody or access rights.[59]

In Quebec, fathers and mothers have rights and obligations with respect to the custody, control, and education of their children as well as an obligation to nourish and maintain them. If the relationship ends, the father or mother of the child may claim custody under article 653 of the *Civil Code of Quebec*.

In cases of adoption, the obligation to inform the natural father and obtain his consent varies from jurisdiction to jurisdiction.[60] For example, in New Brunswick, parental consent is required;[61] however, the court may dispense with it[62] if the parent abandoned the child, obstinately neglected or refused to maintain the child, did not have a parental relationship with the child, or if the delay in finding a home for the child would not be in the best interests of the child. Insofar as the change of name is concerned, the rule says that it is not necessary to obtain the consent of the natural father, although the reverse is true if the parents were married.[63]

■ *Succession Rights*

There is no problem if the child is expressly named in a gift *inter vivos* or in a will.

182

■ *Testamentary Succession*[64]

As a rule, an illegitimate child has the right to petition for support against the father's succession, a conflicting will notwithstanding, provided that there is proof of filiation.[65]

■ *Ab Intestat*

Theoretically, in all Canadian provinces, a child can inherit from its mother. However, among those provinces which maintain the status of illegitimacy, only Alberta, Saskatchewan, and British Columbia give illegitimate children the right to inherit from their fathers. In each case, there are conditions: there must be acknowledgement or recognition of paternity, no lawful issue, or the remedy must be limited to a right to petition for support.[66]

In addition, the right of parents and their ascendants to inherit from their illegitimate children is not always the same as it is in the case of legitimate children.

■ *Tax Law*

Tax laws facilitate certain transactions between taxpayers and their children. In addition, if a child is a dependant or in the taxpayer's custody, the latter is eligible for the child tax deduction,[67] the child care expenses deduction,[68] the child tax credit,[69] and, in Quebec, the availability allowance.[70]

As a rule, a common-law spouse is in the same position as a married taxpayer in terms of benefitting from the provisions regarding children. The word "child" includes an illegitimate child.[71] In addition, the taxpayer may regard as his or her child a person who is wholly dependent or who is, in law or in fact, in the custody and control of the taxpayer. However, the legislation also allows taxpayers to treat their spouse's children as their own. In light of the interpretation of the word "spouse" which was mentioned earlier, this possibility will apply only to married taxpayers. Thus, a common-law spouse who is not the parent of the child will have to establish that the child is in his or her custody or control.

In Quebec, amendments made in 1982[72] following the reform of family law eliminated the expression "of the marriage" which qualified the child in various provisions. At the same time, the rule according to which an illegitimate child is presumed to be wholly dependent on his mother was abolished for purposes of the general child deduction,[73] but retained for purposes of the application of child care expenses.[74] The reverse took place at the federal level, with the presumption being abolished for child care expenses,[75] but retained for purposes of the general deduction.[76]

In practice, these distinctions have little importance, since the authorities rarely require formal proof of custody. The deciding factor is who has assumed the cost of maintaining the child.

It should be noted that although one of the common-law spouses is not eligible for the child tax credit, both are jointly and severally liable for the reimbursement of any overpayment made to the person with whom he or she resides.[77]

For or Against a Greater Legal Recognition of Common-Law Relationships

Now that various aspects of common-law relationships which receive special attention in legislation of case law have been outlined, the question to be posed is whether legislation on common-law relationships should be passed. If so, how far should such legislation go in relation to marriage? Opinions differ. The following are the arguments against a legal framework.

The Principle of Free Choice

It is argued by some that the State should not interfere in the free choice of parties who decide not to marry specifically to avoid the legal consequences of marriage.[78] The flaw in this argument is that the *choice* of not marrying may be unilateral. Nevertheless, both men and women are against the intervention of the State to such an extent that, in Quebec, not a single recommendation of the Civil Code Revision Office on common-law relationships was accepted.[79]

Autonomy of Women

Obviously, the objections raised to the institution of marriage apply to the creation of a similar institution of common-law relationships. The proliferation of rules seeking to protect the weaker party in a relationship are contested by some feminists, who maintain that equality will not be achieved until each and every one of us is truly autonomous.[80] Authors Freeman and Lyon note that identifying common-law relationships with marriage is one means of controlling women, a means of imposing a moral code.[81] This debate has already arisen in other areas of protective legislation:[82] do protective laws help women or are they merely a paternalistic attempt to dominate women by lulling them into a false sense of security?

Commitment of the Couple and Problems of Definition

Another problem concerns the probable duration of the relationship. It is argued that a distinction should be made between couples who are prepared to commit themselves in a more permanent way and couples who are not willing to make the type of commitment that marriage represents.[83] The divorce rate is a good answer to this argument: why give legal recognition to a marriage which lasted four years, and not to a common-law relationship which lasted five years? Nevertheless, there is a problem when trying to establish the duration of a common-law relationship. In the absence of children, even when the couple publicly acknowledges their relationship as that of a common-law marriage, there must be certain types of evidence required to prove that the couple has undertaken a commitment deeper than that of a transitory or convenient relationship. Thus, what must be determined is the criterion of permanence or the degree of proof required for the other factors. In addition, a criterion of permanence implies that both the starting point and the continuity of the relationship must be established. The diversity of the criteria used at the present time in the various jurisdictions, and even within the same jurisdiction, but for different purposes, is an indication of some arbitrariness in this area. One way of avoiding this problem is to base any acknowledgement solely on the presence of children,[84] a solution which may, however, raise other problems and which would necessarily be incomplete.

Preservation of Marriage

Would more widespread acknowledgement of common-law relationships threaten the institution of marriage? Apart from the moral issues, it is to the advantage of Western countries to promote a type of family unit which disturbs the persons involved as little as possible, defines the obligations of support placed on the parties and their children, and has a positive impact on the birth rate. The current problem is that it is not certain that marriage, as we know it, fulfils these functions, as the proliferation of common-law relationships would seem to indicate. As discussed earlier, even in the absence of legislative rules, the courts are tending to apply the stereotypes of marriage to common-law relationships in order to remedy unjust situations. The magnitude of the phenomenon may explain this trend. Who does not know someone living in a common-law relationship? Scarcely 15 to 20 years ago such a relationship was the exception to the rule, and more often than not, was kept quiet.

The following are among the arguments in favour of broader legal recognition of common-law relationships.

Right to Support

It is neither socially expedient nor just to refuse to recognize the rights and obligations to support of persons involved in a relationship which, for all intents and purposes, resembles marriage.[85]

Legislative Policy versus Court Intervention

Would it not be preferable to establish a comprehensive legislative policy on common-law relationships, instead of leaving it up to the courts to follow the evolution of morals? At first glance, comprehensive legislation seems a more coherent solution, but women have to be cautious of policies which often serve only to confine them to the role of "unpaid linchpin" of the family. However, it will take a long time for society to move away from the traditional attitudes reflected, unfortunately, in our legal system. Even in the case of *Marvin v. Marvin*,[86] Mr. Justice Tobriner stressed that the court's decision should not be interpreted as a slight on the institution of marriage.

It is a real dilemma: how is it possible to protect women who have lived or are living in a common-law relationship without, at the same time, creating a legal superstructure that would establish their dependence? Equating common-law relationships to marriage is not the answer, since even the rules governing marriage cannot guarantee women's financial inheritance or their real, daily control of a couple's finances.

Given the divergence of opinions concerning marriage and the reforms needed, it is likely that only compromise solutions — in other words, partial legal recognition of common-law relationships — will be adopted in Canadian jurisprudence.

Consequently, some propose to maintain the distinction between common-law relationships and marriage but at the same time recognize that common-law relationships create an interdependence between the parties and that the State has a duty, if not an interest, in having the parties assume certain obligations, if only to the children of such a relationship.[87]

Others prefer a solution that would rest solely on the right to make contracts. In a written agreement, common-law spouses would specify their choice of either the general legal rules of matrimonial law or some other set of rules agreeable to the parties. This solution warrants particular attention.[88]

Domestic Contracts

As discussed earlier, some jurisdictions make express provision for the right of common-law spouses to enter into domestic contracts concerning various aspects of their life as a couple. Even in the other jurisdictions, the absence of such legislation would not necessarily prevent an agreement of this nature from being as valid as any other contract.

Is this really the way of the future? Experience shows that persons united by sentimental attachments shy away from contracts. Asking for a contract may imply a lack of confidence. In order to overcome this obstacle, it would perhaps be advisable to subject common-law relationships of a certain permanence to a rebuttable presumption indicating that the spouses wish to be governed by the legal rules of marriage.[89] Consequently, spouses would be required to sign a written agreement to the effect that they did not want to be treated as married persons. It is hoped that the exercise would open the door to free discussions on the rights and obligations of each party in the event of the dissolution of the union.

As in the case of married women, it is difficult to take a stand against the integration of female common-law spouses in public and private compensation plans. Obviously, the goal is the financial independence of everyone. However, until this goal is reached, it seems illogical to deny the need for benefits, when, in fact, it exists.

The Royal Commission on the Status of Women in Canada did not examine the issue of common-law relationships.[90] The Conseil du statut de la femme du Québec[91] has recommended that common-law contracts be given legal recognition and that the Minister of Justice disseminate information on the necessity of concluding such contracts. In addition, it has recommended that the criteria with respect to the permanence of the relationship within the framework of social legislation be made uniform by using three years for relationships without children and one year for those with children.

It seems that these measures constitute a minimum requirement in each Canadian jurisdiction. The current trend is toward a greater integration of common-law spouses into matrimonial legislation for claims based on economic dependence, but not for claims based on the right to ownership of property. This has the effect of perpetuating the subservience created by support rather than addressing the problem of the fair division of the assets acquired during the relationship.

Insofar as children are concerned, distinctions based on the conditions of the child's birth should be abolished and the rights and obligations associated with parent-child relationships should be standardized.

Suzanne P. Boivin *is a partner in the law firm of Mélançon et associés in Montreal. She has also been active in the National Association of Women and the Law.*

Notes

1. E. Groffier, "Les époux de fait dans le droit civil du Québec", in *Marriage and Cohabitation in Contemporary Societies: Areas of Legal, Social and Ethical Change — an International and Inter-Disciplinary Approach*, eds. J.M. Eckelaar and S.N. Katz (Toronto: Butterworths, 1980), p. 236.

2. The author prefers the terms "common-law relationship" and "common-law spouses" for the reasons given by E. Groffier, *ibid.*

3. See in particular: F. Engels' work *The Origin of Family, Private Property and the State* (New York:International Publications, 1942).

4. For example, homosexual or polygamous relationships; for an overview of the options involved in these types of relationship, refer to J. Payne, "Maintenance Rights and Obligations: A Search for Uniformity", *Family Law Review* (1978), at 2.

5. This paper will not dwell on the distinctions between legal marriage and so-called "common-law" marriage or on the other legal aspects of a putative marriage. See: M.D.A. Freeman and C.M. Lyon, *Cohabitation Without Marriage. An Essay in Law and Social Policy* (Aldershot, England: Gower, 1983), p. 3; and W.H. Holland and D.K. McNair, *Unmarried Couples — Legal Aspects of Cohabitation; Tax Aspects* (Toronto: Carswell, 1982), pp. 9-28.

6. For example, articles 768 of the *Civil Code of Quebec*, repealed in 1980, restricted the rights of common-law spouses with respect to gifts *inter vivos*; see: N. Balla's study, "Consequences of separation for unmarried couples. Canadian developments", 6 *Queen's Law Journal* 72 (1980).

7. See: *infra*, n. 23, for an analysis of the criterion "of some permanence"; there is no "cohabitation" where a woman lives with a man under the same roof but is financially independent: see: *Re Stokiewicz and Filas* (1978), 21 O.R. (2d) 717, 7 R.F.L. (2d) 366, 92 D.L.R. (3d) 129.

8. *Louis v. Esslinger; Dumphy v. Esslinger*, (1981) 121 D.L.R. (3d) 17 (B.C.S.C.); and in the fiscal field, decisions cited in *infra*, n. 40.

9. For a detailed study of provisions applicable in common law jurisdictions, see: Holland and McNair, *supra*, n. 5.

10. *Workmen's Compensation Act*, R.S.Q. 1977, c. A-3, s 2, which defines the word "consorts" as a man and a woman who are married and who live together or who live together as husband and wife and who at the time of the accident had been living together for three years or for one year if a child was born of their union and who were publicly represented as consorts. This definition also applies for the purposes of the *Act to promote good citizenship*, R.S.Q. 1977, c. C-20, s 1; the *Act respecting the protection of persons and property in the event of disaster*, R.S.Q. 1977, c. P-38.1, s 44; the *Act respecting indemnities for victims of asbestosis and silicosis in mines and quarries*, R.S.Q. 1977, c. I-7, s 11; the *Automobile Insurance Act*, R.S.Q. 1977, c. a-25, s 1.7; and the *Act respecting labour standards*, R.S.Q. 1977, c. N-1.1, s1. A broader definition is given in the *Act respecting work income supplement*, R.S.Q. 1977, c. S-37.1, s 1, which requires only that persons live together and are married or live together as husband and wife for at least one year, and in the *Act respecting income security for Cree hunters and trappers*, R.S.Q. 1977, c. S-3.2, s 1, which defines "consort" as "a person who lives with another person, as husband and wife, taking into account native customs." With regard to retirement, refer to the *Act respecting the Quebec Pension Plan*, R.S.Q. 1977, c. R-9, s 91. See also: the *Act respecting the Government and Public Employees Retirement Plan*, R.S.Q. 1977, c. R-10, s 44; the *Act respecting the Teachers Pension Plan*, R.S.Q. 1977, c. R-11, s 46; the *Act respecting the Civil Service Superannuation Plan*, R.S.Q. 1977, c. R-12, s 77; and the *Act respecting the conditions of employment and the pension plan of the Members of the National Assembly*, R.S.Q. 1977, c. 52.1, s 54.

11. For example, the Quebec *Regulation respecting the application of the Legal Aid Act*, R.R.Q. 1981, c. A-14, r 1, amended by Order in Council 943-83, (1983) 115 G.O. II 2343, p. 2344 which stipulates in section 6 that a person applying for legal aid must provide information concerning the "... person with whom he forms a couple."

12. S. 102.1 and 102.2 of the *Act respecting the Quebec Pension Plan, supra*, n. 10, since January 1, 1978.

13. In Quebec, see: article 2507 a) C.C.L.C.; for the applicable legislation in other jurisdictions, see: Holland, *supra*, n. 5, at p. 181.

14. The main legislation is as follows:

    Alberta: *The Domestic Relations Act*, R.S.A. 1980, c. D-37; *Matrimonial Property Act*, R.S.A. 1980, c. M-9; *Family Relief Act*, R.S.A. 1980, c. F-2;

    British Columbia: *Family Relations Act*, R.S.B.C. 1979, c. 121;

    Prince Edward Island: *Family Law Reform Act*, S.P.E.I. 1978, c. 6 (R.S.P.E.I. 1974, c. F-2.1);

    Manitoba: *Family Maintenance Act*, S.M. 1978, c. 25 (c. F-20 of the Continuing Consolidation of the Statutes of Manitoba);

    New Brunswick: *Marital Property Act*, S.N.B. 1980, c. M-1.1 and the *Child and Family Services and Family Relations Act*, S.N.B. 1980, c. C-2.1;

    Nova Scotia: *Family Maintenance Act*, S.N.S. 1980, c. 6 (c. F-22 of the Consolidated Statutes of Nova Scotia);

    Ontario: *Family Law Reform Act*, R.S.O. 1980, c. 152;

    Quebec: arts. 497-517, 521-524, 529-535 and 556-559, C.C.Q. (the former provisions 1266(r)-1267(d) and 1338-1383 C.C.L.C. remain in effect for a transitional period);

    Saskatchewan: *Deserted Wives' and Children's Maintenance Act*, R.S.S. 1978, c. D-26;

    Newfoundland: *Maintenance Act*, R.S.N., 1970, c. 223; and *Matrimonial Property Act*, S.N. 1979, c. 32;

    Northwest Territories: *Domestic Relations Ordinance*, R.O.N.W.T. 1974, c. D-9;

    Yukon: *Matrimonial Property Ordinance*, R.O.Y.T. 1979 (2d), c. 11, amended by *An Ordinance to Amend the Matrimonial Property Ordinance*, R.O.Y.T. 1980 (2d), c. 15, as amended.

15. *Pettkus v. Becker*, [1980] 2 S.C.R. 834, 19 R.F.L. (2d) 165 (S.C.); in Quebec, doctrine accepts that this possibility exists since the repeal of art. 768 C.C.Q.; A. Lareau, "Les transferts de biens et les paiements de soutien entre concubins : une analyse des dispositions fiscales", (1983) 24 C. de D. 177; M. Guy, "Les accords entre concubins et entre époux après la loi 89", (1981) 1 C.P. du N. 165; and J. Sylvestre, "Les accords entre concubins", (1981), C.P. du N. 197; E. Groffier, *supra*, n. 1, at p. 238, except perhaps in jurisdictions which specify that unmarried couples can enter into an agreement in contemplation of their marriage to each other which is, however, unenforceable until after the marriage; see, for example: *Matrimonial Property Act*, R.S.A. 1980, c. M-9, s 37 (2).

16. This reservation was expressed in the California decision of *Marvin v. Marvin* (1976), 18 Cal. (3d) 660, 134 Cal. Reptr. 815.

17. See: Holland and McNair, *supra*, n. 5, at pp. 74ff.

18. In Quebec, see: arts. 449-452, C.C.Q.: protection includes household furniture used by the family.

19. For example, in Manitoba, this type of order can be requested if the union lasted one year and if a child was born of the union, *Family Maintenance Act, supra*, n. 15, s 10.

190

20. Such as the reserve which was proposed in Quebec by the Civil Code Revision Office in the *Report on the Quebec Civil Code*, vol. I, book 3, arts. 59 ff., and which, incidentally, applied only to married couples.

21. Notwithstanding the provisions adopted by British Columbia and Manitoba to recognize support obligations after dissolution of the relationship, the validity of such measures was questioned in Alberta and Quebec; Alberta Institute of Law Research and Reform, *Working Paper on Matrimonial Support 113* (June 1974); Civil Code Revision Office, *supra*, n. 20, vol. II, title 1, book 2, at p. 208.

22. In *Donheim v. Irvin* (1979), 6 R.F.L. (2d) 242, an eleven-month relationship was recognized as having the degree of permanence required; see also: *Re Labbé and McCullough* (1979), 23 O.R. (2d) 536 (Prov. Ct.). The same criterion applies in the Yukon, *Matrimonial Property Ordinance*, *supra*, n. 15, s 30.6.

23. See, however: *Succession Law Reform Act*, R.S.O. 1980, c. 488, s 57 (d) (i). The definition of "common-law spouse" (s 57 (b)) is the same as that given in the *Matrimonial Property Act*.

    Estate Administration Act, R.S.B.C. 1979, c. 114, s 86. The surviving spouse must establish that the deceased had supported her for at least two years prior to his death.

    Dependants of a Deceased Person Relief Act, R.S.P.E.I. 1974, c. D-6. The definition of a dependant includes a person of the opposite sex who, for a period of at least three years immediately prior to the date of the death of the deceased, lived and cohabited with the deceased as the spouse of the deceased and was dependent upon the deceased for maintenance and support.

    Dependant's Relief Ordinance, R.O.N.W.T. 1974, c. D-4, if there was cohabitation for one year prior to death.

    Dependant's Relief Ordinance, O.Y.T. 1980 (2nd), c. 6, if there was cohabitation for three years.

24. (1975) 1 S.C.R. 423, (1973) 41 D.L.R. (3d) 367.

25. See: *supra*, n. 15. Even in those provinces which have adopted reforms which include common-law spouses, such as Ontario, Prince Edward Island, British Columbia, and the Yukon, common-law spouses are not referred to in family law reform provisions dealing with the division of property. See: Macdonald et al., *Law and Practice Under the Family Law Reform Act of Ontario* (Toronto: Carswell, 1980), vol. 1, pp. 1-16 to 1-18.

26. *Rathwell v. Rathwell*, [1978] 2 S.C.R. 436, 83 D.L.R. (3d) 289; *Pettkus v. Becker*, [1980] 2 S.C.R. 834, 117 D.L.R. (3d) 257; *Beaudoin-Daigneault v. Richard*, [1984] 2 S.C.R.

27. In *Pettkus v. Becker*, Dickson J. reiterated the criteria he had previously outlined in *Rathwell, supra*, n. 26.

28. *Supra*, n. 26.

29. Compare *Rathwell and Murdoch, supra*, n. 27 and 24.

30. Motion for leave to appeal granted on January 22, 1985.

31. *Cantin v. Comeau*, [1972] C.A. 523; *Labelle v. Légaré*, [1978] C.S. 1033; *Beaudoin-Daigneault v. Richard*, [1984] 1 S.C.R. 2, reversed [1982] C.A. 66.

32. *Richard v. Beaudoin-Daigneault, supra*, n. 31, at p. 79 (Lajoie J.), at p. 77 (Monet J.).

33. For a comparative study, see: P. Girard, "Concubines and Cohabites: A Comparative Look at Living Together", 28 *McGill L. J.* 977 (1983).

34. See: the decision of Dickson J. in *Pettkus v. Becker, supra*, n. 28, at p. 850; see also: the comments of Freeman and Lyon, *supra*, n. 5, at p. 210.

35. In *Beaudoin-Daigneault*, Paré J. of the Court of Appeal assessed the contribution at $6,379.15 while the claim, allowed by the Supreme Court, called for half of the property valued at $60,000.

36. *Income Tax Act*, S.C. 1970-71-72, c. 63, as amended, referred to below as I.T.A.

37. *Taxation Act*, R.S.Q. 1977, c. I-3, as amended, referred to below as T.A.; the comments apply as a general rule to the part of the act dealing with taxes on gifts and to the provisions of the *Succession Duty Act*, R.S.Q. 1977, c. D-13.2.

38. The courts decided that the word "spouse" refers only to a married spouse. See: *No. 673 v. M.N.R.*, 60 D.T.C. 21; *Schapira v. M.N.R.*, 66 D.T.C. 157; *Sokil v. M.N.R.*, 68 D.T.C. 314; *The Queen v. Taylor*, 84 D.T.C. 6234. This interpretation would be confirmed by the recent amendments which refer to a common-law union without using the term "spouse".

39. At the federal level, s 73 (1) (d) I.T.A., added by S.C. 1980-81, c. 48, s 39 (1), applicable to goods transferred after 1979 and Regulation 6500; in Quebec, s 454 (d) and Regulation 454 R.I., R.R.Q. 1981.

40. S. 56 (1) (c. 1) and s.60 (c. 1) I.T.A., added by 1980-81-82-83, c. 140, s 26 (4) and 28 (2); s 336.1 (b) and 312 (b) T.A., amended by 1982, c. 5.

41. Lareau, *supra*, n. 15, at p. 218.

42. In accordance with the right to "equal protection"; *Levy v. Louisiana* (1968) 391 U.S. 668; *Trimble v. Gordon* (1977), 430 U.S. 762.

43. Ontario, *Children's Law Reform Act*, R.S.O. 1980, c. 68; New Brunswick, *Child and Family Services and Family Relations Act*, S.N.B. 1980, c. C-2.1; Quebec, art. 594, C.C.Q., added by S.Q. 1980, c. 39, s 1; the Yukon, *The Children's Act,* Statutes of the Yukon Territory, 1984, c. 2, passed on May 17, 1984; Manitoba, *Family Maintenance Act*, S.M. 1978, c. 25, amended by 1982-83-84, c. 54, adding s 11.2.

44. For example, art. 574, C.C.Q. stipulates that if a child is born during a marriage or within three hundred days after its dissolution, the husband of the child's mother is presumed to be the father, unless the child is born after the remarriage of the mother (art. 576, C.C.Q.).

45. See, in particular: section 8 of the Ontario Act and section 103 of the New Brunswick Act, *supra*, n. 43.

46. Subsection 103 (3).

47. In New Brunswick, the father of the unborn child also has a support obligation toward the pregnant mother for the costs of the birth of the child, s 112 (2).

48. *Family Maintenance Act*, S.N.S. 1980, c-6, s 11; *Family Law Reform Act*, S.P.E.I. 1978, c-6.

49. In British Columbia, even when there is no cohabitation, the father could be ordered to pay support if he contributed to maintaining the child for at least one year, s 1 (b) (ii), *Family Relations Act*.

50. The statutory criterion is a settled intention to treat the child as a family member. *Barlow v. Barlow* (1978), 8 R.F.L. (2d) 6 (Ont. Prov. Ct.); *Snedker v. Snedker* (1978), 6 R.F.L. (2d) 213 (Ont. Prov. Ct.).

51. See, in particular: New Brunswick, *supra*, n. 43, s 1.

52. *Sayer v. Rollin* (1980), 16 R.F.L. (2d) 289 (Ont. C.A.).

53. Such agreements can also be entered into in other jurisdictions which allow domestic contracts.

54. *Brulé v. Plummer*, [1979] 2 S.C.R. 343.

55. *Louis v. Esslinger, supra*, n. 8; the legislation which abolished the status of legitimacy contains corresponding provisions setting out how contracts and statutes are to be interpreted; see, in particular, s 11.3 of the *Family Maintenance Act* of Manitoba , *supra*, n. 14.

56. *Family Allowance Act, 1973*, 1973-74, c. 44, s 2. The act defines "parent" as an individual whose principal responsibility is the maintenance of a child.

57. Alberta, *Domestic Relations Act*, R.S.A. 1980, c. D-37, s 47; British Columbia, if the natural parents did not live together, *Family Relations Act*, R.S.B.C. 1979, c. 121, s 27; and in the Northwest Territories, the *Domestic Relations Ordinance*, R.O.N.W.T. 1974, c. D-9, s 28.

58. See, in particular: the New Brunswick Act which defines the criterion.

59. F. Héléine, "Les conflits entre mariage et concubinage ou la rencontre du fait et du droit", 38 R. du B. 679 (1978).

60. See: Holland and McNair, *supra*, n. 5, at p. 174.

61. *Supra*, n. 43, s 76 (1) (n).

62. *Ibid.*, s 78.

63. See: S.P. Boivin, "The Name of the Married Woman and of Children", in this volume.

64. See: Holland and McNair, *supra*, n. 5, at pp. 163ff.

65. In particular, *Estate Administration Act*, R.S.B.C. 1979, c. 114; *Family Relief Act*, R.S.A. 1980, c. F-2; *Testators' Family Maintenance Act*, R.S.N.S. 1967, c. 303.

66. *Intestate Succession Act*, R.S.A. 1980, c. I-9; *Intestate Succession Act*, R.S.S. 1978, c. I-131; *Estate Administration Act*, R.S.B.C. 1979, c. 114.

67. S 109 I.T.A.

68. S 63 I.T.A., s 351 T.A.

69. S 122.2 I.T.A.

70. S 357 and 776.2 T.A.

71. According to the definition given in section 252 (1) I.T.A. and section 1 T.A.

72. S.Q. 1982 c. 17, s 47-54.

73. S 699 T.A., amended by S.Q. 1982, c. 17, s 53.

74. S 356 T.A.

75. The previous section 63(4) I.T.A. was repealed by recent amendments which also abolished the deduction criteria based on the sex of the taxpayer, S.C. 1983-84, c. 1.

76. S 109 (3) I.T.A.

77. S 122.2 (2) (b) I.T.A., amended by S.C. 1983-84, c. 1, s 65 (2).

78. Freeman and Lyon, *supra*, n. 5, at p. 198, particularly the reference to the disagreement of Clark J. in the *Marvin* case and the Canadian decisions cited on pp. 198-199; see also: Holland and McNair , *supra*, n. 5, at pp. 103-104; Alberta Institute of Law Research and Reform, *supra*, n. 21.

79. This refers to the repeal of articles 768, C.C.Q. The Conseil du statut de la femme du Québec views the obligation to respect the freedom of choice of the couple as the *objective* of any reform regarding common-law relationships. *Pour les Québécoises : égalité et indépendance*, 1978, p. 161.

80. Freeman and Lyon, *supra*, n. 5, at p. 192.

81. *Ibid.*, p. 159.

82. Particularly concerning labour legislation which stipulated conditions applicable only to women; for example, the obligation to pay for a taxi after a certain hour.

83. Freeman and Lyon, *supra*, n. 5, at pp. 190-191.

84. This approach was adopted in Sweden; see: *ibid.*, p. 164.

85. P. Girard, *supra*, n. 33.

86. *Supra*, n. 16.

87. P. Girard, *supra*, n. 33; see also: the analysis of commentaries collected by the Quebec Civil Code Revision Office, vol. II, *Commentaries*, p. 115.

88. Freeman and Lyon, *supra*, n. 5.

89. The merits of this type of proposal are discussed by J. Payne, *supra*, n. 4, at pp. 3-4.

90. Canada. *Report of the Royal Commission on the Status of Women in Canada* (Ottawa: Information Canada, 1970).

91. *Supra*, n. 79, at pp. 161-162.

The Surname of the Married Woman and of Children[*]

— *Suzanne P. Boivin*

It was customary, although not a legal obligation, for a woman to adopt her husband's surname on marriage, and their children were given their father's surname. Historically, this name change reflected a sort of passing of title from a woman's father to her husband; essentially a woman became her husband's possession.

The author examines the laws and customs surrounding the surname of the married woman and her children, comparing the legislation which varies from province to province. Given the historical context of the change of names and the social realities of the 1980s, the author points out the incongruities between the professed purpose (identification of individuals) and the social effect of the law. The author favours the Quebec legislation which prevents the adoption of a husband's surname by a wife on marriage.

Introduction

The task of writing about the surname[1] of the married woman and of children may, at first glance, seem to be a glaringly easy one: the subject will be quickly dispensed with as it is a technical matter that, in general, boils down to the recording of data.

However, as will be observed from the very first examination of the subject, this initial impression doesn't take into account the impact of

---

[*] Translated from French

customs and laws concerning the giving of surnames on so-called traditional family values. The traditional family unit recognizes the husband-father as head of the family; the wife-mother and the children derive their identity from him.[2]

In principle, laws pertaining to surnames are intended to identify people. Government defends its right to be able to identify its citizens, and even to compile statistics.[3] This is how government justifies keeping records of the surname each person is given at birth and any subsequent name changes.

Even if one were to accept such a justification, current legislation is unsatisfactory since it goes far beyond the stated purposes. What is clear is government's desire to control the family unit by relying on traditional values. The following examples bear witness to this desire. First, the choice of a newborn child's surname cannot be made freely; in most cases, the father's surname must be given. In some instances, a married person cannot change her/his surname without making a similar application for her/his spouse and their children. Finally, some provisions restrict the right of married women to change their surname, while others set out clear-cut rules for changing one's own surname and that of one's children in cases of divorce, widowhood, and remarriage. Rules of this type are not needed if the sole purpose is to identify people.

This study examines two elements of Canadian law on surnames: the rules governing the surname of the married woman, and those pertaining to the surname given a child either at birth or through a subsequent application for a change of surname.

It will be seen that reforms have been adopted to take into account the increasingly widespread desire of married women to retain their own identity, and of parents to have greater scope in choosing the surname of their child in order to recognize the mother's lineage.

Nevertheless, discriminatory provisions still remain and the reforms, although they do respond in part to the desires expressed, have been unable to eliminate the patriarchal principle sustained by the relevant legislation.

In conclusion, this study illustrates how access to women's equality within the context of legislation concerning the surname depends on questioning the legislative policy itself rather than reforms within the scope of existing legislation.

The Surname of the Married Woman

A Brief Background[4]

The use and giving of a surname has, throughout history, raised many questions. Does the individual hold a property right to her/his surname such that she/he can forbid its use by third parties? Is the surname of so little importance that it can be changed at will? What criteria must govern the choice of a surname? What social values justify the giving of the same surname to a group of individuals? It is interesting to note that surnames have not always been a function of a blood tie or a marriage tie. They have often been used to indicate ownership: consider, for example, the surnames of Roman or American slaves.

Questions related to the surnames of married women have been the focus of much attention. The legal framework used to decide these questions varies from one society to another. Historically,[5] in civil law jurisdictions, the woman keeps the surname she was given at birth; in Germanic jurisdictions, she acquires the family name of her husband; in common law jurisdictions, it is customary for her to adopt the surname of her husband although the woman is free to keep or take back her own surname or even choose an entirely different surname.

In Canada, all jurisdictions have passed more or less detailed legislation concerning surnames. Most of these laws have provisions that pertain specifically to the surname of the married woman.

It should be noted, however, that regardless of the applicable legislation, the custom of taking the husband's surname has become very widespread. How can this be explained? Some authors[6] state that it is a logical result of the legal incapacity of the married woman. Why cling to an identity separate from that of one's husband when the law states that husband and wife form a single unit and that the husband exercises the rights of that unit? Added to this are such reasons as convenience and prestige. Thus, even in cases where the married woman had legal status, it often happened that she used her own surname for legal transactions and her husband's surname in her social life.

This use of the husband's surname is so deeply rooted that the legal situation has become confusing. Does a woman have an obligation to take her husband's surname on marriage? If they divorce, does she have to stop using her husband's surname? What happens if she took her husband's surname but wants to begin using the surname she was given at birth? These and other questions have been raised before the courts. In some cases, the married woman claimed the right to use her own surname; in others, the ex-husband would try to stop the ex-wife from using his surname; in still others, an error in the designation of the married woman was invoked as grounds for invalidating a legal instrument. Mixed in with all this were such factors as social class, morality, financial interest, culture, and religion.[7]

An examination of the present state of Canadian law will make it possible to answer these questions for women living in Quebec under civil law, or in other provinces or territories of Canada under common law.

The State of Canadian Law

■ *Quebec*

In Quebec,[8] every woman who married on or after April 2, 1981, keeps the surname she was given at birth after marriage and *must* exercise her civil rights under this name. Obviously, the legislator cannot prevent a woman from using her husband's surname in her social life. But wherever a legal relation is involved, for example any registration, any contract, or the practice of her profession, the woman has not only the right but the *obligation* to use only her own surname.

In fact, the solution adopted by the Civil Code Revision Office (CCRO) merely entrenches the rule that already existed, that is, the legal surname of any individual is the surname given at birth. However, the custom of taking the husband's surname was so widespread that it had acquired force of law.[9] The effect of the new law was to invalidate the custom. Thus, women no longer have the option of using their husband's surname when exercising their civil rights. Nor can they add their husband's surname to their own, as had frequently been done for a number of years. The CCRO based its choice on the principle of the permanence of the surname stating that the new rule takes into account the equality of both parties.[10]

This solution, simple and unique in Canada, received support from women's groups in Quebec.[11] The rule makes it possible to avoid the proliferation of rules found elsewhere in Canada respecting the surname of the married woman.

■ *Common Law Jurisdictions*

The common law rule, stated in the *Cowley v. Cowley*[12] decision, is that an individual may adopt the surname of his or her choice provided the choice is not made for fraudulent purposes or with the intention of misleading. This principle of free choice applies to the married woman who has the right, but not the obligation, to adopt the surname of her husband, and, where applicable, to continue to use her husband's surname following dissolution of the marriage and even after re-marriage. However, she also has the right to keep the surname she was given at birth.

The common law rule is not, however, the only legal regulation that applies. Consideration must be given to the legislation passed in all Canadian jurisdictions. With the exception of the Act passed in Prince Edward Island,[13] all the laws set out criteria for surname changes and refer specifically to the married woman. When the provincial and territorial Acts on changes of surname were passed, there were questions as to whether the common law rule had been rescinded, either in whole or in part.[14] Since no Canadian law requires a woman to take her husband's surname, it is accepted that a married woman may continue to exercise her civil rights under her own surname. This option is implicitly recognized in Alberta,[15] Manitoba,[16] and New Brunswick.[17] In two jurisdictions — British Columbia[18] and Saskatche-wan[19] — this right is now subject to a formal declaration.

Recent amendments to the British Columbia and Saskatchewan Acts stipulate that a woman who is getting married and who, after marriage, wishes to use the surname she was given at birth, must produce a declaration to this effect. If she fails to produce such a declaration, it is assumed that she has taken her husband's surname. Other jurisdictions do not require a declaration of this type.

Although the married woman has the right to keep her own surname, she also has, in each jurisdiction, the option of taking her husband's surname. This choice is guaranteed in different ways: an express exemption to the applicable procedure for changing one's surname,[20] an express declaration that the common law rules have been maintained, or silence on the part of the law, which has the same effect. (It is accepted that an express provision is needed to withdraw rights granted under common law.)

The Newfoundland Act[21] offers the most complete range of options affecting both spouses. They can adopt the surname of either spouse or even a surname composed of both of their surnames.

What about the right to change surnames during marriage? For example, suppose that a woman adopted her husband's surname at the time of their marriage but wishes to take back her own surname. Another example would be the case of a woman who produced a declaration in British Columbia or Saskatchewan stating that she would be keeping her original surname. Can she change her decision? The response varies from one jurisdiction to another. Here again, the Newfoundland Act is the least restrictive. Each of the spouses can take back their original surname during the marriage without having to go through any legal or administrative procedure.

In Saskatchewan,[22] the woman who sends a notice stating that she wants to use her own surname can ultimately opt through a formal procedure to adopt the surname of her husband. Furthermore, no delay is stipulated for the sending of the declaration concerning use of one's original surname, and it might be argued that the right to opt for one's own surname exists at any time during the marriage. In British Columbia,[23] any woman who has not sent her declaration at the time of marriage or who wishes to change her surname must follow the legal procedures. The husband's consent is not required. But, unlike the husband, the wife is limited in her choice of surname during the marriage.[24]

In the Northwest Territories[25] and the Yukon,[26] the woman cannot change her surname as long as her husband is living. In Manitoba,[27] the woman must obtain her husband's consent or notify him of the change unless she can establish that she is separated.

When the Act does not expressly mention the right of the married woman to take back her own surname during the marriage, without formal procedure, it would seem that the woman must follow the usual procedures for applying for a change of surname.[28]

Such is the case with the Ontario Act. In the case of *O'Connell Hord v. Hord*,[29] it was ruled that, as the Ontario Act specifically allows the retaking of one's original surname following dissolution of the marriage, it must be concluded that this option does not exist during the marriage. Thus, the woman must make application for a change of surname in accordance with the Act. The Ontario Act now allows the married woman to institute proceedings to change her surname, but this may prove difficult to do as, in principle, the woman must make a subsequent application with respect to both her husband and her children. This mandatory binding of other family members also exists in other jurisdictions[30] and leads to obvious obstacles when the sole aim of the woman is to take back her own surname.

The courts in Ontario have examined the situation, just as absurd, of the married woman who has never taken her husband's surname and wishes to change her own surname. In *Re Vabalis*,[31] the wife wished to change her name from Vabals to Vabalis. Her husband was agreeable to this but did not wish to change his own name despite the clear provision that reads as follows:

> 4(1) A married person applying for a change of surname shall also apply for a change of surname of his or her spouse and all unmarried minor children of the husband or of the marriage.

The Ontario Court of Appeal invoked the rule of interpretation to the effect that it must be presumed that the law does not wish to create an absurd or unjust effect. Expressing the view that a literal interpretation of section 4(1) would produce such an effect, the Ontario Court decided that the section in question should be applied only in cases where the spouses had the same surname. It therefore granted a change of surname for the woman only.

The *Re Czudyjowycz*[32] decision achieved a similar result. This time, it was the husband who wished to change his surname while his wife bore a different surname. In deciding that the husband's request could be granted without having any consequence on his wife's surname, the judge relied on the following provision:

> 16(3) An order made under this section may provide for such changes of names as the court considers proper having regard to the nature of the application, the relationship and status of other persons mentioned in the application and all other relevant circumstances, and every order has effect according to the tenor thereof.

A similar provision exists in most of the Acts.

These examples taken from legal decisions demonstrate that the Ontario Act is not consistent with the growing trend among women not to take their husband's surname. For this reason, the courts have had to resort to the use of interpretation to get around provisions which assume that all members of one family must have the same surname.

What happens upon dissolution of the marriage? Several jurisdictions expressly allow the woman to take back her own surname without formal procedure upon dissolution of the marriage.[33] There is a growing tendency to grant the judge pronouncing the dissolution of marriage, either by a decree absolute or an annulment, an ancillary power over the right to change surnames.[34] In Ontario, it has been recommended that such a provision be adopted as, according to its drafters, it would avoid any temptation on the part of the mother having legal custody of the children to change their surname without notifying the father.[35] In any event, the courts have already decided that, pursuant to the *Divorce Act*, they have jurisdiction to rule on conclusions regarding a change of surname, at least with respect to the children.

Furthermore, the obligation to include the children in the application does not, as a rule, exist in the case of the divorced woman but remains in certain jurisdictions with respect to the widow.[36]

Conclusion

The right of the married woman to retain her own surname upon marriage or to take it back on the dissolution of marriage does not pose any legal difficulty in Canada. If, however, the married woman adopts the surname of her husband at the time of marriage, and later decides to take back her own surname, she may encounter obstacles with respect to either her right to do so or the procedures to be followed.

Furthermore, in all jurisdictions in Canada except Quebec, the custom according to which the married woman may take the surname of her husband survives, although it is not mandatory. Recent amendments by the legislatures of British Columbia and Saskatchewan continue to give precedence to this custom. Is the maintenance of this custom desirable? The words of a judge ruling on an application for a change of surname regarding a young girl are revealing in this regard:

> The child is a female and in all likelihood will marry and lose whatever surname she has at that time, so why should one be concerned with her surname at all?[37]

Only Quebec's solution fully answers this question; henceforth, the fact of contracting marriage no longer has any effect on the surname of the individual.

The proposal may seem radical but the experience of Quebec shows that it has not led to revolution. It also has the advantage of avoiding absurd situations that result from stopgap legislation. As the *O'Connell Hord* decision illustrates, legislative reform intended to be progressive may have a negative impact. It seems that instead of attempting to anticipate the whole range of possible circumstances — tax legislation shows that this form of legislation can be very costly — it would be preferable to reduce the principle to its simplest form of expression, even if this would require a transition period.

The author believes this is not only the most consistent, but also the fairest solution. It is true that the new options under consideration in Newfoundland, which have been the subject of favourable recommendations in Ontario and British Columbia, have the advantage of emphasizing that the change of surname should not be a matter limited to women. But do these options not leave open the possibility of emotional blackmail by the new spouse, or even by the community, in the form of pressure brought to bear on the woman to follow tradition? The Quebec Act eliminates this obligation to negotiate which proves so difficult in the matrimonial relationship, a situation recognized by the feminist groups that have supported the adopted solution.[38]

Thus, in the face of restrictive or discriminatory provisions, one must wonder whether it is sufficient to extend the provision to both spouses or whether it would not be preferable to demand more fundamental reform. The same question arises with respect to the surname of the children.

The Surname of Children

There is some legislative control in all jurisdictions as to the surname of a newborn child[39] (except in Newfoundland) and as to the possibility of subsequently changing this name[40] (except in Prince Edward Island).

Surname Given at Birth

Analysis of the relevant provisions shows that parents have the utmost discretion in the choice of their child's given name(s)[41] but that their options as to the child's surname are limited, even nonexistent. With only a few exceptions, the rule is still that the father's surname is given unless the child is born out of wedlock, in which case the rule is that she/he is given the mother's surname. Thus, most of the Acts perpetuate the link to the father's family while maintaining an arbitrary distinction between the children according to the civil status of their parents.

To evade the rule whereby the child is presumed to be the husband's child and is given his surname, the married woman must produce a declaration to the effect that she was not living with her husband at the time of conception and that her husband is not the father of the child. Only with the consent of the natural father may she register the child under the natural father's surname and designate him as the father. His consent must also be obtained if the unmarried mother wishes to depart from the rule whereby she must give the child her surname, in order to give him or her the surname of the natural father.

In Quebec, Ontario, Manitoba, and Alberta, it is now possible for parents, married or unmarried, to give the child a compound surname.[42] The choice is not totally free as the surname must include the surnames of the parents, and, in Ontario, the Act requires that the same surname be given to all subsequent children of the union. Fortunately, the arbitrary requirement of the Ontario Act to the effect that the father's surname must appear first has been abolished.[43] However, even in these jurisdictions, except Quebec, the general rules stated earlier apply if both parents do not consent to the giving of a compound surname.

Finally, only Quebec and Manitoba allow the mother's surname to be chosen. The Quebec provision states that, where applicable, the parents jointly decide between the father's surname and that of the mother. In Manitoba, the Act does not clearly state who makes the choice and it would seem that the individual who completes the declaration would have full latitude in this regard.

What do these criteria mean? Everything hinges on the intended purpose. As indicated in the report of The Uniform Law Conference of Canada, if the purpose of the Act is to register individuals accurately, the most effective solution, though disruptive of social values, would be to give the child a name and number.[44] Current legislation places the emphasis on the paternal line. Obligatory connection to the father is no more appropriate than any other means to identify individuals. The same may be said of the new, more balanced provisions, which offer the option of using a compound name. They provide greater equality, but raise questions of application. Where there is no agreement between the parents, who will choose from among the various options? Is it desirable for all children born of the same union to have the same surname? This practice is a factor which links them to each other but can still maintain distinctions within a family when the children are offspring of different parents. Can compound surnames be compounded *ad infinitum*? These questions illustrate the need to re-evaluate the philosophy which underlies the current legislation.

Change of Surname

Parents have control over the surname of their children, not only at the birth of the children but also while the children are minors. All jurisdictions, except Prince Edward Island, provide for specific circumstances in which parents may request a change of surname for a child who is a minor. It is unusual for the children themselves to apply for a change of surname, but if they are 12 years of age or older their consent is required.

As a rule, the husband and wife have the same rights and obligations with respect to a change of surname of their children whether during the marriage or following dissolution of the marriage by divorce or the death of either party. The exceptions are British Columbia, the Northwest Territories, and the Yukon which stipulate that, during marriage, only the husband may apply to change the surname of the children. In British Columbia, this right even extends to children of his wife born prior to the marriage, the wife's involvement being limited to consent.

What is striking in the various legislation is the emphasis on the civil status of the mother and her right to give the surname of her successive husbands to her children. Most of the laws refer specifically to the marriage of the unmarried mother, or the remarriage of the widow or the divorced woman.

In Newfoundland[45] and Alberta,[46] the mother may request that the child bear the surname of her common-law spouse, even if he is not the father of the child. The underlying premise of these provisions is that the woman will want to adopt the surname of the new spouse and that it is desirable for all family members to bear the same surname. This is also the purpose of the criteria for the mandatory linking of the children and spouse discussed earlier.

Once again, rather than allow for an easy system for identifying individuals, the Acts in question tend to reinforce the social values related to the family unit. Should the civil status of parents have this influence on the surname of their children? Is this not a means of treating the children as private property to be transferred at will? From the feminist point of view, don't these provisions maintain the image of the man as the head of the family?

The courts, swamped with litigation concerning the right to change the surname of children, have a tendency to recognize here, as in other areas, the criterion of the child's best interests.[47] The impact of the loss of the father's surname in favour of that of the new spouse is balanced against the *symbol* of the surname as a sign of affection.[48] Should the surname serve as a sign of affection or rather as a means of identification? Isn't the real function of the surname to identify an individual rather than to serve as a sign of affection?

Conclusion

As long as our society opts for identification by the surname and given names, we must find a mechanism for determining the surname at birth. There is no reason to deprive parents of this responsibility which is also part of the freedom of choice. Legislative policy may, then, either offer a free choice, forbid any choice, or even impose criteria for choosing. If the intended purpose is to identify the individual in question, it would seem that free choice would be every bit as acceptable as the current solution.[49]

However, from the perspective of an eventual agreement, the current reforms which permit the use of a compound surname are more equitable since both lines are recognized and both parties are involved in the decision.

The change of name legislation is more questionable as it perpetuates the desire to link the child to a man even when dealing with powers granted to the mother.

Proposals for Reform

We have seen that change of name legislation contains some discriminatory provisions. The most flagrant case is that of laws which do not allow the married woman to drop her husband's surname during the marriage. The Yukon Act, which includes such a provision, was challenged in court after section 15 of the Canadian *Charter of Rights and Freedoms* came into effect on April 17, 1985. The Yukon Supreme Court declared that the provision in question was contrary to the equality rights guaranteed by section 15.[50]

It is to be expected that women will use the Charter to invalidate legislation that clearly goes against the equality rights guaranteed by section 15. However, in addition to trying to invalidate particular discriminatory clauses, the more basic question of the legislative policy which underlies change of name laws must be examined. In other words, the question must be asked as to what type of legislation is needed to provide a true guarantee of the right of equality and autonomy of women.

In common law provinces, efforts to ensure equality have so far translated into amendments that offer a number of choices to both the man and the woman. For example, the Newfoundland Act allows a man to take his wife's surname. In reality, a provision of this type is merely wishful thinking. How many men will take advantage of it? The social pressure against making such a decision is still very strong.

Thus, the Act appears to be neutral but in fact is powerless in the face of a custom which favours men.

Even the solution of a compound surname to be taken by both spouses — and, eventually, by their children — is not without problems. Here again, one must accept the fact that this option will be used by only a minority of couples. This solution only multiplies the adjustments that must be made if the marriage is dissolved. It must not be forgotten that in today's world, a person often has more than one union in her/his lifetime. Are people prepared to add or remove parts of their surname — and even the surnames of their children — with each successive relationship? Such action would be detrimental to an effective system for identifying people.

The main problem consists of allowing surname changes not as a function of personal change, but as a function of a change in marital status. This legislative philosophy, coupled with the dominant social customs, creates an inefficient system lacking in equality. In order to solve this problem, the purpose of legislation on surnames must be re-examined.

In the author's view, its purpose should be limited to the identification of people. A person's marital status should have no bearing on her/his name. To eliminate the impact of social pressures that serve to reinforce the concept of the family centred around the husband-father, the author recommends that the law clearly state that the legal surname of any person — man, woman, or child — is the original surname given at birth. Such a stipulation would not prohibit subsequent surname changes, but it would relieve the woman of the obligation to automatically change her surname to that of her partner.

The only problem created by the proposed system is that society would have to become accustomed to the fact that people living under the same roof do not all have the same surname. Already, the general public is becoming more aware of this notion. If we accept the fact that a surname is a means of identification and not a symbol of affection or family ties, the process should not be too difficult.

Suzanne P. Boivin is a partner in the law firm of Mélançon et associés in Montreal. She has also been active in the National Association of Women and the Law.

Notes

1. This study is concerned with what is commonly referred to as the surname, not the given name(s). We have used the expressions "own surname" or "original surname" which are preferable to the common expressions "maiden name" and "patronymic". It would be senseless to speak of a "family name", as we are arguing that members of the same "family" should have different names.

2. See, notably: the comments of the Ontario Law Reform Commission, *Report on Changes of Name* (Toronto: Ontario Law Reform Commission, 1976), p. 3.

3. According to one decision, the purpose of the acts concerning civil status statistics is to record ". . . the changing status of individuals for statistical purposes". *Vaughn-Hulbert* and *Vaughn-Hulbert*, 50 B.C.L.R. 110 (Sup. Ct.).

4. See in general: N.W. Palmier, "The Married Woman's Name", thesis for a master's degree in law, McGill University, 1977.

5. *Ibid.*, p. 25.

6. D.E. Pask, "The Game of the Name: The Surname of a Married Woman", *L'Égale: A Journal on Women and the Law*, p. 2; McCaughan, *The Legal Status of Married Women in Canada* (Toronto: Carswell, 1977), pp. 43-44; P.M. Bromley, *Family Law*, 6th ed. (London: Butterworths, 1981), p. 113.

7. See the cases cited in: E.J. Bander, *Change of Name and Law of Names* (Dobb's Ferry, N.Y.: Oceana Publications, Inc., 1973), pp. 45-59; *Cowley v. Cowley*, [1901] A.C. 450 (titles); *Thrasher v. Thrasher-Brown* (1984) 2 D.L.R. (4th) 542.

8. Art. 442, C.C.Q. and *An act to establish a new Civil Code and to reform family law*, L.Q. 1980, c. 39, section 7.

9. G. Brière, "Les effets du mariage", (1982) 5 R.G.D. 10-11.

10. *Rapport sur le Code civil du Québec*, vol. 2, title 1, p. 35, taking into account the equality of the parties.

11. An ad hoc committee on "La femme et son nom" (the woman and her name). The Fédération des femmes du Québec strongly supported this provision in its report entitled *Mémoire sur l'attribution du nom de la personne*, 1979, p. 12; however, see G. Brière, "La réforme du droit du nom et du domicile", (1975) 6 R.G.D. 471.

12. [1901] A.C. 450; according to this rule, recognized in recent case law, the woman may informally adopt, for herself and her children, a name of her choosing: *Hoodekoff v. Hoodekoff* (1976) 25 R.F.L. 8 (B.C.S.C.); *Zumpano v. Zumpano* (1979), 7 R.F.L. (2d) 328 (B.C.S.C.); *Re Gloade* (1980), 37 N.S.R. (2d) 445 (Co. Ct.); *Thrasher v. Thrasher-Brown* (1984) 2 D.L.R. (4th) 542; *O'Connell Hord v. Hord* (1982) 129 D.L.R. (3d) 368, pp. 370-371.

13. *Change of Name Act*, R.S.P.E.I. 1974, c. C-3, amended by 1974 (2nd), c. 65, section 8.

14. Pask, *supra*, n. 6, at p. 6; J. Bankier, "Change of Name and the Married Woman", 21 *Chitty's Law Journal* 302 (1973); R.B. Sirkis, "The Importance of Being Ernestine", 38 *Man. Bar News*, at 215-217.

15. *Change of Name Act*, R.S.A. c. C-4, sections 8 and 9.

16. *Change of Name Act*, S.M. 1982-83-84, c. 56, section 12.

17. *Change of Name Act*, R.S.N.B., c. C-2, subsection 4(2).

18. *Name Act*, R.S.B.C. 1979, c. 295, subsection 3(2).

19. *The Change of Name Act*, R.S.S., c. C-6, amended by *The Change of Name Amendment Act*, S.S. 1980-81, c. 14.

20. British Columbia, *Name Act, supra*, n. 18, subsection 2(a); New Brunswick, *Change of Name Act, supra*, n. 17, subsection 2(1); Ontario, *Change of Name Act*, R.S.O. 1980, c. 62, section 2; Saskatchewan, *The Change of Name Act, supra*, n. 19, section 3; Newfoundland, *The Change of Name Act*, 1978, S. Nfld., c. 57, amended by S.N. 1982, c. 28, subsection 3(2); Northwest Territories, *Change of Name Ordinance*, c. C-2; Yukon, *Change of Name Ordinance*, c. C-3, subsection 3(2); Manitoba, *Change of Name Act, supra*, n. 16, section 12.

21. *The Change of Name Act*, 1978, *supra*, n. 20, subsection 3(2).

22. *Supra*, n. 19, subsection 19(4).

23. *Name Act, supra*, n. 18, subsection 3(5)(b).

24. She may change her name to take her husband's name, or to take back her original surname or the name she bore prior to marriage, subsection 3(5).

25. *Supra*, n. 20, subsection 4(3).

26. *Supra*, n. 20, subsection 4(3), the provision was recently contested, see *infra*, p. 19.

27. *Supra*, n. 20, subsection 2(13).

28. In particular, the husband's consent may be required.

29. 129 D.L.R. (3d) 368 (Ontario Unified Family Court).

30. In the Nova Scotia, *Change of Name Act*, S.N.S. 1977, c. 6, amended by 1984, c. 55; in New Brunswick; in Alberta.

31. (1984), 2 D.L.R. (4th) 382.

32. 28 O.R. (2d) 222; the same problem arises when a parent wishes to change the surname of the children without changing their own name, *Re Cormack and Howell* (1980), 29 O.R. (2d) 798; *Re Demers* (1981) 32 O.R. (2d) 351 (which underlines a situation of inequality experienced by the natural father).

33. Northwest Territories, the Yukon, Ontario, New Brunswick, Newfoundland, and Manitoba. As a rule, the acts contain provisions aimed expressly at the widow and the divorced woman.

34. British Columbia, *supra*, n. 18, section 4; Nova Scotia, *supra*, n. 32, section 7. In Ontario, the Ontario Law Reform Commission recommended the adoption of a provision of this type, see *supra*, n. 2, at p. 20.

35. *Bryson v. Bryson*, 20 R.F.L. 351 (B.C.S.C.).

36. See, for example: the Alberta Act which distinguishes between the widow who *must* include the children and the divorced woman who *may* include them.

37. *Re Gloade* (1980), 37 N.S.R. (2d) 445 (Co. Ct.), p. 450.

38. See: *supra*, n. 11.

39. Quebec, sections 56, 56.1, and 56.2, C.C.B.-C.; Alberta, *Vital Statistics Act*, R.S.A. 1980, c. V-4; British Columbia, *Vital Statistics Act*, R.S.B.C. 1979, c. 425; Prince Edward Island, *Vital Statistics Act*, R.S.P.E.I. 1974, c. V-6; Manitoba, *Vital Statistics Act*, L.R.N.B., V-3;

Nova Scotia, *Vital Statistics Act*, R.S.N.S. 1967, c. 330; Ontario, *Vital Statistics Act*, R.S.O. 1980, c. 524; Saskatchewan, *The Vital Statistics Act*, R.S.S. 1978, c. V-7; Newfoundland, *The Registration (Vital Statistics) Act*, R.S.N. 1970, c. 329; Northwest Territories, *Vital Statistics Ordinance*, Ordinance of the N.W.T., c. V-4; Yukon, *Vital Statistics Ordinance*, Ordinances of the Yukon, c. V-2; as amended.

40. Quebec, subsections 56.3 and 56.4 C.C.B.-C and, *Change of Name and of other Particulars of Civil Status Act*, L.R.Q. 1977, c. C10; for other jurisdictions, see the change of name legislation cited above.

41. See: *Vaughn-Hulbert* and *Vaughn-Hulbert,* 50 B.C.L.R. 110 (Sup. Ct.), in which the parents wished to attribute the given name "God's Loving Kindness" to their child.

42. In Saskatchewan, following an amendment to the *Change of Name Act*, the parents may *change* the surname of the child to give the child a compound surname. No subsequent amendment was made providing for attribution of a compound surname at birth. See: *The Change of Name Amendment Act*, 1983, S.S. 1983, c. 15 amending subsection 6(3). Amendments to allow for this option were proposed in Vancouver (Eleventh Report of the Royal Commission on Family and Children's Law, *Change of Name*, June 1975) and in Ontario (*supra*, n. 2).

43. 1978, c. 81, following recommendations of the Ontario Law Reform Commission, *supra*, n. 2, at p. 10.

44. Proceedings of the Sixty-Fifth Annual Meeting, Quebec, 1983, Appendix O, p. 282.

45. *The Change of Name Act, 1978, supra*, n. 20, subsection 10(4).

46. *Change of Name Act, supra*, n. 15, subsection 11(4). It is surprising that section 13 of the Act prohibits a person living in a *de facto* union from applying to adopt the surname of their *de facto* spouse.

47. See: *Bryson v. Bryson* (1975), 20 R.F.L. (B.C.); *Hoodekoff v. Hoodekoff* (1976), 25 R.F.L. 8 (B.C.S.C.); *Zumpano v. Zumpano* (1979), 7 R.F.L. (2d) 328 (B.C.S.C.); *Comrie v. Comrie* (1980), 13 R.F.L. (2d) 146 (Man. Q.B.); *Re Britton* 23 R.F.L. (2d) 101 (N.W.T.S.C.).

48. *Re Stephen*, 9 R.F.L. (2d) 36 (N.S. Co. Ct.). This is indicated in the grounds for change of surname recognized in Quebec subsection 56.3 C.C.B.-C. and in the criteria that allow for the change of the children's surname without their father's consent, for example, if he has failed or neglected to provide maintenance. The attribution of the compound surname changes nothing. While completing this study, the author received a call from a woman who wished to submit a petition to amend the Quebec Act. She wished to remove without formal procedure the father's surname, which had been included in the compound surname of the child.

49. In Ontario, persons questioned by the Ontario Law Reform Commission showed little interest in this option. See: *supra*, n. 2, at p. 10. Furthermore, the fact that it involves a perfectly legitimate solution is recognized by the report of The Uniform Law Conference of Canada, *supra*, n. 47, at p. 283 and the Civil Code Revision Office, *supra*, n. 10.

50. Decision handed down May 14, 1985, by the Yukon Supreme Court in the case of Suzanne Bertrand.

Women and the Reproductive Technologies

— *Bartha Maria Knoppers*

Reproduction has become the object of major technological advances, with techniques for genetic screening, pre-natal diagnosis, and overcoming problems of infertility. However, there is virtually no legislation to regulate the use of these techniques despite their profound social and ethical implications. As a greater understanding of these techniques develops, legislation will have to be carefully drafted to ensure that it gives clear guidelines yet does not inject a moral tone into something which should be a matter of free choice.

From a feminist perspective, there is concern that women will lose control over reproduction with this increased medical intervention. Women must ensure that the law protects the autonomy of their bodies.

Introduction

Almost 15 years ago, Shulamith Firestone in her famous book, the *Dialectic of Sex*,[1] argued for the freedom of women from the tyranny of reproduction. She envisaged that artificial conception, like contraception, would allow women to choose the method of creation and development of their children. Now that alternative modes of conception are a reality, however, more and more women are seeing this new technology not as a source of freedom and power but of oppression.[2] Indeed, the availability and use of reproductive technology could lead to the economic and social exploitation of women.[3]

Thus, the feminist dilemma is a complex one. Is individual freedom increased by separating sexual relations from reproduction? Or does the possibility of scientific analysis of the well-being of the embryo or of the foetus, from conception to birth, intensify the possibility of control? Will there be an increased pressure on childless couples to use donated genetic material or the womb of another so as to make child-bearing possible? Finally, does the arrival of these techniques serve to emphasize the importance of reproduction and women as the source of that reproduction, though no longer the sole source?[4]

Due to the novelty of these techniques, such political and social questions cannot as yet be answered, but reflection and reaction are of the greatest necessity. Already, in its usual incremental and yet organic fashion, the law has begun to deal with some of the implications or repercussions of different aspects of modern birth technology.

For example, the traditional legal presumption of paternity within marriage, which guarantees the legitimacy of the child, can now serve as a coverup for a different scientific reality. Moreover, hastily drafted legislation to protect the status of children born after artificial insemination by donor semen is preventing biological fathers from claiming their paternity following surrogate arrangements. In addition, a decade of liberalized abortion laws undermined by funding or restricted-access policies is now being followed by the medicalization of those pregnancies being carried to term. This leaves women a limited freedom to abort but also renders them liable for the less than perfect child should they choose not to.

The numerous legal contradictions and conflicts cannot be understood without a preliminary grasp of the scientific possibilities for conception raised by reproductive technology. Reproductive technology must be studied in terms of its implications for women as participants, donors or surrogates, as married or single women seeking access to these techniques, as pregnant women, and as mothers responsible for their children.

Scientific and Medical Aspects

Artificial insemination by donor (A.I.D.) has long been practised in cases of male sterility, particularly since World War II. During the war, men could arrange to have deposits of their sperm frozen in sperm banks before leaving for war. In contrast, *in vitro* fertilization (I.V.F.) in cases of female infertility produced its first successful birth only in

1978 and involved a married couple using their own genetic material. Artificial insemination by donor introduced the possibility of a third party contributing genetic material to be used immediately or at a later date if frozen, whereas *in vitro* fertilization, where the sperm and the egg are cultivated outside of the woman to be replaced a few days later, introduced the possibility of fertilization outside of the body.[5]

Surrogate parenting, known since biblical times, emerged as an alternative to infertility only when artificial insemination by donor became more widespread. Thus the insemination of a surrogate with the sperm of the biological father became a means of bypassing his wife's infertility, or any inability to carry a child to term or any genetic contra-indications.

More recently, in those cases where conception is impossible but a woman can carry a child to term, the technique of artificial embryonation by lavage is used. This procedure involves flushing out the embryo five days after conception and implantation in a second woman (possibly the wife of the man who donated the sperm) to be carried to term by her. Finally, the knowledge gained from the freezing of sperm has enabled scientists to go one step further and freeze the excess embryos after I.V.F. for future use by the donating couple. This avoids further surgical interventions on the female partner or donor for the removal of the ova. Ironically, although this myriad of scientific possibilities is of great help to the infertile, it can also create pressure on persons to make use of these techniques as opposed to accepting or choosing childlessness.

These variations have to some extent alleviated the social stigma attached to female infertility. Parallel to the development of these variations on the traditional biological "reproductive roulette", however, has been the concurrent expansion of post-conception diagnostic techniques. These techniques enable physicians to determine the genetic and physical health of the unborn while it is still in the womb.

One of these techniques, amniocentesis, involves the removal by aspiration through the abdomen of a small amount of amniotic fluid during the sixteenth week of pregnancy in order to determine chromosomal or genetic defects. Because it takes a few weeks to determine the results of this particular test, women are often 18-20 weeks pregnant before another test can be done to affirm a positive result or before a decision with respect to abortion can be taken.[6] Amniocentesis may soon be bypassed, however, by the newer experimental technique of chorionic villi biopsy. Under this technique, foetal cells can be withdrawn via the woman's cervix as early as the eighth to tenth week of pregnancy and examined for chromosomal or genetic defects.[7]

Pre-conceptual testing now enables couples intending to conceive to determine whether they have been exposed to environmental, drug-induced, or occupational hazards, and also to avoid unnecessary exposure to these hazards. As well, it permits genetic testing, thus increasing the decision-making powers and responsibilities of the couple planning to conceive.[8]

This concurrent development of reproductive technologies and diagnostic tools would not have been possible without the extensive use of ultrasound, a sonar device enabling television screen pictures of the womb. Ultrasound, seemingly the most innocuous and beneficial of techniques in terms of knowledge concerning foetal health, confronts women with the early visualization of the foetus, a bonding effect that makes procreative decision making all the more stressful and difficult.[9]

This brief overview avoids a description of the more futuristic techniques[10] such as cloning, parthenogenesis, gene therapy, and the creation of an artificial womb, to concentrate instead on the very real and present possibilities of conception as faced by women today. The impact of the current technologies on the laws affecting Canadian women will be examined chronologically, beginning with the procreative autonomy of the woman as the donor or recipient of genetic material or as surrogate, to decisions and choices open to her during pregnancy and birth, and then to maternal liability for the exercise of such choice. In conclusion, the wider political and sociological implications will be studied.

Women and Procreative Autonomy

Figures ranging from 10 to 15 per cent have been given as national infertility rates.[11] One recent survey has noted an 83 per cent increase, between the years 1965 and 1979, in infertility in married couples. This increase is due as much to sexually transmitted diseases later affecting fertility and producing reduced sperm counts in men, as to environmental, occupational or chemical factors.[12] Moreover, the decreasing number of babies available for adoption, the widespread use of contraception and abortion, the postponement of child-bearing to a later age, as well as the premium placed on the number, spacing, and health of each child have made human procreation into a quasi-science. Equally important is the gradual and insidious acceptance of medical intervention in the reproductive process.

Overriding these developments is the question of the costs associated with infertility and its treatment. The laboratory work, testing, storage, and transfer procedures may or may not be covered under provincial health schemes. Thus access may be limited for financial reasons, not to speak of those areas of the country where treatment may not be available at all, depending on government priorities in the allocation of health resources.[13]

As increasing numbers of persons turn to medical technology to alleviate infertility problems, the issue of whether there is a right to procreate by whatever manner is scientifically possible becomes paramount. If such a right does exist, to whom is it granted? In other words, are single women, single men, surrogates, or homosexual individuals included within this right? Furthermore, if the individual is married, does his or her participation as donor, recipient, or surrogate require spousal consent?

The Right to Procreate

No court has yet addressed the question of whether the notion of procreative autonomy includes the right to have children, that is, the freedom to reproduce. While the issues of contraception, sterilization, and abortion have long assumed constitutional proportions in the United States, the court decisions dealt mainly with the right to marry and the right to bear and beget or raise children as a liberty right but not specifically with the legality of "how" to have children.[14]

American decisions in this area have included the notion of privacy within the constitutional right to liberty. This personal right of privacy also includes the freedom to obtain an abortion, but a recent decision in Illinois illustrates how elusive this privacy right can be.[15]

In 1979, the state of Illinois enacted the *Illinois Abortion Law* of 1975 under which a physician who fertilized a human ovum and sperm outside the body, that is, *in vitro*, would be deemed to have the care and custody of the child with respect to its health and life up to birth. No Illinois physician has offered *in vitro* fertilization as a result. An infertile couple is challenging the law as a deprivation of their fundamental right to privacy and liberty and as a violation of their right to decide to beget and bear a child.[16]

The first decision in Canada on the question of whether "privacy" falls within the purview of the "liberty and security of the person" under section 7 of the Canadian *Charter of Rights and Freedoms* declined to follow these American precedents. It limited such liberty to physical liberty and security only and did not include protection from

215

State interference with procreative decision making.[17] Thus, it cannot be said with any certainty that there is a right to reproduce by whatever means possible under Canadian law. Even so, the recognition of such a "right" may, according to one author, serve only to underscore a pro-natalist attitude that could be detrimental to the recognition of the worth of women. The right to reproduce should instead simply be framed as the right not to be prevented from having children.[18]

Reproduction and Civil Status

It is ironic that while adoption laws are being relaxed in order to permit unmarried individuals of either sex to adopt, social prejudices are preventing single women from having access to techniques that would enable them to bear and give birth to children that may in some cases be at least 50 per cent genetically their own.

Any legislation that does exist in Canada[19] or the United States[20] with respect, for example, to artificial insemination by third party donor concentrates on the consent of the husband so as to ensure the filiation, legitimacy, and inheritance rights of the child. Thus while not explicitly prohibitory, such statutes have the effect of limiting artificial insemination to married couples, effectively barring single individuals and those of different sexual orientation from access. As a result, only 10 per cent of physicians practising in the area of infertility use A.I.D. to fertilize single women[21] and most *in vitro* centres will accept only married couples or those in stable long-term unions.[22] Nevertheless, it is questionable whether such social criteria would stand up against a challenge based on human rights legislation.[23] Finally, not only is marital status relevant, but couples are usually judged on their ability to nurture, their age, and the origins of their infertility (such as previous abortions, infertility following venereal disease, or previous sterilization), considerations which do not determine the right to bear children in the general population.

Spousal Consent

For those couples who meet these preliminary criteria, the request for the consent of the spouse prior to treatment or donation is a requirement based on dubious legal grounds.[24] Some jurisdictions even require the consent of the spouse of the married sperm donor.[25] Although egg retrieval is at present a surgical procedure involving a general anaesthetic, spousal consent has never been a legal requirement for other medical treatment or even organ donation. In fact, the negation of the spousal role is based on the principle of the autonomy of the freely consenting capable individual.[26]

By analogy, then, the consent of the spouse of the nine-month surrogate, of the egg donor, or of the one transferring an embryo at five days should not be necessary. Yet should the surrogate decide to keep the child or should the transfer fail, such a spouse would be presumed to be the father and would be liable to pay support.[27] Similarly, the sperm or egg donor would be liable should the resulting child be in need.

It could be argued that requirement of spousal notification or consultation for the donation or receipt of genetic material should be sufficient rather than the requirement of consent. If the woman is free to abort or to be medically treated without spousal consent, the same principles should apply to those using reproductive technologies. Finally, once past the consent and treatment stage and if the infertility treatment is successful, it is during the actual pregnancy and birth that the lifestyle and personal freedoms of the pregnant woman may be the most severely circumscribed.

Maternal Lifestyle and Birthing

Women who are accepted for these modes of alternative conception are closely monitored. Indeed, because of the stress and pressure to become pregnant, combined with the investigatory procedures, the doctrine of informed consent prior to treatment can easily become meaningless for these couples who are so anxious to achieve a pregnancy at any cost. Pre-natal or even pre-conceptual diagnosis, while permitting greater knowledge, makes for difficult choices both prior to and after conception. Should malformations be discovered and abortion be ruled out, foetal surgical techniques have now made possible the correction of certain defects *in utero*. Finally, in this area of "premium" conceptions, birthing options are often determined only in light of the best interests of the child, the final step in what certain critics of this high technology reproduction would label the incubation status of women.[28]

Pre-Conception and Post-Conception Choices

Knowledge of the relation between environmental or occupational hazards and birth defects has been documented elsewhere.[29] What is disturbing is that the ensuing legislation, meant to protect women and the unconceived, or the foetus, has also resulted in restrictions in hiring and career advancement for women.[30] Similarly, as such information concerning pre-conceptual and pre-natal influences expands, metabolic or dietary controls both prior to and after conception are being suggested in certain circumstances, for example, for diabetic women or women with hereditary diseases.[31] Artificial conception programs would obviate some of these restraints, particularly where a surrogate is used to carry the embryo of another couple allowing for normal foetal development during pregnancy or where artificial insemination is used to avoid genetic disorders. It is in fact possible to pre-select healthy ova or sperm for fertilization; unhealthy embryos are already being discarded rather than implanted.

Once implanted, pre-natal diagnosis permits not only the detection of abnormalities but also permits sex selection through selective abortion. Moreover, reproductive technology has made sex selection possible even prior to implantation through sperm-washing techniques and the testing of embryos. In this way, the perpetration of certain social biases in favor of male children may become a reality.[32]

If the viability of the foetus is assumed and parental choice concerning abortion is foregone, foetal therapy in the form of *in utero* surgery can be offered.

Foetal Therapy

Management of foetal medical conditions can include pre-natal blood transfusions, high dosages of vitamins or medication, and lately, foetal surgery. So far, doctors have inserted catheters to remove deadly urinary-tract and head blockages. At this point, the foetus with a treatable birth defect may well be considered a patient by the medical profession.[33] The inconsistency between the freedom to abort defective foetuses, where such freedom exists,[34] and the encouragement to treat these same foetuses is self-evident.

While some would advocate separate representation for the interests of the foetus, physicians working in this area have encountered a different problem, that of restraining women from submitting themselves to experimental foetal surgery carrying a greater risk to their health and life than the risk the defect poses to the foetus.[35] As the legal recognition and protection of the foetus moves further back in time, with artificially assisted viability currently at 20 weeks, the freedom to consent to, or to refuse, such foetal therapy will soon be open to

218

question. More importantly, can a society that encourages the treatment of the foetus even prior to viability allow abortion? Recent decisions of conflicts of rights at birth do not augur well for the principle of freedom of choice.

Birthing Options

Under the *Criminal Code* of Canada, a child only becomes a human being "when it has completely proceeded in a living state from its mother" (art. 206(1)). In a recent British Columbia case[36] involving a charge of criminal negligence against a midwife, the court held that such a charge applied to pre-birth negligence. A child carried to term, in the process of being born, was thus equated with a person.[37]

Furthermore, in the United States, there are two reported cases of forced caesareans granted by the courts on the basis of State protection of the unborn.[38] Another example of post-viability protection of the unborn is found in the practice of placing brain-deceased pregnant women on life-support systems in order to continue the life of the foetus until birth.[39]

The medical profession is involved in the conception of life outside the womb: in the determination of optimal conditions for storage, growth, and implantation; in the supervision of a medically controlled pregnancy; and in the choice of method of giving birth. One author has gone so far as to ask whether by engaging in sexual intercourse, the woman waives the right to her body in favour of the foetus.[40] The answer to that question, particularly in the area of artificial conception, demands some understanding of more than the choices, or lack thereof, a woman has. It also necessitates an understanding of the possible maternal duties rendering the woman legally liable after birth for the exercise of such choices.

Maternal Freedoms and Liability

Family law has been structured on the basis of patriarchal lineage, the presumption of paternity serving socially and legally to legitimize the child. Now that a child can have five parents (a sperm donor, an ovum donor, the woman who gestates the child, and the couple who raise it), traditional notions of paternity, filiation, and inheritance are becoming obsolete. The freezing of human sperm and embryos makes post-mortem insemination and conception possible, further undermining family law structures and particularly those based on paternal filiation and legitimacy.

Decisions concerning filiation and legitimacy must now take into account the fact that the gestational mother (the woman who carries the child) may well be a married or unmarried surrogate. Surrogacy in itself can run afoul of the prohibition of payment under adoption laws. Enforcing the prohibition of payment and the questionable legality of such a contract for public policy reasons raise additional problems.

Furthermore, these scientific and medical possibilities prior to or following conception may well imply a certain duty to ensure as much as possible the health and well-being of the child to be conceived or to be born. Will the "negligent" woman be liable for foetal abuse and subject to State intervention prior to birth or to suits by her own child after birth?

Filiation and Legitimacy

Even supposing that proper records are kept and genetic lineage could be traced,[41] the deficiencies of a legal system based on biological presumptions of paternity as opposed to scientific reality is pointed out by the short-sightedness of existing legislation dealing with artificial insemination. Legislatures in 22 American states[42] and in the province of Quebec[43] have adopted laws providing that the child conceived by artificial insemination is the child of the sperm recipient and her consenting husband. These laws are designed to relieve the sperm donor from parental obligations such as support, or rights such as visitation or custody. They also prevent biological fathers from using married surrogates and then claiming paternity other than through laborious adoption procedures. This application of artificial insemination legislation to surrogate parenthood is presently being challenged in California as a negation of the privacy right to make procreative decisions.[44]

Only four Canadian provinces have eliminated the stigma of illegitimacy.[45] Thus, depending on the marital status of the parties involved, the child born after artificial insemination may fall outside of benefits accruing to legitimate children.

What of the status or control of stored or frozen genetic material? This was precisely the issue in a dispute before a French court where a widow was claiming her husband's frozen sperm as her inheritance[46] and also in another case after the death of the embryo donors in Australia.[47] While the notion of "ownership" is a property concept better left out of the human context, the issue of control and disposition of genetic material is particularly relevant to the surrogate contract.

Surrogacy

When a female ovum donor is used or a woman receives an embryo, will the woman who gives birth still be the mother of the child and be obligated to assume parental obligations[48] or have visitation rights?[49] With regard to any arrangements made between the biological and the social parents, the law is silent.

While most jurisdictions either explicitly, or as a matter of public policy, prohibit payment to a surrogate, it is unclear what would fall under allowable expenses,[50] such as those received by sperm donors,[51] and what would be considered baby-buying as forbidden under adoption laws.[52] Is surrogate parenting a commercialization of child-bearing, an exploitation of needy women, or a legitimate occupation?[53] Should egg donors or five-day surrogates receive an equivalent or higher fee than sperm donors considering the greater inconvenience and limited supply? Furthermore, would the very participation in these treatments and the assumption of risks by the mother or surrogate prevent the child from suing after birth not only for support but also against its own mother(s) for lack of pre-conceptual or pre-natal care? The limits of control over the freedom of the pregnant surrogate can be decided only within the context of the freedom of any pregnant woman and her possible liability after birth for the exercise of that freedom.

Maternal Liability

The importance of the pre-conceptual and the pre-natal environment for the health of the foetus has already been described. To this date, pregnant women have been free to care for their health and that of their future child within the usual confines of the physician-patient relationship. This autonomous decision making is now subject to three limiting influences: that of the spouse, that of the State, and that of the child.

Spousal intervention has been most noticeable on the question of abortion. Third parties have been given standing to challenge abortion legislation[54] or intervene in abortion decisions.[55] In Canada, individual spouses can now question the exact compliance of accredited therapeutic abortion committees with the requirements of the *Criminal Code*.[56] Furthermore, one American decision records an attempt by a spouse to obtain a court order during the pregnancy for a surgical intervention on his wife to prevent miscarriage.[57]

With respect to State intervention under its duty to protect the child, two Canadian decisions involving drug[58] and alcohol[59] abuse during pregnancy authorized the immediate removal of the children from the mother at birth. This was done on the basis of anticipated deprivation under child abuse laws by extending backwards in time the definition of child so as to include the foetus.

In a California case, a prosecutor wanted to take custody of the foetus by incarcerating the mother, a heroin addict.[60] In Maryland, in another case of drug addiction, a woman was ordered to attend a drug rehabilitation clinic and to submit to laboratory tests for the last two months of her pregnancy.[61]

Finally, in a case that threatens parental immunity, if not the social fabric of the family, a child through his father was given leave to sue his own mother after his birth with discoloured teeth, for her failure to seek pre-natal care, to request a pregnancy test, and to inform her physician that she was taking tetracycline, an antibiotic.[62] The case was remanded to trial court to determine whether the mother had acted reasonably.

Prospective parents prior to conception, pregnant women, and parents after birth may soon have their decisions subjected to the same test of "reasonableness" that applies to third parties under general negligence law, reasonableness also being the limit placed on the exercise of Charter rights. The conflicts of rights issue is perhaps not the framework for this reproductive maternal-foetal debate, as the real issue is seeing women as morally responsible agents faced with difficult choices.[63] A brief review of the commissioned studies or of the proposed reforms in the area of reproductive technology reveals a move towards a greater restriction of reproductive freedom, and thus, the diminution of what little choice remains.

Conclusion

Infertility is a socially stigmatizing condition; the language reflects this in terms such as blighted ovum, incompetent cervix, habitual aborter, infantile uterus, and hostile cervical mucous.[64] The values inherent in the use of these terms may provide some insight into the failure of the proposed reforms to deal with the fundamental problems of access and decision making in reproductive technologies.

Most reforms or proposed reforms are mainly concerned with questions concerning the protection and status of the child. The proposed reforms in Canada, and the legislation enacted in Quebec, deal with the status of the child born as a result of artificial insemination after birth. Furthermore, both the 1975 British Columbia Royal Commission on Family Law[65] and the 1981 federal report on the storage and utilization of human sperm[66] attempt to limit access to these techniques by granting the physician the authority to decide the ability to nurture of the married couple applying, a criterion not applicable to the general population. Only the 1981 Saskatchewan proposals, which recognize such practices to be in contravention of human rights legislation, recommended that marital and economic criteria not be legislated although the physician would remain free to use his social judgement.[67]

Although one Australian state,[68] as well as a recent English report,[69] recognized *de facto* couples, not one other jurisdiction has recommended in their commissioned studies or legislative bills that single individuals have access to artificial insemination. Stable two-parent families are considered necessary for the well-being and best interests of the child. Generally, surrogacy has not been ethically approved or even legislated on or controlled. Some studies, realizing that the practice is growing, recommend that the woman giving birth be regarded as the mother[70] leaving the biological father and the "invisible"[71] social mother to flounder in the maze of contract law, family law, and adoption law.

Once past these initial barriers, most would recommend legislating the necessity for spousal consent[72] and forbidding payment other than reasonable expenses for the donation of genetic material.[73] Donors must renounce their rights or duties to any child conceived from their genetic material[74] while at the same time being assured of anonymity.[75] Donation of an embryo by lavage of a five-day surrogate has not been widely approved.[76] The use or growth of donated genetic material for experimentation or transplantation is generally controlled or prohibited[77] and embryos are usually scheduled to be re-implanted after 14 days *in vitro*.[78] Donated material that is frozen is subject to the donor's control.[79]

Most studies after lengthy consideration avoid the futility of the legal "personhood" debate (on the question of when life begins) to concentrate instead on protection mechanisms (with regard to storage, experimentation, and donation) respectful of human life.[80] The same concern extends to the legitimacy, filiation, and inheritance rights of children born of these techniques.[81]

No study has dealt with the freedoms of the five-day or nine-month surrogate mother, a discussion that might have shed some light on maternal freedoms during pregnancy.[82] This is particularly important in that embryo transfer or embryo freezing can run afoul of provincial vital statistics acts or public health acts defining "delivery" or "birth" as expulsion, or extraction, or removal of a "product of conception" and a stillbirth as the delivery of such a "product" weighing under 500 grams or under 20 weeks.[83] Would embryo transfer or foetal surgery involving the temporary removal of the foetus constitute a "birth" of a person or "stillbirth" even though alive? Similarly, definitions of "child" under these same statutes or under child protection legislation raise equally problematic issues. If child by definition includes the unborn child as is the case in New Brunswick,[84] or is loosely phrased to include "anyone" under the age of 18 irrespective of gestational age, suits for foetal abuse are more than just a hypothesis and in fact have become a legislated reality in the Yukon.[85]

Finally, recourse to these techniques may itself be considered unreasonable as well as the decision not to submit to special diets or medical controls, or, paradoxically, not to make use of donated genetic material where one is known to be at risk for giving birth to a defective child. The "reasonableness" standard of negligence law will extend to pre-conception choices and pregnancy decisions, and thus to measuring the reasonableness of all parents in procreative decision making as judged by their offspring[86] or others deciding the best interests of the child prior to or after conception.

More awesome a task than contemplating the ramifications of such potential legal liability is the immediate issue of control and the avoidance of exploitation. Should the State license sperm banks or clinics offering artificial conception?[87] Should control of genetic material after a limited time pass to the State?[88] The answer lies in the social acceptance of disabilities, in human choice and error, and the freedom to make mistakes; for, as stated in a recent book entitled *Test-Tube Women*, ". . . (i)t seems that in gaining the choice to control the quality of our children, we may be losing the choice *not* to control the quality, the choice of simply accepting them as they are."[89] Accountability does not necessarily mean legal liability but rather an insistence on moral responsibility and on respecting the integrity of women as responsible decision-makers.[90]

If the inherent difficulty of these choices, or lack thereof, with regard to procreative decision making were to be recognized and respected, if indeed the biological, economic, social, psychological and ultimately, moral burden of such choices were to be realized, then perhaps those that are so quick in the name of protection, of medical feasibility and of societal control to intervene, would hesitate or refuse to do so. True freedom for women as morally responsible decision-makers would be grim and awesome, but also, humbly human.

Bartha Maria Knoppers is a professor of law at the Université de Montréal. Her doctoral thesis is on the comparative aspects of artificial conception and she has written numerous articles on related topics.

Notes

1. Shulamith Firestone, *The Dialectic of Sex* (New York: Bantam, 1970).

2. Susan Rae Peterson, "The Politics of Prenatal Diagnosis: A Feminist Ethical Analysis", in *The Custom-Made Child? Women-Centered Perspectives*, eds. Helen B. Holmes, Betty B. Hoskins, and Michael Gross (New Jersey: Humana Press, 1981), p. 95. At p. 103:

   > It is both a curse and a blessing that only women bear children. It is historically and economically a source of women's oppression. Yet the overwhelming significance of species survival through reproduction has guaranteed women a source of great potential power in the sense of ability rather than control. So on the one hand some see freedom from reproduction by medical technology as oppression, while others are reluctant to give up the only value women clearly have in a patriarchal society, i.e., as reproducing machines.

3. "(I)n the growing usage of procreative technology there can be seen an economic exploitation of the normative desire to bear genetic offspring as well as an expression of political and legal disingenuity", as quoted in: Joanne Finkelstein and Patricia Clough, "Foetal Politics and the Birth of an Industry", *Women's Studies Int. Forum*, vol. 6 (1983), p. 395, at p. 396.

4. Elizabeth Moen, "Women's Rights and Reproductive Freedom", *Human Rights Quarterly* (1981), p. 53.

5. For a clear and detailed description of these techniques, see: Lori B. Andrews, *New Conceptions: A Consumer's Guide to the Newest Infertility Treatments* (New York: St. Martin's Press, 1984). See also: Jalna Hanmer, "Reproductive Technology: The Future for Women?" in *Machina Ex Dea: Feminist Perspectives on Technology*, ed. Joan Rothschild (New York: Pergamon Press, 1983), p. 189.

6. For a discussion of this conflict with abortion law, not to speak of the trauma associated with such late abortions, see: Ruth Hubbard, "Personal Courage is Not Enough: Some Hazards of Childbearing in the 1980's", in *Test-Tube Women: What Future for Motherhood?*, eds. Rita Arditti, Renate Duelli Klein, and Shelley Minden (London: Pandora Press, 1984), p. 331. Questions of access are directly related to the resources made available to clinics or hospitals with the result that usually only women over 35 or those who can pay will be given this test on demand.

7. *Ibid.*, p. 335.

8. Margery Shaw, "The Conditional Prospective Rights of the Foetus", *Journal of Legal Medicine*, vol. 5 (1984), p. 63.

9. Hubbard, p. 335.

10. See generally with respect to these techniques: Peter Singer and Diane Wells, eds., *The Reproductive Revolution: New Ways of Making Babies* (Melbourne: Oxford University Press, 1984).

11. *Ibid.*, p. 26; Finkelstein, p. 397.

12. Andrews, pp. 2-3.

13. Singer and Wells, pp. 20-30. For example, see: Quebec's *Law Respecting Health Services and Social Services*, L.R.Q. S-5, art. 4, which reads in part:

    > Every person has the right to receive adequate, continuous and personal health services and social services from a scientific, human and social standpoint, taking into account the organization and resources of the establishments providing such services.

14. According to George P. Smith and Roberto Iraola, "Sexuality, Privacy and the New Biology", 67 *Marquette Law Review* 263 (1984), at 289:

    . . . a woman's fundamental right to privacy or procreation does not encompass a right to A.I. or to surrogation . . . The state's desire to raise children in the *traditional* family setting and, at the same time, promote the institution of marriage and the family is an unquestionably permissible, if not laudable, objective.

    In the same vein, with respect to surrogacy in Canada, see: Philip Epstein, "Surrogate Motherhood: Legal, Social and Practical Aspects From an Ontario Viewpoint", *Canadian Bar Association, Ont., Continuing Legal Education* (1983). See also: P.A. Wright, "The Right to Parenthood", 2 *Family Law Review* (1979), at 173; *Contra:* Helen B. Holmes, "A Feminist Analysis of the Universal Declaration of Human Rights" in *Beyond Domination: New Perspectives on Women and Philosophy*, ed. C. Gould (New Jersey: Rowman & Allanheld, 1984), p. 250.

    An example of the "duty to procreate" is found in the recent anti-abortion law in Romania making it the duty of every Romanian woman to have four children. All married women undergo tests once a month to determine if they are pregnant (Moen, p. 57).

15. *Smith v. Hartigan*, 82C4324 (U.S.D.C.), February 4, 1983.

16. *Ibid.* The appeal factum claims that:

    . . . (b)y prohibiting in vitro fertilization, the In Vitro provision deprives the plaintiffs, MARY and JOHN SMITH, and the class they represent of their fundamental right to privacy and liberty as guaranteed by the Due Process Clause of the Fourteenth Amendment, in violation of their right to decide to beget and bear a child. (p. 10).

17. *The Queen v. Morgentaler, Smoling and Scott*, (1984) 47 O.R. (2d) 353 (H.C.).

    See, however, the two arguments raised by Peter Bowal in: "Surrogate Procreation: A Motherhood Issue in Legal Obscurity", 9 *Queen's Law Journal* (1983), at 5.

    According to Bowal, the equality before the law argument under the Canadian *Charter of Rights and Freedoms* (art. 15) would serve to sanction an arrangement to reproduce where the couple's childlessness arises from the wife's incapacity (just as A.I.D. helps infertile husbands). Nevertheless, he argues that under the "reasonable limits" of art. 1, the surrogate arrangement could found to be objectionable under the general public interest.

18. Holmes, "A Feminist Analysis . . .", p. 256.

19. For an overview of Canadian legislation (if any) or legislation that would apply by analogy such as contract law, status and welfare of children acts, etc., see: Somer Brodribb, "Reproductive Technologies, Masculine Dominance and the Canadian State", *Occasional Papers in Social Policy Analysis*, no. 5 (OPSPA: OISE, 1984).

    See also: *infra*, n. 43.

20. See: Elizabeth Crabtree, "Protecting Inheritance Rights of Children Born Through *In Vitro* Fertilization and Embryo Transfer: Suggestions for a Legislative Approach", 27 *St. Louis University Law Journal* (1983), at 901.

21. George Annas, "Fathers Anonymous: Beyond the Best Interests of the Sperm Donors", 14 *Family Law Quarterly* (1980), at 1; Barbara Kritchevsky, "The Unmarried Woman's Right to Artificial Insemination: A Call for an Expanded Definition of Family", 4 *Harvard Women's Law Journal* (1981), at 1.

22. For a critique of this position, see: Singer and Wells, pp. 69-71; Brodribb, pp. 8-10; and Kritchevsky, *ibid.*

23. This was expressly recognized by the Law Reform Commission of Saskatchewan, *Tentative Proposals for a Human Artificial Insemination Act*, 1981, at p. 13: ". . . it would appear that if a physician or medical institution which generally offers artificial insemination services to the public refuses to inseminate an unmarried woman solely because of her marital status, *The Saskatchewan Human Rights Code* would be violated."

24. According to the Law Reform Commission, *ibid.*, at pp. 1-3: "There is nothing in existing law which requires a physician to obtain the consent of a recipient's husband; nor is there any prohibition against refusal of artificial insemination on the basis that the applicant's husband has not consented."

    Nevertheless, the Commission held that the requirement of the husband's consent would be too much of an interference in the personal relationship of the parties involved. "The decision whether or not to become pregnant is not one in which the law should play a role." (pp. 1-4).

    The Ninth Report of the British Columbia Royal Commission on Family and Children's Law, *Artificial Insemination*, 1975, at p. 5, recommended obtaining the husband's consent. See *contra:* Bartha Maria Knoppers, "Modern Birth Technology and Human Rights", 35 *American Journal of Comparative Law* 101 (1985), at 107.

25. For example, in France, artificial insemination by donor is viewed as a gift from a fertile couple to an infertile couple. The sperm donor must be married and have fathered two normal children and his partner is required to give her consent to the donation. (See: *L'insémination artificielle*, Actes du XXXVe Congrès International de Langue Française de Médecine Légale et de Médecine Sociale, Dijon, 1977).

26. Knoppers, pp. 122-124.

27. Patricia Kern and Kathleen Ridolfi, "The Fourteenth Amendment's Protection of a Woman's Right to Be a Single Parent Through Artificial Insemination by Donor", 7 *Women's Rights Law Reporter* 251 (1982), at 277.

28. Jalna Hanmer and Pat Allen, "Reproductive Engineering, the Final Solution", *Feminist Issues*, vol. 2 (1982), p. 53. See the frightening but fictional account of such incubation status in: Diane Sautter and Steven Feinberg, "Prima Gravida", *Ms.* (October 1982), p. 45.

29. Shaw, pp. 66-75.

30. *Ibid.*, p. 71; see also: Janet Gallagher, "The Foetus and the Law — Whose Life Is It Anyway?", *Ms.* (September 1984), p. 62.

31. Shaw, pp. 81-89; Peta Lewis Hallisey, "The Fetal Patient and the Unwilling Mother: A Standard for Judicial Intervention", 14 *Pacific Law Journal* (1983), at 1065; "Special Diet May Soon Be Basic to Planned Pregnancy", *The Gazette*, September 7, 1984, p. F-2; Susan Weinberg, "A Maternal Duty to Protect Fetal Health", 68 *Indiana Law Journal* (1982-83), at 531.

32. Jalna Hanmer, "Sex Predetermination, Artificial Insemination and the Maintenance of Male-Dominated Culture", in *Women, Health and Reproduction*, ed. Helen Roberts (London: Routledge & Kegan Paul Ltd., 1981), p. 163; Roberta Steinbacher, "Sex Preselection: From Here to Fraternity", in *Beyond Domination*, p. 274.

33. See generally: Shaw, pp. 78-81; Knoppers, pp. 124-127.

34. Sherman Elias and George Annas, "Perspectives on Fetal Surgery", *American Journal of Obstetrics and Gynecology*, vol. 145 (1983), p. 807, at p. 811:

    We believe that respect for the pregnant woman's dignity and autonomy and the tradition of medicine as a voluntary service require the voluntary and informed consent of the pregnant woman prior to the performance of fetal research or therapy. The right to make a mistake should continue to be the pregnant woman's not the physician's or judge's.

Contra: John Robertson, "The Right to Procreative and In Utero Fetal Therapy", *Journal of Legal Medicine*, vol. 3 (1982), p. 333.

35. Albert Jonsen, "The Ethics of Surgery in Utero", in *Genetics and the Law III*, eds. Aubrey Milunsby and George Annas, New York: Plenum Press (forthcoming, 1985). See also: John Fletcher, "The Fetus as Patient: Ethical Issues", *Journal of the American Medical Association*, vol. 246 (1981), p. 772.

36. *Regina v. Marsh* (1983) 2 C.C.C. (3d) 1, at 8: ". . . The State has a duty to protect unborn children and to preserve their opportunities to be born and to enjoy the rights and obligations normally incident to the status of human kind."

37. *Ibid.*

38. *Jefferson v. Griffin Spalding County Hospital Authority*, 247 Ga. 86, 274 S.E. 2d 457 (1981). The other case was reported in W. Bowes and B. Selgestad, "Fetal v. Maternal Rights: Medical and Legal Perspectives", *Journal of Obstetrics and Gynecology*, vol. 58 (1981), p. 209. For a critique of these decisions, see: Ruth Hubbard, "Some Legal and Policy Implications of Recent Advances in Prenatal Diagnosis and Fetal Therapy", 7 *Women's Rights Law Reporter* (1982), at 201.

39. Margery Shaw, "Should Child Abuse Laws Be Extended to Include Fetal Abuse?", in *Genetics and the Law III* (forthcoming, 1985).

40. Holly Smith, "Intercourse and Moral Responsibility for the Foetus", in William Bondeson et al., *Abortion and the Status of the Foetus* (Dordrecht: Reidel, 1983), p. 229.

41. Martin Curie-Cohen et al., "Current Practice of Artificial Insemination by Donor in the United States", *New England Journal of Medicine*, vol. 300 (1979), p. 585. (Seventy per cent of the surveyed doctors practising A.I.D. did not keep records on donors.)

42. Smith and Iraola, p. 269.

43. The *Civil Code of Quebec* is the only provincial legislation specific to the area of artificial insemination by donor. Art. 586 reads as follows:

> When a child has been conceived through artificial insemination, either by the father or with the consent of the spouses, by a third person, no action for disavowal or contestation of paternity is admissible.

See also: Brodribb, pp. 6-10.

44. *Handel v. California State Dept. of Social Services*, C500854 (filed June 5, 1984).

45. Quebec, New Brunswick, Manitoba, and Ontario.

46. Trib. gr. inst. de Creteil, 1re civ., Aug. 1st, 1984 GAZ PAL 1984, p. 11. See also: Xavier Labée, "L'insémination artificielle pratiquée après la mort du donneur", 1984 GAZ PAL doctr., p. 2.

47. Harry Nelson and Edwin Chen, "Orphan Embryos Raise Legal, Ethical Questions", *Los Angeles Times*, June 19, 1984.

48. Lori B. Andrews, "Removing the Stigma of Surrogate Motherhood", *Family Law Advocate*, vol. 4 (1981), p. 20.

49. In *C.M. v. C.C.* 152 N.J. Super 160, 377 A 2d 821 (1977), while no intercourse took place, the sperm donor was known to the recipient and subsequently, filed an application for visitation rights to the baby. The court said it was in the child's best interest to have two parents whenever possible.

50. Brodribb remarks that the current $10,000 paid for "expenses" related to the pregnancy are equivalent to $1.54 an hour for a nine-month pregnancy and hard labor, well below the minimum wage (p. 18).

51. *Ibid.*: "Semen donors receive from $25 to $75 dollars . . . ."

52. See especially: *Youth Protection Act*, L.R.Q. c. P. 34, art. 135.1.; Andrews, *New Conceptions*, pp. 226-233; Smith and Iraola, p. 271ff.; Epstein, pp. 15-17.

In *re Baby Girl*, 9 *Family Law Reporter* 2348 (April 5, 1983), a Kentucky judge refused to recognize an adoption when a surrogate bore a child, was paid, and turned the child over to the biological father and his wife. See also: *Sykrowski v. Appleyard*, Civ. Action 81, 122 DP (Cir. Ct. Mich. 1981); Aff'd. 1d 122 Mich. App. 506, 33 N.W. 2d 90 (1983).

53. See generally, sources already cited and more particularly: Susan Ince, "Inside the Surrogate Industry", in *Test Tube Women: What Future for Motherhood?*, eds. Rita Arditti, Renate Duelli Klein, and Shelley Minden (London: Pandora Press, 1984), p. 99.

54. *Minister of Justice for Canada et al. v. Borowski*, (1981) 130 D.L.R. (3d) 588.

55. *Re H.*, (1979) 106 D.L.R. (3d) (N.S.).

56. *Medhurst v. Medhurst*, (1984) 7 D.L.R. (4th) 335.

57. *Taft v. Taft*, 388 Mass. 331, 446 N.E. 2d 395 (1983).

58. *Superintendent of Family and Child Services and McDonald*, (1982) 135 D.L.R. (3d) 330.

59. *Re Children's Aid Society of Kenora and J.L.*, (1983) 134 D.L.R. (3d) 249.

This interventionist philosophy is particularly evident in Edward W. Keyserlingk's article, "A Right of the Unborn Child to Prenatal Care — The Civil Law Perspective", 13 *Revue du droit de l'Université de Sherbrooke* (1982), at 49.

See *contra*: W.W. Watters et al., "Response to Edward W. Keyserlingk's article "The Unborn Child's Right to Prenatal Care," *Health Law in Canada*, vol. 3 (1983), p. 32.

60. *Reyes v. State*, 75 Cal. App. 3d 214, 214 Cal. Rptr. 912 (1977).

61. *New York Times*, April 27, 1983, p. 11, col. 4.

In another case emanating from California, a mother convicted of child endangerment for imposing a macro-biotic diet on her children causing them to be hospitalized, was put on probation. One of the conditions of the probation was that she would not conceive children during the five-year probationary period. The California Court of Appeals rejected this condition as too broad, though it did in *obiter* suggest that:

> We believe this salutary purpose can adequately be served by alternative restrictions less subversive of appellant's fundamental right to procreate. Such less onerous conditions might include, for example, the requirement that appellant periodically submit to pregnancy testing; and that upon becoming pregnant she be required to follow an intensive prenatal and neonatal treatment program monitored by both the probation officer and by a supervising physician. If she does bear a child during the probationary period, the court adds, this child "can be removed from her custody and placed in foster care," as was done with her other children. *(State v. Pointer*; Cal. Ct. App. 1st Dist, 2/17/84).

62. *Grodin v. Grodin*, 301 N.W. 2d 869 (Mich. App. 1980).

See generally on the subject of "foetal abuse": Ron Beal, "Can I Sue Mommy? An Analysis of a Woman's Tort Liability for Prenatal Injuries to her Child Born Alive", 21 *San Diego Law Review* (1984), at 325; Weinberg, "A Maternal Duty . . ."; Hallisey, "The Fetal

Patient"; Hubbard, "Legal and Policy Implications"; Gallagher, "The Fetus and the Law"; Robertson, "The Right to Procreate".

63. Caroline Whitbeck, "The Moral Implications of Regarding Women as People: New Perspectives on Women and Personhood", in *Abortion and the Status of the Foetus*, p. 247; Janet Farrell-Smith, "Rights-Conflict, Pregnancy and Abortion", in *Beyond Domination*, p. 265.

64. Barbara Menning, "In Defense of In Vitro Fertilization", in *The Custom-made Child?*, eds. Helen B. Holmes et al., p. 263, at p. 266.

65. Ninth Report, *Artificial Insemination*, 1975.

66. Report of the Advisory Committee to the Minister of National Health and Welfare, *Storage and Utilization of Human Sperm*, 1981.

67. Law Reform Commission of Saskatchewan, *Tentative Proposals*, pp. 1-3 to pp. 1-5.

68. Committee to Consider the Social, Ethical and Legal Issues Arising from *In Vitro* Fertilization, *Report on Donor Gametes in I.V.F.*, Victoria (Australia), 1983.

69. *Report of the Committee of Inquiry Into Human Fertilization and Embryology* (Chairman: Dame Mary Warnock) (London: H.M.S.O., 1984), Cmnd. 9134:

    ... This report takes the term *couple* to mean a heterosexual couple living together in a stable relationship, whether married or not ... (2.6). ... (W)e believe that as a general rule it is better for children to be born into a two-parent family, with both father and mother ... (2.11).

70. *Warnock Report, ibid.*, 6.8; Council for Sciences and Society, *Human Procreation: Ethical Aspects of the New Techniques* (Oxford: Oxford University Press, 1984), arts. 7.3.19-7.3.25.

71. Ince, p. 112.

72. *Warnock Report*, 3.5 in writing; rebuttable presumption of spousal consent, 4.23; *Report on Donor Gametes*, 3.5 in writing; rebuttable presumption of spousal consent, 4.6; *Report of the Ad Hoc Committee on Artificial Insemination*, American Fertility Society, 1981, p. 17; (no A.I.D. without spousal consent). See also: "Insémination Artificielle", Adoption d'une proposition de loi, Sénat J.O. 6 June 1980, 2397, art. 8, requiring writing spousal consent and modifying the original *Proposition de la loi tendant à faire de l'insémination artificielle un moyen de procréation*, no. 47, 26 Oct. 1978 which would have permitted the insemination of single women (art. 9); *Contra*: L.R.C., Saskatchewan, Rec. I (2): "The consent of an applicant's husband should not be a statutory prerequisite to her eligibility for artificial insemination."

73. Royal College of Obstetricians and Gynaecologists, *Report of the RCOG Ethics Committee on In Vitro Fertilization and Embryo Replacement or Transfer*, 1983, 14.4; *Warnock Report*, 4.27 and 6.6; Council for Science and Society, 4.5; *Victoria Report*, 3.10, 3.11; American Fertility Society, p. 12; in France all donation of genetic material must be free, *Proposition de loi*, art. 2.

74. RCOG, 5.3, 14.4; *Warnock Report* 4.22, 6.8; Council, 4.5, 4.11; Victoria, 3.14, American Fertility Society, p. 7; Saskatchewan, 3.19.

75. British Medical Association, "Appendix VI: Interim Report on Human In Vitro Fertilization and Embryo Replacement", *British Medical Journal*, vol. 286 (1983), p. 1594, art. 5; RCOG, 14.4(1); *Warnock Report*, 3.2 and 6.6; *Victoria Report*, 3.36; American Fertility Society, "Ethical Statement on In Vitro Fertilization", *Fertility and Sterility*, vol. 41 (1984), V; Saskatchewan, II-12; *Proposition de loi*, art. 4.

76. *Warnock Report*, 7.5 not recommended as too risky.

77. Committee to Consider the Social, Ethical and Legal Issues Arising from In Vitro Fertilization, *Report on the Disposition of Embryos Produced by In Vitro Fertilization* (Final Report), 6.14: "Embryo research shall be limited to the excess embryos produced by patients in an I.V.F. programme"; BMA, p. 1480; Council for Science and Society, p. 85, 8.7 (i):

> We see no absolute objection to the use in research of unimplanted embryos if they are at an early state (5.7), or to the freezing of embryos for later implantation, or for research for therapeutic purposes (5.8, 7.9.1-4 and 8.3). Each use requires its own ethical justification in the light of potential benefits. However, it would be unethical for fetuses to be used at, or beyond, the state at which their developing nervous systems might be sufficient to provide them with some rudimentary sense of awareness.

78. *Warnock*, 11.22; *Final Report, ibid.*, 3.29, 6.15.

79. American Fertility Society, "Statement", VI; BMA, no. 11; RCOG, 11.3; Warnock, 10.10; Victoria, 6.11.

80. See, for example: Warnock, 11.16: "The human embryo *per se* has no legal status . . ." 11.17. "Nevertheless . . . the embryo of the human species ought to have a special status . . . We recommend that the embryo of the human species should be afforded some protects in law."

81. *Ibid.*, 4.17; 10.14. See also: Saskatchewan, s. 19 (b) and (c); British Columbia, Rec. 1. *Status of Children (Amendment) Act*, 1984; *Report of the Ad Hoc Committee on Artificial Insemination*, American Fertility Society, p. 18.

82. A most interesting bill is the Alternative Reproduction Bill of Michigan (1984) (R. Fitzpatrick, rep.) which would label those parents intending to bring up the child (not necessarily its biological parents) as the societal mother or father. Most importantly, it would permit surrogate parenting while leaving the surrogate herself a 20-day revocation period after birth. With respect to maternal freedom during pregnancy, sec. 14 (1) reads in part as follows:

> (a) That the surrogate mother or the surrogate carrier agrees to submit to any reasonable request by the societal father for a medical, psychiatric, or psychological examination and to authorize the release of the results of the examination to the societal father.

> (b) That the surrogate mother or the surrogate carrier agrees to adhere to the reasonable medical instructions regarding her prenatal health and the prenatal health of the fetus given to her by the physician who performed the insemination or the implantation or any other physician attending her during pregnancy. However, this agreement shall not be construed to require the surrogate mother or the surrogate carrier to abort the fetus.

83. *Vital Statistics Act*, R.S.N.B., 1979, c.V-3; *Vital Statistics Act,*. S.O., 1980, c.524; *Vital Statistics Act*, R.S.M. 1970, c.V-60; *Vital Statistics Act*, R.S.A., 1980, c.V-4; *Vital Statistics Act*, R.S.B.C. 1979, c.425; *Vital Statistics Act*, S.S., 1976, c.V-7; *Règlement d'application de la Loi sur la protection de la santé publique*, 1982 (L.R.Q. c.P-35, a.69), arts. 2 and 9.

84. *Child and Family Services and Family Relations Act*, 1980, c.C-21.

85. *Children's Act*, Statutes of the Yukon Territory, 1984, c.2, art. 134 (1) reads:

> Where the Director has reasonable and probable grounds to believe and does believe that a foetus is being subjected to a serious risk of suffering from foetal alcohol syndrome or other congenital injury attributable to the pregnant woman subjecting herself during pregnancy to addictive or intoxicating substances, the Director may apply to a judge for an order requiring the woman to participate in such reasonable supervision or counselling as the order specifies in respect of her use of addictive or intoxicating substances.

86. Such actions would be possible under, for example, *The Family Law Reform Act*, R.S.O., 1980, c.152, s.66:

> No person shall be disentitled from bringing an action or other proceeding against another for the reason only that they stand in the relationship of parent and child.

See especially: Shaw; Beal; and Hallisey on these types of suits.

87. Warnock, 13.7-13.9; *contra*: British Columbia, *Artificial Insemination*, rec. 2:

> There should be no legislation, either to promote or to prohibit the use of artificial insemination, but rather, there should be the development of a logical series of social policies and professional standards by which to protect the interests of society as a whole and of each individual involved in artificial insemination, i.e., the recipient, her spouse, the donor, the resulting child, the physician, and others who render services in collecting, processing and storing seminal fluid, and in documentation. (p. 9.)

One could ask, however, whether British Columbia's position taken in 1975 would be the same today considering the expansion of reproductive technologies well beyond simple A.I.D.

88. Warnock, 10.10-10.13.

89. Barbara Kati Rothman, "The Meanings of Choice in Reproductive Technology", in *Test-Tube Women*, p. 30.

90. For a discussion of responsibility ethics as opposed to a conflict of rights or adversarial approach, see: Whitbeck, p. 249; Farrell-Smith, p. 269; Hubbard, "Personal Courage . . .", p. 346; Holmes and Peterson, p. 73. See especially: Marjorie Reiley Macquire, "Personhood, Covenant and Abortion", *American Journal of Philosophy and Theology* (forthcoming, 1985).

The Canadian Advisory Council on the Status of Women was established as an independent advisory body in 1973 in response to a recommendation by the Royal Commission on the Status of Women. Its mandate, "to bring before the government and the public matters of interest and concern to women" and "to advise the Minister on such matters relating to the status of women as the Minister may refer to the Council for its consideration or as the Council may deem appropriate", is wide and may be interpreted to cover all Council activities on behalf of Canadian women.

The Council is an autonomous agency that reports to Parliament through the Minister Responsible for the Status of Women. This allows the Council to maintain a voice within Parliament and at the same time maintain the right to publish without ministerial consent.

The following were members of the Canadian Advisory Council on the Status of Women at the time of publication (1985):

Sylvia Gold
President
Ottawa, Ontario

Patricia Cooper
First Vice-President
Calgary, Alberta

Marie-Hélène Boyle
Vice-President
Montréal, Québec

Jean Augustine
Etobicoke, Ontario

Monique Bernard
Mont St-Hilaire, Québec

Shirley Bradshaw
Yarmouth, Nova Scotia

Clarisse Codère
Sherbrooke, Québec

Erminie Joy Cohen
Saint John, N.B.

Jo-Ann Cugnet
North Battleford,
Saskatchewan

Edith Daly
Montague, P.E.I.

Anne Enge
Yellowknife, N.W.T.

Kilby Gibson
Vancouver, B.C.

Marthe Gill
Pointe Bleue, Québec

June Marie Hampton
Faro, Yukon

Alison Hinchey
New Waterford, N.S.

Monica Matte
Montréal, Québec

Robert McGavin
Toronto, Ontario

Jeannette Pelletier
Campbellton, N.B.

Jane Pepino
Toronto, Ontario

Lynn Pitt
Calgary, Alberta

Cécile Rémillard-
Beaudry
Winnipeg, Manitoba

Margaret Strongitharm
Nanaimo, B.C.

Margaret Taylor
Belleville, Ontario

Brigitte Turcotte
La Sarre, Québec

Ann L. Tweddle
Edmonton, Alberta